Managing the Future

A Guide to Forecasting and Strategic Planning in the 21st Century

ONE WEEK LOAN

D1423951

Stephen M. Millett

Published in this first edition in 2011 by:
Triarchy Press
Station Offices
Axminster
Devon. EX13 5PF
United Kingdom
+44 (0)1297 631456
info@triarchypress.com
www.triarchypress.com

A catalogue record for this book is available from the British Library.

Cover design by Heather Fallows ~
www.whitespacegallery.org.uk

ISBN: 978-1-908009-48-7

Contents

Dedicated with much love to my generational futures:
Jennie, Annie, Brandee, Wendi, Ellie, Maggie, Anderson, and Natalie

Introduction

When I was a graduate student in history at Ohio State some 40 years ago, I saw a cartoon that in effect asked: Why study history? There's no future in it! This joke became no laughing matter for me, as I have spent a career using my education in history to explore the future. When I finished my doctorate, I went on active duty with the US Air Force as a humanities instructor at the fully accredited residential School of Engineering of the Air Force Institute of Technology. I think of that assignment as my post-doctoral education, whereby I learned how to think like, and work closely with, scientists, technologists, and mathematicians. I became increasingly interested in applying history to solving problems, too.

In 1979, I resigned my commission and joined the staff of the Battelle Memorial Institute in my hometown of Columbus, Ohio. As the world's largest private, non-profit technology research and management institution, Battelle was somewhat of an odd place for a person with a doctorate in history to land, but my professional education and my Air Force experience served me remarkably well working with engineers, systems analysts, economists, and management consultants on forecasting projects. My earliest scenario projects were with aerospace and defense companies, which closely matched my expertise in American diplomatic, modern European, and Russian history. I went on to apply scenario analysis and other forecasting methods to all kinds of companies that were asking the same types of questions about the future. I consequently spent a career of 27 years at Battelle and managed well over 100 major projects for corporations, non-profit organizations, and government agencies in the US, Canada, Mexico, Europe, India, and Japan. I continue my work today with my own research and consulting company.

As a futurist, I call my type of work "applied history." I taught history as an adjunct instructor at several universities, so I was doing some "academic history" in the traditional sense of teaching and research. I was also publishing in my fields of expertise. My bread and butter employment, however, made me an applied historian. I was applying historical techniques (e.g. primary and secondary research into the past, critical judgment and reasoned speculation, and the consideration of alternative possible pasts – counterfactual history) to the futuring methods of trend analysis, expert judgment, and scenarios. I could use what I had learned about interpreting historical evidence for disciplined speculation about the past to help me think about the future. I could help my clients structure the boundaries of uncertainty and plan for the future within ranges of probabilities. Contingency planning in diplomatic and military history was just as viable as contingency planning for business strategies. I could use both history and futuring to help my clients with their needs in long-term strategic planning, emerging technology assessments, new product development, and risk management.

When explaining to clients what I do, I prefer to use the term "futuring" rather than forecasting. Too often people think that "forecasting" means computer models, formulas, and numbers. It is what statisticians, systems analysts, econometricians, insurance actuaries, and financial analysts do. It is highly quantitative. "Futuring" combines qualitative with quantitative methods and may take the form of stories rather than figures. It also suggests "doing" as well as "understanding," since the purpose of futuring is to form well considered expectations for the future to use in visioning for strategy-making, planning, and acting today to influence (if not make) desirable futures. I did not care for the term "foretelling," which at one time was used by the scenario writers at Shell, as it sounded too much like "fortune telling," which was not at all the mental image that I wanted to convey. In this book, I have used "forecasting" as a synonym for "futuring," but with the understanding that "forecasting" means framing expectations for better tomorrows.

I hate the 1960s terms "futurism" and "futurology." They suggest visions of the future that border on science fiction, which would not typically go over well with corporations in the late 20th and early 21st centuries. I also do not like the work of futurists who rely almost exclusively on visioning to generate highly aspirational, normative, and idiosyncratic predictions without the context of forecasting trends in the external environment. I feel that this approach to thinking about the future relies too heavily on wishful thinking. I do respect the more recent term "foresight" to embrace both the pursuit of likely futures (forecasts) and visioning (preferred futures).

The product of futuring, like forecasting, is a forecast. The result of "futuring" certainly is not "the future," although it could be "a future" as one of several possible futures. The result of visioning is not just the strategic plan but the operations that achieve its goals. The product of visioning may well be "the future" to the extent that one has the capabilities, resources, cooperation, and even good luck of the self-fulfilling prophecy.

The central idea of this book is that managers, especially young and middle-level managers, will increasingly need to be their own futurists in order to become executive leaders in the future. Previously, managers relied on outside consultants and forecasters to provide the forecast as well as the information to support it. Managers in the future, however, will have to acquire their own skills and develop their own expert judgments to generate their own well considered expectations for the future. Therefore, the primary target readership of this book consists of business and management students and young managers who aspire to bigger and better things in the future.

Although this book has a strong bias toward for-profit companies, the theories, methods, and best practices of futuring and visioning, to one degree or another, apply also for managers in non-profits, institutions, other organizations, and government agencies. Although management styles and organizations may vary, they have to be their own futurists, too. So when I say "company" or "corporation," I am thinking of all kinds of institutions and organizations. Every manager responsible for developing human talent, deploying assets, setting goals, and achieving objectives must think about and act upon their expectations for the future.

A secondary and much broader readership for this book is everyday people who have responsibilities for managing their households, families, finances, possessions, and time. The skills of business managers apply to personal business as well as public business. People of all kinds form expectations of all kinds for the future. Some expectations are well considered, but many are not: often leading to disappointments and even despair. We all have to think ahead about our education, careers, loved ones, trips, and retirement. Even a Will is a plan.

Unlike the physical sciences and some of the social sciences, I have found that most futurists have a weak grounding in the philosophy and theories that lie behind their practices. Futurists may employ trend analysis, expert surveys, and scenarios to generate their expectations for the future, but they usually cannot explain the theory that makes their work credible, even prescient. One purpose of this book is to provide philosophical explanations and theories to support the work of futurists. This is very much a blend of theory and practice.

Why would managers need to know the theories in addition to the best practices of futuring and visioning? I learned from my engineering colleagues that you have to understand the first principles of science and technology in order to work problems through to successful completion. You are less likely to find an answer to a troubling question when you do not grasp the fundamentals at hand. Likewise, the successful manager of the future will need to comprehend the basic principles of futuring and visioning to appreciate the prescience of forecasts (or lack thereof), to judge the reliability of the methods used to generate them, to derive robust strategies based on well considered expectations for the future, to draw up inspiring plans, to motivate others to achieve desired objectives, and to recognize changes that require adjustments to plans without abandoning goals.

Toward the goal of establishing a philosophy of futuring and a frame of reference for more closely uniting theory and practice, I offer five futuring principles:

1. The future will be some unknown combination of continuity and change.

2. The future can be anticipated with varying degrees of uncertainty depending upon conditions.

3. Futuring and visioning are different but complementary perspectives of the future.

4. The best forecasts and plans are methodically generated and provide well considered expectations for the future.

5. There is no such thing as an immutable forecast or plan for an immutable future. Forecasts and plans must be continuously monitored, evaluated, and revised according to new data and conditions in order to provide real-time frameworks for making long-term decisions and strategies.

The first five chapters cover these principles, one principle per chapter. The last four chapters concern the best practices of managing futuring, visioning, applications and benefits, and the managing of expectations themselves. They are largely drawn from my own professional experiences supplemented by decades of reading, studying, and thinking.

The numerous experiences related in this book, of course, are my own interpretation of events during my career and do not in any way represent the views, interests, or concerns of the Battelle Memorial Institute, Battelle's clients, the clients of Futuring Associates LLC, or the many individuals with whom I have had the pleasure of working. My views are my own. I have been very careful in this book to omit proprietary information and the names of specific clients, except in cases where the names of such clients have already been made public.

If it takes a village to raise a child, it takes a city to support the career of a futurist. I owe debts of gratitude to so many people – teachers, colleagues, and clients. Most importantly, I remember with great respect what my father, Dr. John D. Millett, taught me about history and how to use it to think about the future. In his own day, he was a highly respected authority on strategic planning in higher education with decades of experience as a professor at Columbia University, a participant in government commissions, President of Miami University, and the first Chancellor of the Board of Regents in Ohio.

I have many colleagues, clients, and friends with whom I have traveled during my professional voyage as a futurist. I owe a great debt to gratitude to my former scientific and technological associates in the Air Force and at Battelle. They very patiently worked with me and taught me more science and engineering than I ever learned in school. I owe a particular debt of gratitude to my mentors at Battelle, including Dr. Hal Fisher, Dr. Gary Stacey, Mr. Andy Massena, Dr. Henry Cialone, and Mr. Ron Cudnik; my closest associates Dr. Bill Huss and E. J. Honton; and my understudy Lennie Rhoades, who assisted me on many futuring projects and went on to successfully apply some of the things that we learned together for a highly successful career in an international corporation. I have had the great pleasure of staying in touch with Bill Huss, now at Babson College, who generously read and commented upon versions of this book in draft.

I also greatly appreciate the support and encouragement of the Columbus Futurists, who have provided excellent feedback on my ideas and earlier versions of this book. In this context, I have greatly enjoyed interacting once again with Dr. Marvin Zahniser, who 40 years ago was my doctoral advisor at The Ohio State University, and Mr. Ron Cudnik, more recently one of my best managers at Battelle. I also have greatly benefited from my association with Dr. David Staley, who leads the Columbus Futurists. Like the best colleagues and clients of the past, David asks the big questions and seeks solutions beyond the conventional. His book *History and Future* counts as a significant contribution to the theory of scenarios as alternative futures.

I owe a large debt of gratitude to Ms. Imogen Fallows, who did an outstanding job of editing my manuscript for publication at Triarchy Press. She proved the point that, although their work remains largely hidden in the shadows of authors' bylines, exceptional editors make writers appear more talented than they really are.

Finally, I wish to acknowledge the huge contribution of my wife, Sherry Richards, in offering continuous encouragement, constructive criticism, and many hours of improving rough manuscripts that only gradually emerged as a coherent and cohesive work. This book is very much hers, too.

Stephen M. Millett
Columbus, Ohio
September 30, 2011

Chapter 1. Continuity and Change

Futuring Principle 1: The future will be some unknown combination of continuity and change.

Several years ago a corporate client of mine asked "Do I really need to think about the future?" After a moment, I somewhat flippantly responded, "No, not if you are willing to accept whatever happens." Perhaps the executive believed that the future was already determined, so he did not need to worry since there was nothing he could do about it. Or perhaps he was taking the opposite point of view that since the future cannot be predicted there was no use in wasting his time thinking about it. In either case, my response was correct, if not politic. As a pragmatist, I urge my clients to think seriously about the future, plan, and prepare for it – and then monitor events and detect changes according to new situations in order to adjust strategies to achieve goals.

It is in the self-interest of companies, especially new and growing enterprises that depend on other people's money, to exude confidence of success in the future. Companies rarely admit a lack of faith in continuous growth. Business people tend to think in linear terms – they think the future will always be better than in the past. They assume that how things are going today will naturally continue into the future. Managers may also believe in business cycles, of course, because they learned them in college and business schools. Too often cycles, however, are rationalizations. When business is growing, complacent managers will claim the credit for themselves; but when business declines, the same managers will attribute reversals to uncontrollable circumstances and complain "How was I supposed to know *that* would happen?"

If market conditions and business operations remained the same for long periods of time, then preparing for the future would be less important than it really is. We would just plan to do more of the same. But time moves in only one direction, and the passing of time introduces variability, or risk. As the saying goes, change happens. Yet the uncertainty of change makes planning more difficult while it makes it more important to do. If we did not know that before, we certainly learned it in the global economic downturn of 2008, often called the "Great Recession".

Astute managers learn quickly that business trends can be upset by changes, not all of them good. They acquire the skills to better anticipate the future and to adjust to it when necessary. With such skills, they are better prepared to deal with uncertainty. What holds for clever managers in particular also holds for clever people in general.

The future, which is still evolving and yet to occur from the perspective of the present, will be a product of both our own design and elements beyond our control that we often characterize as "chance" or "luck." I believe that good luck can be maximized and bad luck can be minimized with forethought, planning, and preparation. There are indeed things coming that will be beyond our control; but if we do nothing to prepare for the future, then we deserve whatever happens to us, good or bad. We may not be able to control the future, but we can steer forward in desired directions.

Bad things have a way of happening on their own, but good things have to be made to happen. I admire students who prepare to do well on exams; young people who plan years in advance by taking courses leading to professions in medicine, law, and teaching; employees who work smart as well as hard by planning ahead; athletes who dedicate huge amounts of time and effort in practices leading to competitive victories; soldiers who plan and train for successful missions; architects who meticulously draw blueprints for highly complex building projects; carpenters and tailors who "measure twice, cut once;" actors and musicians who repeatedly rehearse for perfect performances; and business people who think through a strategy of required investments and actions to achieve their goals.

I have been undertaking forecasting and planning projects for managers and executives in corporations, non-profits, and government agencies around the world for about 30 years. During my career, I have learned many lessons the hard way. I have supplemented my experiences by much reading and thinking about the theories that support the practices. I discovered that my clients took my forecasts more seriously when they understood the principles behind the methods – when they realized that well considered expectations should be acted upon rather than dismissed as just made-up guesses about the future. The purpose of this book, therefore, is to share my thoughts and experiences with both emerging and experienced managers so that they, too, can do a more professional job of anticipating the future.

The two most common mistakes in thinking about the future must be addressed first. One is the common assumption that the future will be all continuity, so that trend projections from the past to the future will nearly always be valid. Such trend projections are typically linear or cyclical extrapolations. The other mistake is the opposite assumption that the future will be mostly changes with little regard for the past and present.

The nub of the first futuring principle is that the future has always been and always will be (most likely) a mixture of both continuity from the past and changes from the present and future. We perceive continuity through our awareness of trends and our recognition that things today are products of the past. Because we cannot know the future in any direct way through our perceptions, we can never be certain exactly what combination of continuity and change will come in the future. Let us first look at the basic science of time to see what it tells us about the nature of the future and how we might better manage expectations for it.

Time's Arrow

In 1927 the British astronomer Sir Arthur Eddington used the term "the arrow of time" to capture the image of time flying in only one direction. He was an early defender of Albert Einstein's theories of relativity, including the concept of space-time. Physicists have long recognized that time is asymmetrical, meaning that it cannot move both forward and backward, only forward. Fundamentally, within the known laws of physics, time travel back into the past is physically impossible, despite the imaginations of such skilled novelists as H. G. Wells. The British physicist Stephen Hawking speculated that if the universe stopped expanding and then started to contract, time would flow in the opposite direction, from the future to the past, so that we would remember the future but we would not know the past. Later, he reversed his position and concluded that time, or at least the human perception of it, would still flow from the past to the future.[1]

One scientific explanation of why time travels in only one direction is the Second Law of Thermodynamics, which says that, in the absence of new energy, the natural state of things (any organization or system of molecules) flows in only one direction, from order to disorder. This process is called entropy. An everyday example of entropy is the well-known fact that heat flows from hot (a higher energy level of molecules) to cold (a lower energy level of molecules), unless an outside force redirects it. In a similar way, time passes from the past, which represents a higher state of order (that which has already occurred), to the future, which constitutes a lower state of order, because so many things could happen relative to what did happen. The uncertainty of the future appears as a lower state of order. No outside force, however, has ever been identified that changes the passage of time from the past to the future. In addition, the principle of entropy states that events flow in a one-way sequential order of cause-and-effect

---

1   Richard Morris, *Time's Arrow. Scientific Attitudes Toward Time*. New York: Simon & Schuster, Inc. (A Touchtone Book), 1986, p. 121; Stephen W. Hawking, *A Brief History of Time. From the Big Bang to Black Holes*. Toronto and New York: Bantam Books, 1988, pp.143-153. Also see Stephen Hawking and Leonard Mlodinow, *A Briefer History of Time*. New York: Bantam Dell, 2008.

relationships, whereby past causes lead to future effects but effects never change the causes that preceded them.[2]

We have many popular expressions that capture similar ideas, such as "A stitch in time saves nine" and "You can't undo the past." In addition, we perceive time's arrow every day in such phenomena as the cumulative effects of physical wear and erosion, decay, and our own aging. What we often fail to see, however, is that business wears out with time, too. We often think that the future will be a continuation of today, but according to the Second Law of Thermodynamics, unless we add new energy to the enterprise, business like all systems of molecules will decay as time moves forward.

An implication of the linear and sequential nature of time is that we cannot know the future through our senses and experience because it has yet to occur. In this regard, our everyday perceptions of time are well aligned with the physics of time. Another implication is that, if time moves in only one direction, then, like a straight arrow, it might have a linear path of certain continuity with the past and present.

Time's Target: The Future

If we use Eddington's metaphor of time's arrow, does that also mean that time has a trajectory toward a designated target in the future? Does linear time lead us to a predetermined destiny? While it is popular to talk about fate, most of us do not realize that everyday notions about time and the future have been highly influenced by thousands of years of religious beliefs and philosophical concepts. There are elements of fatalism in Judaism, Christianity, Islam, Hinduism, and Buddhism. In religious terms, the one way arrow of time is called divine predestination. In the natural and social sciences, it is called determinism.

We hear expressions in our everyday language that reflect fundamental beliefs in predestination and fate, such as:

- Everything will work out OK in the end.
- It was meant to be (or it wasn't meant to be).
- It was fate.
- It is in His hands.
- What will be, will be (*Que sera, sera*).
- It is written.

---

2   In addition to Morris and Hawking, see Stefan Klein, *The Secret Pulse of Time. Making Sense of Life's Scarcest Commodity*. Translated by Shelley Frisch. Cambridge, MA: Da Capo Press, 2006; and Sean Carroll, *From Eternity to Here. The Quest for the Ultimate Theory of Time*. New York: Dutton, 2010.

I once heard a story, allegedly true, about a Protestant bishop a few years ago who was receiving a briefing on trends in his church. The graphs showed many trend lines that were declining over time: membership, attendance, collections, etc. At the end of the gloomy presentation, the bishop sighed and commented, "Well, I guess we're having a bad century." He likely had no doubt that "business" would recover and continue on the path to the Day of Judgment.

Many business people with strong religious beliefs may accept the doctrine of predestination in their private lives but still engage in planning and hard work in their secular enterprises. If you were to draw up business plans and run an enterprise based on predestination, then you would have to accept either success or failure accordingly. We see a lot of fatalism based on wishful thinking in cases of start-up companies and entrepreneurs who are very confident of riches in the future. Very few corporate executives and venture capitalists, however, would accept fatalism as the premise for future business success, especially when large sums of money are at stake. They accept business plans based on business models, management experience, and market trends and opportunities, but rarely on faith alone. If they were to rely upon any divine guidance, it would be the axiom that God helps those who help themselves.

Parallel to the religious beliefs in predestination run purely secular concepts of the future determined by natural forces of physics, chemistry, and biology. Time's arrow can be viewed as a force of nature in the same way as motion is calculated in Newtonian mechanics. Newtonian physics is deterministic in the sense that exact causes will have exact results every time. Statistics are also deterministic in that data are expected to fall with a determined frequency distribution that looks like a bell curve on a graph. The natural determinists say that we do not need God to predict the laws of nature. This line of reasoning leads to the conclusion that we could know the future if only we recognized the natural forces that were carrying us to it.

In the Enlightenment of 18th century Europe, philosophers turned to the logic of Newton to explain social as well as physical phenomena. They searched for the basic forces of history like the laws of motion and gravity. They proclaimed a new arrow of time, and they called it "progress." Their concept was that mankind moved through history according to certain social dynamics that were leading to a state of individual and social perfection. One such advocate was the Marquis de Condorcet, a mathematician and philosopher at the time of the French Revolution. During the winter of 1793-1794, while in hiding under the shadow of the guillotine, Condorcet wrote an essay in which he argued that the methods of science could be applied to the problems of society. He saw time as having but one direction: it propelled people toward the goal of universal human rights and justice. His view of progress became a dominating intellectual force during the radically changing economics, politics, and social relationships of the Industrial Age. The idea of progress from rational philosophy crossed back over into science with the view that evolution was a biological corollary to progress toward greater complexity and higher levels of development. Although Darwin assigned no direction to evolution, many of his followers did. Some went so far as to speculate that evolution was directing the species toward perfection. The so-called Social Darwinists viewed the concept of progress in society as being virtually the same as natural selection in biology.[3]

During the 19th century numerous philosophers, professors, and social experimenters characterized human progress across history as a march toward utopia.[4] Perfection could be achieved on earth in the here and now. The concept of progress as time's arrow was most famously championed in the 19th century by Georg Hegel and Karl Marx. In very simple terms, Hegel built further on the concept of history as a dynamic of human progress. He conceptualized history as inevitably moving through a dialectical process of changes caused by conflicts. He took the concept of the dialectic from a logical to a metaphysical construct. A state of things is called a thesis. The opposition to a thesis is an antithesis. In conflicts between thesis and antithesis, a new state of affairs arises, called the synthesis. This process repeats itself over and over again until a final goal is achieved. Hegel argued that through this dialectic, people advanced across time toward higher and higher states of social progress through reason in history. The end state would be a society of pure reason.

Marx flipped Hegel's concept of the dialectic from the abstract to the material and applied it to the conflict of classes in the industrial society. He called his arrow of time "dialectical materialism." Each stage of history had its own social conflicts between the privileged few and the impoverished many. In the 19th century, the conflict was between the working class (proletariat) and the middle class (bourgeoisie) that profited from the surplus value of labor in factories, mills, and shops. In advanced stages of development the conflict between classes would ignite a great revolution through which the proletariat would achieve its own state of perfect social order in which all people would work according to their abilities and receive from society things according to their needs. The perfect order, or the

---

3   Condorcet's views of social progress stimulated one of many disagreements between Harvard biologists and arch rivals Edward O. Wilson and Stephen Jay Gould. See Edward O. Wilson, *Consilience. The Unity of Knowledge*. New York: Vintage Books, 1998, pp. 15-22; and Stephen Jay Gould, *The Hedgehog, the Fox, and the Magister's Pox. Mending the Gap Between Science and the Humanities*. New York: Harmony Books, 2003, pp. 196-197.

4   An excellent overview of the "utopian socialists" as well as Marx's theories can be found in Robert L. Heilbroner, *The Worldly Philosophers. The Lives, Times, and Ideas of the Great Economic Thinkers*. New York: Touchstone/Simon & Schuster, 1999 (1953), pp. 105-169.

end of history, would be a social order that Marx and his collaborator Friedrich Engels called "communism."

One famous assault on Marxism came from the 20th century philosopher Karl Popper, who dismissed all concepts of historical forces as Newtonian mechanics as "historicism," a pseudo-science. He rejected the whole idea of history as a manifestation of hidden forces moving mankind to any naturally determined destiny. "...Is it within the power of any social science to make such sweeping historical prophecies?," he posed rhetorically. "A careful examination of this question has led me to the conviction that such sweeping historical prophecies are entirely beyond the scope of scientific method. The future depends on ourselves, and we do not depend on any historical necessity." Popper found no rational basis in either philosophy or science for the concepts of inevitability, destiny, or predetermination of any kind in the history of human affairs. Popper found nothing inevitable about any totalitarian regime like Nazi Germany or Communist Russia, except that freedom will most likely die where the open exchange of information and opinions are repressed. His conclusion was that the freedom of inquiry must exist in politics as well as in science so that the validity of any proposition can be tested only through evidence, criticism, and continuous validation. To Popper's eye there is no arrow of time or target in history.[5]

A new period of natural determinism emerged in the late 20th century with scientific breakthroughs in genetic research. As more and more laboratory research connects specific genes with specific human conditions, some experts conjecture that human behavior may be largely if not solely determined by DNA. Our fate, some would say, lies not in the stars but in our chromosomes. As early as 1875, Darwin himself presented the idea that both human and animal behaviors may have evolved along with anatomy and physiology.[6] It was only a short intellectual leap from Darwin to the present hypothesis that evolutionary behavior could be predictive of future behavior. This thought has given rise to new fields of study called evolutionary psychology, evolutionary sociology, and evolutionary history. As in generations before them with their analogies to physics, some experts have gotten carried away applying new biological laws to human trends. There may be, they would argue, a genetic basis for the ancient concept of innate knowledge, or at least an evolutionary explanation for intuitive human thought patterns and instinctive survival strategies. This model of biological predestination, when carried to extremes, sounds a lot like a new form of natural predestination.

---

5 Karl R. Popper, *The Open Society and Its Enemies*. Princeton, NJ: Princeton University Press, 1950; quote on p. 4.

6 Charles Darwin, *The Expression of the Emotions in Man and Animals*. Chicago: Phoenix Books/The University of Chicago Press, 1965 (1875).

Determinism, beyond its apparent rational content, may have a strong emotional appeal. When people are frustrated, disappointed, and in pain, they may take comfort in the explanation that fate, not individuals, determined what happened. Often feelings of fatalism go with the sense of having been victimized by unexpected events. It relieves us to dismiss misfortune by saying "I could have done nothing to prevent it" or "I could not have done other than what I did." This may be a form of fatalism as a psychological defense mechanism. It is far easier to accept fate as circumstances beyond our control than to assume the heavy weight of responsibility, and potential blame, for making the future happen as though we enjoyed complete free will.

Again, as in the case of religious predestation, if natural determinism were to be proven, then the future would have a destination determined by forces beyond human control. Time's arrow would be flying toward a target and the future would be highly predictable and consistent with the experiences of the past and with a belief system or mental model of the future. While I believe that some trends are very strong and likely to continue in the future, no trend or target is so predetermined as to have a 100% probability of occurrence.

As strong as some trends may be, we continue to be surprised by unexpected events, which the statisticians dismiss as "outliers" because they do not fit a preconceived pattern. Many business managers continue to place great reliance on linear extrapolations of past to future business performance as though time and business dynamics were indeed linear. They also find attractive the idea of periodic business and economic cycles, which we should examine next.

A variation on the linear is the cyclical approach to predicting the future. Time as a natural phenomenon may move in only one direction, but events over time in human activities may move in waves, curves, and cycles rather than in straight lines. The concept of cycles certainly has much intuitive appeal because we have all experienced mood swings, good and bad days, and career ups and downs. Human societies have always been strongly influenced by the cycles of day and night, the months, and the seasons of the year, which are highly predictable. The underlying assumption is that long-term, repetitious patterns reflect driving forces that may be deterministic. For every up there will be a corresponding down, and vice versa. The idea further suggests periodicity, or a regular timing for the ups and downs of a cycle; if so, then cycles would be predictable. Some thinkers have taken cycles very literally, but others have argued that they should be seen as metaphors. In either case, cycles pose the possibility that if the past influences, if not exactly determines, both the present and the future then knowledge of the present and the past reveals foreshadowing of the future (under the conditions of a closed system or a fixed set delineated by boundaries).

One of the earliest theorists of the cyclical nature of history was the great Muslim historian and philosopher Ibn Khaldun, who lived in North Africa and Moorish Spain during the 14th century. He saw a pattern to the rise and fall of ruling dynasties. A dynastic cycle would begin when a rather primitive people with great energy toppled a well-established, but weakening culture. Having conquered a more sophisticated culture, the new rulers slowly adapt to the ways of the conquered. They learn and expand upon the previous culture, rising to new levels of refinement, but also decadence. During the cycle, the state is formed with three goals: the good of the rulers, the good of the ruled, and the good of the ruled in the world to come (consistent with Islam). Further stages see refinements in the arts, crafts, and science, but sophistication ultimately leads to vulnerability to more aggressive, primitive people. A full dynastic cycle was estimated to be roughly three generations of about 40 years each (a biblical generation), or a span of about 120 years. Ibn Khaldun was particularly concerned with the transitions of societies, as he argued in his own lifetime that one epoch of Muslim culture largely based on Arab ways was declining relative to the rising power of others, such as the Turks from Central Asia.[7]

Arguably the most prevailing ideas about cycles have arisen from economics and business. Today we hear many economists and business people explain market ups and downs as though they were forces of nature. The concept of business cycles arose in the early stages of European industrialization. Building upon the work of previous economists, the French physician and statistician Clement Juglar developed as early as the 1850s a model for explaining and perhaps predicting periodic economic cycles. While others had commented on economic crises as peculiar events, Juglar found a statistical pattern of phases of prosperity, crisis, and liquidation. He studied the statistics of banking loans and saw that commercial crises occurred along with monetary crises. He also saw what he characterized as periodic abuses in the use of credit, probably motivated by excessive speculation akin to reckless gambling. He was hesitant to assign exact causes to particular events, but he made a medical metaphor of general physical to economic health – when normal conditions are compromised, the market body becomes more susceptible to illness. Juglar was also cautious not to claim that the cycles had any regular periodicity, although the data suggested roughly 10 year intervals. In subsequent debates, other economists jumped to cycles with regular

---

7   Ibn Khaldun, *The Muqaddimah*. Translated from the Arabic by Franz Rosenthal. Edited and abridged by N. J. Dalwood. Princeton, NJ: Bollingen Series/Princeton University Press, 1967. Also see Muhsin Mahdi, "Ibn Khaldun" in David L. Sills, ed., *International Encyclopedia of the Social Sciences*. New York: The Macmillan Company & The Free Press, 1968, Vol. 7, pp. 53-57; and Dimitri Gutas, "Ibn Khaldun" in Robert Audi, General Editor, *The Cambridge Dictionary of Philosophy. Second Edition*. New York: Cambridge University Press, 1999, pp. 410-411.

periods, making them more predictable, but Juglar refused to go that far – the cycles were general and could vary with the particular circumstances of the times. While economic cycles had many similarities over time, no two cycles were ever exactly the same. Juglar also asserted as a hypothesis that cycles would continue to occur, but each time the return to a state of market equilibrium would be at a higher level than before, so that the string of cycles moved in a generally upward linear direction.[8]

The 20th century champion of the concept of cycles was Joseph Schumpeter, whose book *Business Cycles* appeared in two volumes of over 1,000 pages in 1939. His monumental work of business history showed intervals of Kitchin cycles of 40 months, Juglar cycles of 8-10 years, and Kondratieff cycles of 50-60 years. Yet, Schumpeter admitted his own doubts, as had Clement Juglar some 80 years before him, whether the periods of the cycles had regularity and whether they were predictive in practice as well as in theory.[9]

Economists have pursued predictable business cycles for over 70 years since Schumpeter's treatise and some have made predictions that were close, but never precise. It is always easier to see the cycles after they happen. Even then, it is difficult to fit (with a straight face) tons of economic data into neat curves, let alone lines. For example, it was after the brutal bear market on Wall Street from September 2008 to March 2009 that economists said that the US had gone into a recession, although the data later showed that the recession actually began as early as December 2007, but we did not have real-time data and did not know exactly what was happening at the time. Some economists claimed after the recession that they had predicted it, but I never heard or saw their predictions, and neither did far more clever investors than I.

Business people in particular rely too heavily upon the determinism of economic and business cycles. They can rationalize a downturn in sales by saying "It was bound to happen – it's just another business cycle and we will recover." Of course, when sales are going well nobody likes to say that "it's bound to go down in the future."

Like many futurists, I believe in cycles – sort of. I suffer from the same doubts that troubled Juglar. As with many theories, I like the concept better than I like the mathematics behind it. If cycles are predictive at all, like the linear extrapolations of continuity, then they are general but not precise indicators of the future.

---

8 Daniele Besomi, "Clement Juglar and the transition from crisis theory to business cycle theories," conference paper, Paris, December 2, 2005, posted at www.unil.ch/webdav/site/cwp/users/neyguesi/public/D._Besomi_

9 Thomas K. McCraw. *Prophet of Innovation. Joseph Schumpeter and Creative Destruction.* Cambridge, MA: The Belknap Press of Harvard University Press, 2007, pp. 251-278.

Perhaps cycles explain variations in human behavior within the boundaries of a system or context. When we see cycles, we may be witnessing an action-reaction phenomenon of hope leading to greed, as Juglar suggested, or from physical exertion to fatigue, or from hunger to satiety. Schumpeter was prescient in general without being predictive in particular by recognizing recurring phases of economic behavior characterized as innovation, growth, peaking, crisis management, and recovery. These are various positions within a relatively closed system but still vulnerable to exogenous variables and surprise events. In addition, much like linear projections, cycles fail to anticipate significant departures from the past, such as a technological innovation or a structural shift in markets.

Continuities in trends, however, do exist. We do not have to embrace predestination or determinism to see that history has patterns of many kinds, not just linear or cyclical. The continuities are not caused by the hand of God (necessarily) or the social forces of nature, but rather by repeating patterns of human behavior over time. These patterns we call trends, and trend analysis, which takes many qualitative as well as quantitative forms, is a principal category of futuring methods. Trends are all about continuities and they provide foresight to the extent that continuities existed in the past and remain in the present. In periods of stability with strong continuity and little change, we can rely on trends to provide much information about the future; but when continuity is seriously disrupted by changes, then trends provide only limited clues to the future. We have to consider changes, too, in addition to trends.

Chaos, Chance, and Randomness

Having just reviewed points of view on the linear or cyclical nature of time, we must also recognize that there is an opposite perspective that time has no direction at all. Time may move in only one direction, but that fact of physics tells us nothing about the human future. Rather than history being all continuity with predictable outcomes in the future, maybe history counts for little when considering the future, which may be inherently unpredictable because it's all about change. Maybe there are no patterns and things just happen. Perhaps time lines and curves are only human perceptions of otherwise random phenomena.

From earliest times, in sharp contrast to the religious and philosophical arguments for determinism, some philosophers and scholars have concluded that human life has little or no order in it and that most, if not all, events are random acts. Life is nothing more than a crap shoot, determined by the chance of the roll of the dice or the draw of the cards rather than by any determining force or intent. Therefore, the future is unknowable and cannot be predicted because of fundamental randomness and chaos. Whether people like it or not, change rules over continuity. Yet, there remains much confusion over such terms as "chaos" and "randomness" as they are used by our language let alone our minds. For example, contemporary chaos theory is often mistaken to be randomness, but it is not. In fact, it is technically called *deterministic* chaos. The basic premise is that very small deviations in starting points can result in vastly different results. The oft-given example is the flight of the butterfly in Africa that starts a motion of air that, through an exponential acceleration of events, results in a major hurricane in the Caribbean. There are patterns within chaos, once the starting point has been identified. So chaos theory looks a lot more deterministic than its name suggests to most people.[10]

In currently used terms, randomness is more chaotic than chaos. It is commonly assumed that randomness is the total lack of order. Things just happen by chance with no pattern or purpose. Historically, randomness has been most closely associated with games of chance. Yet, chance ends up being relative to the players or conditions and not absolute in nature. The study of probabilities reveals patterns in the throws of dice and the distribution of cards from a standard deck. All games of chance have boundary conditions both in the physical medium and the rules of the game. As any tourist to Nevada quickly learns, randomness to the gambler is profit for the house.

Randomness may or may not occur in nature, but it is very much dependent upon one's point of view in a human perceptional sense. A long string of numbers, for example, might look random to one person while presenting a non-obvious pattern to a more trained eye.

The concept that change dominates human affairs can be dated back as far as the Greek philosopher Heraclitus of Ephesus, who lived in a Greek community on the eastern shore of the Aegean Sea before the time of Socrates in Athens. Heraclitus observed that no one ever stepped into the same river twice. This dictum became the argument for continuous change. Heraclitus has been credited with such aphorisms as "The cosmos, at best, is like a rubbish heap scattered at random" and "Everything is in flux and nothing is at rest." This point of view was sharply criticized by another Greek philosopher, Parmenides, who argued that nothing changes in essence so the future must be all continuity rather than change. In an odd way, the philosophy that the future will be all change is just as deterministic as the view that it is all continuity. Some 2,400 years later, Popper categorized Heraclitus as one of the earliest historicists: "But in the Heraclitean philosophy one of the less commendable characteristics of historicism manifests

---

10   The most popular treatment of Chaos Theory remains James Gleick, *Chaos: Making a New Science*. New York: Penguin Books, 1987.

itself, namely, an overemphasis upon change, combined with the compleme belief in an inexorable and immutable *law of destiny*."[11]

A major debate since the earliest times of civilization has raged between believers in predestination and those who totally reject it and instead embrace the concept of human free will. While some philosophers and theologians preached about God's omnipotence and design for the universe, including the future, others expounded a point of view that God had given people the power to control their own actions. However, with free will came a fear that it could, if unchecked by morality, lead to randomness of behavior, with everybody doing exactly as they pleased on the whim of the moment, and no consideration given to consequences and impacts on other people.

A philosophical synthesis emerged when some philosophers and theologians reached the middle ground called "compatibilism," which reasons that people have choices and the freedom to go one way or another, but within a set of rules and circumstances. For example, in a liberal democratic system of government, the people may be free to pursue their personal interests as long as their behavior stays within the confines of the law, socially acceptable standards, and the framework of the prevailing culture. Since everybody enjoys rights, nobody has the right to trample on the rights of others. Laws and regulations set boundary conditions that permit free enterprise for all individuals without market-destructive behavior (misrepresentation, fraud, cheating, lying, etc.) by any one individual.[12]

Perhaps no endeavor has received more attention by modern trend analysts, mathematical model builders, and forecasters than trying to predict the future of financial markets, especially the New York Stock Exchange. Yet, the financial markets come as close to randomness as almost any other business activity. Investing, as Juglar argued, is gambling at a higher level. Many traders and analysts have claimed to have predicted various ups and downs in the markets, but no one has yet come up with a widely accepted quantitative model or a qualitative theory that consistently and precisely predicts the variations in market prices. The reason for this is that the buying and selling of assets and securities on public exchanges is done in seconds by millions of players who have little or no direct contact with each other and who claim to have (more or less) equal access to information but in reality work from different sources of information overlaid with individual intuition, personal goals and preferences, and expectations for the future. The sudden spikes in optimism and pessimism seem almost like free will gone wild.

---

11 Popper, *The Open Society*, pp. 14-20; quote on p. 16 with italics in the original; "Heraclitus" in the *Stanford Encyclopedia of Philosophy* at http://plato.stanford.edu/entries/Heraclitus

12 Tomis Kapitan, "free will problem," in Audi, ed., *Cambridge Dictionary of Philosophy*, pp. 326-328.

In addition, the boundary conditions in respect to technologies, regulations, taxes, economic conditions, the news, and personalities are continuously changing.

Two popular works on randomness appeared in the early 21st century, one by an admired financial trader and one by a highly respected scientist. In the first, Nassim Nicholas Taleb characterized low probability, high consequence events as "black swans" in a book with the same title. He had been a highly successful trader in financial derivatives, the kind of trading that is generally known as "hedging" and "speculating." That very kind of activity rewards small bets with large potential payoffs. It is a market that thrives on unpredictability and spectacular events. With this kind of background, in 2007, before the great bear market, Taleb repudiated virtually every kind of economic trend analysis and financial forecasting. He was particularly harsh in his criticism of traditional statistics with deterministic bell curves. He argued that all through history people have been swung one way or another by unforeseen great events, characterized as black swans (but also known as disruptive events, wild cards, and outliers). He argued that it is virtually impossible to predict the future, but it is possible to prepare for it by expecting the worst to happen. He correctly observed that people generally overrate the likelihood of the present continuing into the future and therefore underestimate the powers of random chance and luck. He offered as general financial advice that one should invest according to the potential size of the payoff rather than the probability of occurrence.

Taleb's tone of voice is harsh. Yet, in several places, he tempers his diatribes against conventional forecasting with remarkable subtlety. For example, he observes that "In practice, randomness is fundamentally incomplete information… Randomness, in the end, is just unknowledge. The world is opaque and appearances fool us."[13] This implies that reality may not be random, but have some order, but we do not have enough information about the phenomena to see patterns. Just five pages later, Taleb advises his reader: "Do not try to always withhold judgment – opinions are the stuff of life. Do not try to avoid predicting… What you should avoid is unnecessary dependence on large-scale harmful predictions – those and only those." In the second edition of his book in 2010, Taleb somewhat backs off by admitting that some traditional forecasting methods are valid when used in the right circumstances.[14]

---

13   Nassim Nicholas Taleb, *The Black Swan. The Impact of the Highly Improbable.* New York: Random House, 2007.

14   Taleb, *The Black Swan*, quotes on pp. 198 and 203, respectively. Nassim Nicholas Taleb, *The Black Swan. The Impact of the Highly Improbable*. Second Edition. New York: Random House Trade Paperbacks, 2010, p. 362.

I agree with Taleb on many points, especially in lamenting the blind reliance on models, trends, and time series statistics that project more or less linear extrapolations of the past into the future. He is right to identify the importance of so-called black swans, his metaphor for rare but highly impactful events that perturb trends. I disagree with him, however, on some points of emphasis. Based on my experiences of futuring for corporations around the world, I think Taleb underestimates the importance of trends and the continuities that they represent. In his own world of financial trading, a system with great volatility, Taleb may be spot on, but he may also be misleading managers who deal with market environments that are much more stable. His book might even discourage some managers from using any forecasts or plans for the future which might be interpreted as a suggestion to just rely on chance or the will of God. Taleb attributes too little importance to continuity and trends in many aspects of our lives, including a great deal of day-to-day business.

In addition, I think Taleb overplays the role of black swans in most cases. After all, as the name implies, black swans are very rare. While changes occur all the time, many of them are small and do not permanently change the continuities of systems or customs. Even catastrophic moments in American history, such as the Japanese attack on Pearl Harbor on December 7, 1941, and the Muslim terrorist attacks on New York City and Washington, DC, on September 11, 2001, as impactful as they certainly were, did not change *everything*. Yet, I give full credit to Taleb for emphasizing the central point that black swans do occur, that trends do not always describe the future as well as they do the past, and that we always must superimpose expert judgment on top of trend analysis when thinking about the inherent uncertainties of the future. In short, what makes Taleb angry is not so much expectations for the future, especially those that are well considered, but rather those that are poorly considered. What constitutes "well considered" expectations for managers who want to improve their foresight is very much the point of this book on futuring.

The importance of chance in the lives of people and nations is further explored in a second, similar book by physicist and mathematician Leonard Mlodinow. He argues that people generally overrate their ability to track cause-and-effect relationships that lead to predictable consequences; rather, they should appreciate more fully how lives are impacted by random events and luck. "Random events often look like nonrandom events," Mlodinow asserts in basic agreement with Taleb. "Though it has taken many centuries, scientists have learned to look beyond apparent order and recognize the hidden randomness in both nature and everyday life." Yet, he admits that randomness is not exactly the same as disorder in all circumstances. In some cases, social and economic trends reveal statistical patterns when individual behavior appears random. Even so, where patterns emerge the meaning of them may vary greatly due to subjective interpretation. He categorically rejects the concept of determinism, including historicism, in the popularized metaphor of time's arrow precisely because of unforeseeable changes.[15]

As a professionally educated historian and experienced futurist, I know plenty of examples of apparently random events that below the surface had a long build-up of trends and were not random at all. Randomness, like surprise, is a point of view based on what we know and don't know about history and current affairs before we think about the future. Using the Great Recession as a recent example, when the financial system teetered on the precipice of the bottomless money pit, the extent of years of financial risk (sub-prime home mortgages, derivatives, and hedge funds) was known to very few insiders at the time but can be reconstructed in retrospect to explain the events of September 2008.

One might incorrectly conclude from the works of Taleb and Mlodinow that business planning would be futile in the face of the randomness of the future. Each day we would just "go with the flow" or "fly by the seat of our pants." In our personal lives, we would not save for our children's college educations or invest for retirement. Yet neither Taleb nor Mlodinow go that far. "Plans fail because of what we have called tunneling, the neglect of sources of uncertainty outside the plan itself," Taleb observes. "We cannot truly plan, because we do not understand the future – but this is not necessarily bad news. We could plan *while bearing in mind such limitations*. It just takes guts."[16] Likewise, Mlodinow admits: "I believe it is important to plan, if we do so with our eyes open… We ought to identify and appreciate the good luck that we have and recognize the random events that contribute to our success."[17] In other words, we can make plans for the future but with the reservation that unforeseen conditions may force us to change them. There may be trends, but trends may be trumped by black swans. Therefore, we have to learn to deal with uncertainty. I can live with that.

Time as Both Continuity and Discontinuity

I take a middle position between the extreme propositions that a) time and history are all continuity, and because the future will be much if not exactly the same as the past, trend analysis and time-series projections will tell us much if not everything about the future, and b) time is all about change, ranging from extreme

---

15 Leonard Mlodinow, *The Drunkard's Walk. How Randomness Rules Our Lives*. New York: Pantheon Books, 2008; quote on p. 20; also see in particular his discussion of patterns and randomness on pp. 169-191; also see pp. 194-195.

16 Taleb, *The Black Swan*, quotes on pp. 156 and 157, respectively. Italics in the original.

17 Mlodinow, *The Drunkard's Walk*, p. 219.

to minor discontinuities, so the future cannot be predicted and planned for – that thinking about the future and planning are largely wasteful, even dangerous because they set up false expectations.

While I accept the extensive scientific evidence that time moves in only one direction, from the past to the present and on to the future, I cannot prove or disprove divine predestination by the tools of scientific inquiry. I also seriously question natural determinism and historicism. The metaphor of time's arrow is very descriptive in some respects, but deceptive when we assume that the arrow has a target. Time is linear, but whether or not the future is predestined, continuities in human affairs (at least over the past 7,000 years or so of civilization) have always existed and will always exist. We can study these continuities by calling them trends and applying the methods of trend analysis.

Historical trends tell us a lot about the past, but they are imperfect, although useful, indicators of the future. The past may or may not be prologue, but it certainly provides ample precedents. There are situations in which trend projections may be prescient:

- When we know all the variables in the system and they remain constant within certain tolerances.

- When we know the relationships among the variables and they remain relatively constant.

- When we have nearly complete and accurate time series data.

- When the time horizon for forecasting is reasonably short (maybe one to three years).

- When no black swans or other species of disruptive events arrive.

I see trends in economics, politics, social structures and relationships, and war as repeating patterns in human behavior.[18] As Shakespeare's Julius Caesar said to his future assassin, "Men at some time are masters of their fates: The fault, dear Brutus, is not in our stars, but in ourselves."[19] The things that men and women did in the past provide us with indications of what could happen in the future based on our understanding of historical behavioral patterns while recognizing that historical conditions provide the context for specific acts. Repeating behavior does not require the same act in the same way; it may only be an expression of something familiar in the past but fresh in its moment.

---

18   Stephen M. Millett, "Trend Analysis as Pattern Recognition," *World Future Review*, Volume 1, Number 4 (August-September 2009), pp. 5-16.

19   William Shakespeare, *Julius Caesar*, Act I, Scene 2, line 135.

Trends reflect the continuities of human behavior. Continuity does not mean "sameness" in the sense that nothing changes. Continuity implies a strong carry-over from one day to another, although every day is different in some regard (and certainly unique on the calendar). Trends do not imply homeostasis and trend lines can have any number of different angles and shapes rather than just being horizontally flat.

The sources of continuity and the trends that represent it include at least the following:

- Repeating patterns of human behavior (trends).
- Tradition, culture, and customs.
- Belief systems, worldviews, and mental models, both religious and secular.
- History and precedents.
- Routines and habits (both individual and institutional).
- Conventions, procedures, protocols, and processes (political, legal, social, commercial, industrial, etc.).
- Institutions, organizations, associations, and governments.
- Constitutions, laws, regulations, rules, policy, and treaties.
- Contracts, commitments, promises, and obligations.
- Legacies and inheritances from past generations.
- Buildings, physical assets, and infrastructure from the past.
- Codes of conduct, morality, and ethics.
- Memories of past experiences.
- Family relationships and ways.

Some trends are very strong with long periods of duration, while other trends are weak and subject to changes. Some trends are so strong that they absorb changes and continue more or less the same, while other trends are weak and may change suddenly and profoundly. One of the biggest challenges to the futurist is to identify the trend momentum that is justified by historical information and present data and to recognize which trends are strong and which are weak.

Earlier, I mentioned two historical events of great importance, historical black swans if there ever were any, but asserted that they did not change everything. Let us now briefly discuss those two dramatic moments in American history.

On the morning of Sunday, December 7, 1941, Japanese naval airplanes apparently coming out of nowhere flew over and extensively bombed American warships at dock and military targets on the ground at Pearl Harbor in Hawaii. The news of the Japanese attack came as a complete surprise to the American people, including the President and his administration. The conventional wisdom in Washington was that the Japanese theoretically could, but would never attempt to, attack Pearl Harbor. They worried more about a Japanese attack on the Philippines. On the morning of December 7, 1941, the Navy was totally in the dark about Japanese intentions to hit Pearl Harbor. After the event occurred, however, numerous investigations and histories reconstructed the trends and events that led up to Pearl Harbor. The Japanese airplanes that appeared to Americans to have come out of nowhere had actually come from Japanese aircraft carriers that had crossed the western Pacific and positioned themselves within striking distance of Honolulu, apparently undetected by American intelligence. What came as a complete surprise to the Americans was a carefully planned operation by the Japanese.

Another historical example of an apparent black swan, much like Pearl Harbor, was the Al Qaeda conspiracy to attack the two towers of the World Trade Center in New York City and targets in Washington, DC on the morning of September 11, 2001. Could the 9/11 attacks have been anticipated? In fact, to one degree or another, they had been. Several forecasts, including ones that I had worked on in 1985 and 1991 for both a defense company and for the Pentagon, had foreseen a general rise in terrorism across the world. We never discussed, however, even the possibility that acts of foreign terrorism could occur in our own country. Other forecasts later in the 1990s did speculate that there could be terrorist attacks upon the US itself, which many experts admitted was possible but thought very unlikely. It is alleged that some futurists even identified the likelihood of a terrorist attack using hijacked commercial airlines crashed into tall buildings. Nobody with access to high government authorities predicted the specific attacks of 9/11. We were completely surprised and entirely unprepared to deal with these sudden events. For virtually everybody, the terrorist attacks of 9/11 became the very definition of a black swan – that high consequence, low probability event that cannot be predicted.

So, the actual events of September 11, 2001 could theoretically have been foreseen. But only under very constrained conditions. We would have had to have known that Al Qaeda leadership in Afghanistan was planning a major attack directly on the US rather than just a continuation of bombings of American targets abroad. We would have had to have known about the Al Qaeda operatives inside the US. We would have had to have known that terrorists were taking pilot lessons and making elaborate plans for suicide missions. It was discovered that one apparent terrorist tried to take flying lessons, but only wanted to learn how to fly while in the air, with no interest in learning how to take off or how to land a plane. Yet, this information, which looks so critically important today in light of what did happen on 9/11, was dismissed at the time as merely curious.

As shocking and unexpected as the attacks of 9/11 were, in fact there were many trends and events leading up to the moment that could be reconstructed after the fact. Numerous government agencies and investigating journalists dug deeply into the origins of 9/11. While they could not document the moment or place when the decision was made by Al Qaeda to attack New York City and Washington, DC, investigators did find evidence of the entry of the conspirators into the US and their various preparations for the attacks. They could all be identified. A special commission was empowered by Congress (much like the Warren Commission formed after the Kennedy assassination) to conduct a thorough investigation and make recommendations for preventing such catastrophes in the future. It issued volumes of evidence. Historians will continue to study the records of 9/11, and they will likely uncover new details, but they will not likely find evidence to substantially revise the work of the 9/11 Commission.

I have two points to make from the historical examples given above. The first point is that the events seemed at the time to have come totally out of the blue with no antecedents, exactly like random events or black swans. They were shocking and seemed to have changed all that had come before them. Yet, in each case, when we knew what occurred, we could substantially reconstruct the trail of evidence that led up to the events. In the study of history, there will always be gaps in our knowledge of the past and there will be controversies about the evidence and the conclusions drawn from them, but historians can always find a trail leading up to events that occurred. No event has ever happened totally spontaneously without prior trends, although recognizing patterns is much easier looking backward than viewing forward. Like the medical analogies drawn by Juglar, the trends are the historical preconditions and the disease is caused by particular events within the context of preconditions.

As I will say several times in this book, surprise is often a point of view; one person's surprise may be another person's plan. I will also add that the shock of a black swan is most acute when it occurs, but fades with time. The ultimate black swan would be the long-awaited end of time and the world. People will adjust to adversity and move on with their lives; so, too, will whole societies.

Trends do exist. Past behavior, history, investments in buildings and infrastructure, institutions and organizations, and culture provide enduring legacies for the future. In addition, there are well-known cause-and-effect sequences of events in history like the sequences of entropy. One example is that a country may respond under certain conditions to a national insult by declaring war, much as an insulted individual might call for a duel as an act of honor. The insult may be mon just verbal: it may be a physical transgression, like an attack that calls counter-attack. It may be in many respects like the egg that falls from a kitchen countertop to the floor and breaks such that it can never be put back together again (so familiar to us in the story of Humpty Dumpty). Once the insult has been made, it is hard to retract and often leads to an over-reaction, even violence. Such sequences provide a basis for foresight, but alone they cannot help us anticipate the future with absolute certainty.

The second point is that highly unexpected, disruptive events certainly occur, too, in addition to trends. Dramatic disruptive events are rare, but many little and persistent changes occur all the time. Because of changes, trend analysis alone, especially when called "history" after the fact, is never sufficient to project what will happen in the future because trend analysis can only identify continuities and cannot possibly identify discontinuities. So, just as trends exist, black swans, and many less exotic birds, also exist. Thinking about the future with more rigor is likely to lead to more prescient expectations, but you have to consider both trends and possible changes.

In both historical case studies above, dramatic events occurred that caused great changes to known trends. Yet, just as no black swan occurs with no antecedents, no black swan changes history completely. Changes may be radical, but they do not wipe out all the trends and continuities of the past. The Japanese attack on Pearl Harbor, as shocking as it was, did not result in a long-term change in the naval hegemony of the US in the Pacific. Just six months after Pearl Harbor, American aircraft carriers and planes virtually terminated the temporary Japanese naval supremacy in the area. Oddly, the Japanese admirals thought that the future naval domination of the Pacific would be determined by battleships, which they targeted at Pearl Harbor. They used aircraft carriers to pull off their surprise attack and then they grossly underestimated the potential retaliatory attack of American aircraft carriers, which broke the back of Japanese naval power at the Battle of Midway. There was no Japanese invasion of the mainland US, as widely feared at the time, and the Japanese assault on Pearl Harbor did not result in the Japanese winning World War II. It could be argued with the knowledge of events that occurred after December 7, 1941, that the event of Pearl Harbor was more of a long-term black swan for Japan than for the US.

Likewise, as shocking and devastating as the 9/11 terrorist attacks of 2001 were, they did not cripple the American economy, as apparently the terrorists hoped that they would. They had no direct impact on long-term trends in American military power. Within months, the US launched a retaliatory attack on Al Qaeda and their

Taliban supporters in Afghanistan, which in turn led to the American invasion of Iraq in March 2003.

So trends count, but so, too, do changes.

Like the previous list of continuities, we can make a list of some potential sources of changes in the future:

- Challenges, threats, fear, and anxiety (both individual and institutional).
- Boredom and the longing for refreshing differences.
- Hunger, thirst, fatigue, and impatience.
- Acts of anger, violence, and revenge – including acts of terrorism and wars.
- Illness and death.
- Marriages and divorces.
- Pregnancies and births.
- Accidents and mistakes.
- Equipment failures.
- Loss of property, liberty, a job, or a loved one.
- Aging, decay, and erosion.
- Creativity, innovation, and inventions.
- New knowledge, exploration and discovery, and technology breakthroughs.
- Ups and downs of the economy.
- Corporate acquisitions and mergers.
- Reorganizations and switches of managers, bosses, and other types of personnel changes.
- Elections and new political directions.
- Weather conditions, including storms, and climate changes.
- Natural disasters.
- Genetic mutations.

A further examination of this topic leads us to the conclusion that there are at least three kinds of changes:

1. Those that are relatively minor variations on trends within a macro-structure (a long-term, stable paradigm or system).

2. Those that cause major changes in trends, even creating new trends coincident with previous trends, but within the same macro-structure.

3. Those that are relatively sudden and huge in their impacts, even shifting the boundary conditions of macro-structures (black swans).

People, whether they like it or not, adjust to changes all the time. Some changes are inconvenient and annoying, but people recover quickly to return to their normal habits and routines. Some changes are merely deviations from existing trends. But obviously some changes are monumental, even catastrophic, ending previous trends and beginning new ones. Monumental unexpected changes that do not fit previous patterns are called "outliers," "disruptive events," "wild cards," "game changers," "paradigm shifters," and "black swans." Given sufficient time and resources, people can adjust even to paradigm-shifting changes. The alternative may be death.

Although no future condition can be predicted with a 100%, *a priori*, probability of occurrence, Futuring Principle 1 comes about as close to absolute certainty as anything can be. It is theoretically possible that there might be no changes at all, so that the future could be all continuity. This outcome seems possible for very short time horizons, but very unlikely for extended lengths of time in the future. Although big changes are relatively rare, small changes are happening all the time. It is also theoretically possible that the future could evolve so that it contained no continuity and constituted absolute change. This would be something like the end of days, the collapse of the universe, and the termination of time.

While the future cannot be predicted with 100% certainty because of the possibility of changes, it can be anticipated with varying degrees of uncertainty because of long-term continuities, which we call "trends." However, there must always be some uncertainty even when the trend momentum may be strong. Although we cannot predict these changes, we can imagine what they might be and account for them in our expectations for the future. This observation links Futuring Principle 1 with Futuring Principle 2, which will be treated in the next chapter.

To conclude this discussion of my first principle of futuring that the future always has been and always will be an unknown combination of continuity and change, I would like to relate a case history of my own involving futuring as a decision-making tool for an American corporation.

A Case Study: Continuity and Change in the European Union

In 1987 an American company asked me to help them generate scenarios on the future of the European Union (EU). The firm was a global corporation that manufactured equipment and provided support services to retail stores and banks. They had completed a major transformation from electro-mechanical devices to computers, and they had repositioned themselves as a global leader in business-to-business information technologies (IT). The company had traditionally been strong in marketing, but faced a major challenge with customers in Western Europe. The challenge was the emergence of the EU, which had set for itself certain unification goals by 1992. The firm asked me to generate scenarios so that it could better understand how likely it was that the EU would achieve their goals and what the implications would be for business. The specific question addressed whether a cohesive EU would become a "Fortress Europe" with protectionist trade policies and whether the American-based company would have to invest billions of dollars in new plants within the EU.

I understood the company's need to make a major investment decision and how they would use the scenarios. We formed a project team and rapidly agreed upon a topic question to guide our work. We held several expert focus groups in the US and Europe to enable the most knowledgeable people to tell us what were the most important descriptors (trends, issues, factors, elements, or variables) for consideration in the scenarios. We performed extensive research on the descriptors and their relationships with each other in order to imagine alternative states (outcomes) for each descriptor by 1992, their apparent probabilities of occurrence, and their impacts upon each other as displayed in a cross-impact matrix. A personal computer (remember them before laptops?) with a scenario-generating software program performed calculations of probabilities using *a priori* (judgment) probabilities and cross-impact values, and generated a distribution of logically consistent but alternative outcomes (scenarios).

We learned from the scenarios that a Fortress Europe could emerge as a result of the EU achieving its 1992 goals, but that the circumstances for it were unlikely relative to other possible outcomes. The most likely scenarios showed a future in which the EU would achieve most, but not all, of its EU goals by 1992 and then continue working on further cohesion issues throughout the decade. The hardest issues for unification would be currency and banking. In international trade policy, the key issue would be reciprocity rather than protection. The implications drawn from the scenarios were that the company would not have to build more factories in Europe due to EU protectionism as long as the US and EU treated each other as equal partners in trade and investments. It was possible, but very unlikely given the strong "free trade" trends in American-European economic relations, that the

US would erect trade barriers against the EU or vice versa. On the other hand, Japanese corporations, because of Japanese trade policies concerning foreign imports into Japan, would likely have to invest heavily in manufacturing within Europe rather than risk a trade war between them and the Europeans.

My client company already had some manufacturing presence in Europe, and they decided to expand that base for a number of reasons, but not in fear of a future trade war between the US and the EU. The scenarios emphasized the emerging importance of post-market service, therefore the company would need to invest more heavily in service centers and networks rather than in factories. The client did so over the next decade and enjoyed growth in its European sales.

As the most likely scenarios foretold, the EU did achieve many, but not all of its cohesion goals in 1992. Currency and banking uniformity remained difficult to attain. The UK decided to keep its own currency, but most members of the EU transitioned to a common Euro. Banking unification was hard to achieve, but progress toward the goals was made step by step. Our scenarios had successfully framed well considered expectations in Europe for the client. The unification of the EU was a major game-changer in world economics, but the changes were planned, announced, and gradually implemented. Such changes proved not particularly disruptive to the long-term continuity of trade relations across the Atlantic.

However, some big disruptive events, definitely black swans, occurred most unexpectedly. To the amazement of the West, the Berlin Wall came down in November 1989, the Communist regime in East Germany collapsed, and German re-unification occurred in October 1990. It seemed unbelievable at the time that such stupendous changes could occur and virtually nobody predicted them. Even more startling was the collapse of the Communist Party of the Soviet Union and the dissolution of the USSR in 1990-1991. A new government in Moscow declared in favor of a Western-style democracy and a free enterprise economy. The Cold War was suddenly over!

My client in the US was closely following the news from Europe. They called me up on the telephone and asked how the end of the Cold War was going to change our scenarios on EU unification. In the original scenarios, we had a descriptor on Soviet-Western relations, and the prevailing state was the continuation of détente and generally more friendly relations in the future than in the past. A return to old Cold War tensions in Europe was not likely. We got that part right, but we completely failed to foresee the end of the Cold War altogether. Even if we had foreseen such a dramatic event, I wonder who would have believed us. The nice thing about having a cross-impact model from which to generate scenarios on a computer was that we could change any number of inputs and run new simulations based on new information. I went back to our scenario software program and entered the fall of the Soviet Union as a disruptive event and cross-impacted it upon the descriptors already in our model.

The scenario simulations led us to the conclusion that the headaches of EU unification would be increased by the prospect of EU expansion to include a new unified Germany and the former Communist countries of Eastern Europe that were desperate to realign their new market-driven economies with the West. We gained sufficient foresight to conclude that the EU unification goals were likely to prevail, but they would be slower to achieve with the new difficulties associated with folding the former Communist countries into the EU. The implications of the scenarios for the client did not change their business plans within the EU, but they encouraged the client to begin to explore new business opportunities in Eastern Europe and the new Russia.

I am often asked whether my forecasts have ever come true. The simple answer is "yes." A far more difficult question, however, is how to evaluate scenarios as alternative portraits of the future. When we do trend projections and time-series forecasts that produce a specific number, like the annual GDP rate, we can check what we said with what happened. I don't like doing that kind of forecasting, and on this score I agree with the strongly held views of Taleb. I don't believe that there can be only one future in the future, so I think in terms of alternative futures. I believe that trend analysis provides a knowledge base for understanding the future, but I recognize that trend analysis can capture only continuities, which are important but rarely a true representation of the future. You have to consider discontinuities, too. In this one case history, the baseline scenarios provided views of the future that emphasized the continuities and relatively minor deviations from them. The simulations of the baseline scenarios with hypothetical or real disruptive events gave us a more complete picture.

So, in this particular case history, like many others that I could share, the real question was whether the scenarios got the basic story right, provided a useful framework for setting expectations for the future, and gave managers sufficient foresight to make wise investment and business strategy decisions. The answer is still "yes." We were successful in sorting out the approximately correct mixture of continuity and change relative to the question asked by the client.

Like the client who initiated the scenario forecast of the EU, what questions should you be asking now about potentially stable or changing market conditions that would help you make wiser decisions in the present about investments, strategies, R&D, and personnel to achieve your corporate and organizational goals in the future?

My practical advice to you based on this chapter is to respect the trend lines of continuity but not to trust them blindly without also considering potential changes and their impacts. To what extent do you think the future of a market or customer base will likely stay the same or change, and, if it changes, how radically? Think in terms of alternative futures (scenarios) and not just end points on a graph.

Chapter 2. Anticipating the Future

Futuring Principle 2: The future can be anticipated with varying degrees of uncertainty depending upon conditions.

In Chapter 1, a review of science tells us that the arrow of time as a physical property in the universe moves in only one direction and that the future has not occurred yet because it follows the present in a sequential order of events. The sequence of events in time follows the Second Law of Thermodynamics, or entropy (the movement of molecules from higher to lower energy and levels of order). Although it is possible, we remain highly skeptical that the sequence of events in time follows a predetermined path toward an ideal goal, like the fixed target of time's arrow. Therefore, we cannot know the future with absolute certainty. These scientific observations, however, do not preclude us from thinking and speaking about the future in meaningful ways – they mean that we can recognize trends and use disciplined imagination to see the possibilities of the future. If the future cannot be predicted with certainty, it can be anticipated with uncertainty. This is the second principle of futuring.

The second principle states that all forecasts and plans for the future are not really predictions but rather expectations and they are conditional based on the circumstances at the time the forecasts and plans were generated and at the target date in the future. Any forecast or plan is a working hypothesis for the future, as it is with so many scientific experiments beyond the determinism of Newtonian mechanics (which are certain only within well known conditions), and should be expressed in terms of probabilities rather than absolute certainty.

Again, a look at science and its uncertainties helps us better understand the inherent uncertainties of the future and how we can more effectively manage them.

Uncertainty in Time and the Future

In 1926, a year before Eddington coined the term "the arrow of time" in the realm of cosmology, a German physicist made a startling discovery in the realm of quantum mechanics. Werner Heisenberg found that in his research into the world of the very small he could not detect at the same time both the position and the velocity of an electron, or for any other particle for that matter. His finding became the Heisenberg Uncertainty Principle. You can determine the position of a particle, but then you have to estimate with probabilities the momentum of the particle, and vice versa. In addition, the very act of investigation and measurement may interrupt the phenomenon so that it can never be known for certain in its theoretically natural state. Such a principle would have confounded Sir Isaac Newton and didn't do much to comfort Albert Einstein, either.

What could be more uncertain than the future? There's a popular proposition that nobody can predict the future. I agree if we define "predict" as knowing the future with absolute certainty as though we had already experienced it. Yet, there are some things that are so certain that we can predict them with more than 99% certainty – like the sun will rise tomorrow morning and set in the evening. Sometimes the momentum of trends and the cause-and-effect relationships are so compelling that we can anticipate things in the future with a very high probability. And then there are the more or less mundane things that we do every day. I can predict the things that I will do when I have the resources and the will to do them. I can make some plans and fulfill them. But, of course, what people want to predict are the very things that are most difficult to predict: daily ups and downs of the stock market, GDP growth, returns on investments, future happiness, etc. When we hear someone say "you can't predict the future," we should modify that statement by asking "predict what?" and "with what degree of certainty and why?"

While it is obviously true that each dawn brings a new day, it is also apparent that each new day brings with it a lot of baggage from previous days. Tomorrow would look very much the same as today if there were no changes occurring, and changes both great and small will happen if for no other reason than just the entropy of the Second Law of Thermodynamics.

I particularly object to the saying "you can't predict the future" when it is extended to also mean "...and so there is no point to thinking about, anticipating, or planning for the future." You most certainly can, and should, even for the most complicated things in the future. You may not be able to predict the future with precision, but, to use the Heisenberg metaphor, you can anticipate likely outcomes in the future with varying degrees of judgment probabilities. You can learn what has happened in the past (to the extent that evidence of the past exists today) and you can know where we are in the present, but you cannot know through our limited perceptual capabilities what will happen in the future with certainty. However, you can estimate.

Some 160 years prior to Heisenberg's discovery, the Royal Society of London published a paper on another kind of uncertainty. The paper had been written by the Rev. Thomas Bayes before he died in 1761. He developed an approach to calculating probabilities using prior (*a priori*) information (even if only expert judgment in place of data) as a starting point and new information to recalculate probabilities (*a posteriori*). The calculation of probabilities was a continuous learning process until the end state was achieved. Bayes more or less originated conditional probabilities, whereby potential events in the future could be estimated according to pre-existing conditions and information about them. Such was the beginning of Bayesian probabilities and information theory.[20]

What is unique about Bayes' approach is the consideration of the probability that a hypothesis or an expectation for the future might be useful even when based on incomplete data and possibly wrong ideas and expectations. Then new data force us to reconsider the probabilities. In Bayesian terms, the *a priori* probability is prior knowledge, judgment, or even a hunch and only a starting point for further calculations of continually adjusted *a posteriori* probabilities.

Many statisticians have objected to Bayesian calculations because they begin with subjective premises. But where else would you start when considering the future, for which nobody has data? If you used only historical (time series) data and no judgment about the future, you would merely capture the continuities of trends and totally miss the possibility of changes, as explained in Chapter 1.

A statistician from Italy shocked everyone in 1935 when he concluded that *all* probabilities are subjective, and he proved it mathematically. Bruno de Finetti used the term "exchangeability" to express the thought that people generally expect the future to be much like the present, so they use (exchange) past data as a substitute for future data. In addition, he identified examples of subjective decisions made by statisticians in picking variables and methods to use. He urged statisticians to admit their biases openly so that they could be reviewed and scrutinized: "…when one pretends to *eliminate* the subjective factors one succeeds only in *hiding* them…but never in avoiding a gap in logic."[21]

An attractive aspect of the Bayesian approach to futuring is that it allows us to get away from trying to predict a single future, as though it were inevitable. If we cannot be 100% certain about a particular outcome in the future, then we can think of alternative outcomes each with its own *a priori* probability. Thinking of the future as alternative outcomes, with varying degrees of uncertainty, allows us more flexibility and subtlety in our decision-making today and more adaptability to unknown but possible changes in the future.

---

20   Leonard Mlodinow, *The Drunkards's Walk. How Randomness Rules Our Lives.* New York: Pantheon Books, 2008, pp. 104-123; David Malakoff, "Bayes Offers a 'New' Way to Make Sense of Numbers," *Science,* Vol. 286, 19 November 1999, pp. 1460-1464; and Sharon Bertsch McGrayne, *The Theory That Would Not Die.* New Haven: CT: Yale University Press, 2011.

21   Bruno de Finetti, "Foresight: Its Logical Laws, Its Subjective Sources," *Annales de I'Institut Henri Poincaré'*, Vol. 7 (1937), reprinted in Henry E. Kyburg, Jr., and Howard E. Smokler, eds., *Studies in Subjective Probability.* New York: John Wiley & Sons, Inc., 1964, pp. 93-158; quote on p. 147.

Another advantage of the Bayesian approach to futuring is that we can build a model of our expectations for the future and simulate different outcomes by adjusting *a priori* probabilities. The models can be both quantitative and qualitative, digital and analog. With a model, we can do simulations to see what conditions will likely produce what results in the future. This is not the same thing as saying that the future will be as I want it to be; it is saying that I can reasonably expect desired outcomes by identifying what sets of conditions would most likely produce them. Now I have a tool for making strategy (affecting conditions) to fulfill goals (outcomes) with more certainty than just wishful thinking. This is as close as we can get to empirically knowing the future.

My experience has taught me that all forecasts, whether qualitative or quantitative, whether single point or multiple outcome (scenario) forecasts, are expectations for – and not predictions of – the future. Well considered or not, all forecasts are predicated upon implicit assumptions or explicit expectations of future sets of conditions. Following the advice of de Finetti, we have to make the underlying assumptions and expected sets of conditions for the future as open as we can and subject them to peer review.

We make forecasts in the present, so there is no way that we can know for sure whether they are prescient or not until events unfold in the future; but I know what I can and cannot successfully defend before the skeptical minds of CEOs who have to make major decisions today that will not likely pay off for years to come.

When we are generating forecasts and plans for the future, we are highly influenced by the problems of the present. In many cases, forecasts do a better job of describing the conditions of the present than of the future. I will elaborate on this point further in Chapter 4 in a discussion of the Recency Effect, which is one of the major reasons why forecasts and plans fail. A huge challenge of futuring and visioning is to foresee a combination of continuity and changes (Futuring Principle 1) that make up a set of conditions in the future in which any outcome is expected. Every forecast and plan is dependent upon the economic, business, political, social, demographic, technological, ecological, weather, and whatever, conditions that will likely exist in the future.

Forecasts, as the product of the process of futuring, take at least two forms. One is an expectation for a certain outcome in the future. Every forecast, whether a number or a description, must provide explicit conditions to explain how and why. Then we can monitor those conditions and we can change the forecast as conditions change. This is futuring as learning. The second is to identify the conditions of the future and to draw inferences about what outcomes we should expect to see given those conditions. Because the past and present are not perfect predictors of the future, we have to attach *a priori* probabilities to both the conditions and the outcomes associated with them. Some trends and expected conditions for the future may seem very likely, but never with an *a priori* probability of 100% as though variables were parameters. Other trends and expected conditions are very uncertain, volatile, and highly speculative due to an acknowledged lack of information, and they should be so identified with low *a priori* probabilities of occurrence.

I am frequently asked by clients and friends to express my expectations about the future on the fly. I am always tempted to just give them a quick answer without boring them with the various conditions and caveats. But when I have the time and energy, I will state my expectations for future conditions and then give a qualitative forecast based on them. I also try to give not just one but alternative outcomes, wrapped in different sets of conditions (scenarios) for the future. After all, I am not a clairvoyant or corporate fortune teller. I should always say, "It depends upon circumstances. If the Dow Jones Industrial Average rises so that people have new confidence in their investments and their retirement funds… if the unemployment rate goes down… if companies offer consumers exciting new products… if consumer confidence is restored…, then…"

Theoretical Sources of Predictability

Upon what grounds could we ever claim prescience for our expectations, let alone predictability, of future conditions and outcomes? If we cannot rely solely upon trend extrapolations for our expectations for the future, what should we rely upon? I want to now explore various theoretical sources of predictability, but with the understanding that even if the abstractions were valid, the practice of them could never achieve 100% certainty due to errors, chance, and so-called black swans. As you will see, there is a range of predictability from low to high among these potential sources. Each has its own limitations, meaning that we can talk about but rarely achieve consistently accurate predictions. Some of them, however, explain why we can anticipate likely and potential futures by using the best practices of futuring and visioning.

Revelation and Divination
These are the most problematic and the least reliable of all possible origins for predictability. In Chapter 1, I briefly mentioned religious beliefs in predestination in the context of time being linear and having a destination. Predestination also suggests certainty in the future, as time itself and human activities through history have been planned and managed by God. If the future were predestined, then predictability would approach absolute certainty if we only knew what the will

of God was and could correctly identify his revelation of it. We cannot know predestination directly, but only indirectly through scripture, teachings, and the belief in signs. But this approach is based on faith, not facts. It is religion, not science and it cannot be validated by the methods of empiricism.

A prevalent tenet of faith shared among Judaism, Christianity, and Islam is that God reveals his plans for the future to selected messengers through the medium of dreams and signs. A well-known example is the story of the ancient Hebrew slave Joseph, who interpreted the dream of the Egyptian Pharaoh that predicted a forthcoming seven-year famine. Because Joseph correctly interpreted the dream, the Pharaoh was warned and consequently prepared for the inevitable famine. Another famous story tells of Daniel, who read the divine writing on the wall predicting the fall of the Babylonian empire. Arguably the most famous of divine revelations is the Book of Revelation at the end of the New Testament. It predicts in highly allegorical and symbolic language, which is subject to many possible interpretations, a sequence of terrible events culminating in the Last Judgment and the end of the world as we have known it.

For thousands of years, people have believed that their strange dreams had meanings. Some people in the 21st century, for all of our alleged sophistication, still think that the future can be revealed to them in dreams. Dr. Sigmund Freud, however, gave the significance of dreams a whole new interpretation: they may reveal our anxieties and wishes for the future, but they cannot predict events beyond our own mental and physical powers. If a dream about the future were to come true, then it is because we believe and act upon it ourselves.

Astrology is one of the oldest forms of fortune telling, a secular and occult approach to revelation, or divination. It was held in the highest regard in Babylon. The belief was that the position and alignment of the stars in the heavens reflected an order that foretold the fate of humans in the future. People have been looking to the stars since ancient times for guidance as to what they must do. Daily horoscopes remain popular reading in newspapers around the world, although no scientific evidence has ever proven their efficacy. In addition to astrology, there are the occult methods of predicting the future from cards, hands, tea leaves, animal entrails (yuck!), omens, and other mysterious media. What they all have in common is the presumption of fate that has already been set for the future.

If divine predestination or non-religious fate were to exist, then reading their signs might provide a very powerful futuring method. But the supernatural approaches to anticipating the future have been long abandoned, although popular remnants continue. To paraphrase Shakespeare's Julius Caesar, human behavior rather than the stars determines our destiny. I respect religious beliefs in predestination and concede that they *might* be right, but if you presented a forecast based on faith who would believe you? I do not recommend pursuing religious signs for the future. Nor the signs of the occult. While I am fascinated with horoscopes, Tarot cards, palm readings, and omens, I enjoy them as forms of entertainment, not scientific inquiry. You may also enjoy them, but I wouldn't recommend taking them seriously for the purposes of either forecasting or planning.

Laws of Nature

The secular version of divine predestination is natural determinism, commonly called the "laws of nature" or the "laws of physics." As discussed briefly in Chapter 1, Newton revolutionized natural philosophy, or what we call science, with the publication in 1687 of his monumental work *Principia*. He identified consistent forces of nature, such as inertia, momentum, and gravity, although he could not explain what caused gravity. Newtonian mechanics work; they are highly predictive of specific cause-and-effect relationships within specified boundary conditions. Since Newton, scientists have continued to pursue the laws of nature in all branches of science. So, too, have philosophers, economists, sociologists, and historians. If the affairs of people were driven by forces like Newtonian mechanics, then we could predict future economic booms and busts, revolutions and wars, and social upheavals.

In 1935, the philosopher Karl Popper published *The Logic of Scientific Discovery*. He argued that no scientific theory can be proven to be absolutely correct under all conditions; it can only be proven provisionally correct (consistent with observations and data) pending further information and experiments. In this line of reasoning, Popper extended the observation made by the Scottish Enlightenment philosopher David Hume about two hundred years earlier that just because something has been true in the past does not mean that it has to be always true in the future. Popper further asserted that a scientific theory, although never absolutely verified, can be absolutely nullified by future discoveries. When we are right, we are only provisionally right, but when we are wrong we are totally wrong. Of course, some phenomena are so common that exceptions would be extremely rare, but we can never be 100% confident of much of what we think we know for certain, especially about the future.[22]

The physicist Niels Bohr, a contemporary of Einstein and Heisenberg, allegedly said something to the effect that it is hard to make predictions, especially about the future. At first blush, this remark sounds witty, like an oxymoron (which is why the same quote has also been attributed to famous baseball sage Yogi Berra). But at a deeper level, to give Bohr his due, the remark may draw a distinction

---

22 Karl Popper, *The Logic of Scientific Discovery*. London: Routledge Classics, 2002; David Hume, *A Treatise of Human Nature*. Edited by Ernest C. Mossner. London: Penguin Classics, 1985.

between anticipating well established and uniformly consistent behavior of phenomena such as Newtonian mechanics on Earth's surface as opposed to predicting "the future," especially of people. Bohr knew well that even the most common principles of science, even with all the uncertainties of science, did not apply also to the vastly complicated realm of human behavior in economics, politics, love, and war.

There is no doubt that humans live within the conditions of a material environment (the planet Earth) and must continuously adjust to the so-called laws of nature – physical, chemical, geological, and biological. We are subject to gravity, momentum, and entropy just like all living and inanimate objects. When designing desirable systems or making plans for the future in the context of visioning, we cannot willfully violate the laws of physics. As the popular saying goes, "keep it real." In the context of futuring, the laws of nature provide plenty of room for disciplined imagination: if something has happened in the past, then it can happen again, and if something is physically possible within the laws of nature, even if it has never happened before, then it could happen in the future.

Trend Momentum
As previously discussed in the first futuring principle, there may be continuities, or trends, that are so well established and carry so much historical inertia (a metaphor) that they provide the basis for anticipating the future. This is the commonly held idea that tomorrow will be much like today because today is so similar to the day before. It is also the idea that the past and present, to one degree or another, shape the future – and that the future will be a reflection of the past. The past and present have much to tell us about the future, and the future will tell us much about the past. To use a simile from Newtonian mechanics, some cultural and social trends are so deeply rooted in tradition and habit, the structure of human activities, that they are like a force (F=ma) propelling people knowingly or unknowingly into the future. Trend momentum, of course, can be changed, but only with considerable new sources of energy.

Trends are the stuff of continuity across time. This present discussion of trend momentum is a continuation of the earlier treatment of continuity in Chapter 1. It focuses on trends as a source of predictability – why trends tell us things, but not everything, about tomorrow. I will cover the concept of trends as pattern recognition and say something about the mechanics of trend analysis in Chapter 3.

The 19th century transcendentalist Henry David Thoreau observed that every day he took the same route between his cabin and Walden Pond. His steps wore a path through the grass and underbrush. From this very simple, everyday experience he extrapolated a generalization about all human activities: "The surface of the earth is soft and impressible by the feet of men; and so with the paths which the mind travels. How worn and dusty, then, must be the highways of the world, how deep the ruts of tradition and conformity!"[23]

Trends are historically stable patterns of social behavior (culture, traditions, customs, rituals, religious beliefs and churches, social institutions, political systems, economic systems, etc.) and life-long patterns of individual behavior (habits, biases, education, jobs, experiences, past decisions, etc.). History may or may not be prologue, but it does provide enduring precedents for the future. The culture of an organization, institution, or corporation can have as conforming an influence as any other "highway of the world." Another source of trend momentum may be the investments of the past. Large investments in infrastructure, buildings, and plants provide a momentum of their own. Just think of the legacy of the buildings that we use today, some of them dating back centuries. And then there are the physical structures that have lasted thousands of years, such as the pyramids of ancient Egypt. In our own times, so as to not "under-leverage assets," corporations as well as governments tend to keep using facilities much longer than was anticipated at the time of their construction.

In our day-to-day language, we often hear people talk about "the wave of the future," which is an allusion to perceived trend momentum. Likewise, business people are referring to trend momentum when they talk about economic, technological, and market "trajectories." We understand trend momentum through trend analysis, or the continuities that will in part account for what happens in the future.

The analysis of trends and their momentum will likely remain the single most popular futuring method. Trend analysis can provide well considered expectations for the future based on historical experience and observed patterns in human behavior, but it will not provide flawless predictions of the future. The practitioner must recognize both the advantages and drawbacks of trend analysis. The drawbacks include the temptation to assume that the future will be very much like the past and the present; but we know from prior experience that changes of all types and magnitudes can happen and change trends. We discussed this matter in Chapter 1. Trend analysis can capture only continuities, and it cannot by its very nature show the discontinuities of the future. Hence, we see every day in business an uncritical reliance on linear projections and historical time-series methods, including the ever popular regression analysis, for sales and profit forecasts.

---

23 Henry David Thoreau, *Walden and Other Writings*. Edited by Brooks Atkinson. New York: The Modern Library, 2000, p. 303.

Trend analysis and time-series projections can provide remarkably predictive forecasts of the future under certain circumstances, such as when:

- Historical trend information and present data are virtually complete and error-free.

- The most important trends have been identified and included in the analysis – no important trends have been omitted and no minor or redundant trends have been included.

- Trend relationships and interactions are known and constant for the time horizon of the forecast.

- No disruptive events, "wild cards," or black swans occur.

- The time-frame of the forecast is relatively short-term, thereby minimizing if not eliminating the potential for variability, which is uncertainty, or what the financial sector calls "risk."

Conversely, trend analysis, when taken too literally and quantitatively (as opposed to using similes, metaphors and analogies), is not so effective under other conditions, including when:

- Historical trend information and present data are incomplete and error-prone.

- The most important trends are not included in the analysis.

- Redundancy of variables (issues, trends, etc.) in models or formulas skews the forecast.

- Trend relationships and interactions are not well understood or shift over time.

- Disruptive events, "wild cards," or black swans occur.

- The time frame is relatively long-term, allowing more opportunities for variability, uncertainty, and risk.

When the appropriate situations for applying trend analysis and time-series projections, including various statistical methods like regression analysis and mathematical modeling like econometrics are known, many short-term projections turn out to be correct (within a margin of error) and many plans are successfully fulfilled. Conversely, when the appropriate situations for forecasting methods and tools are not known at the time the prediction is made, most long-term projections and plans turn out to be wrong, even wide of the mark. The best that you can do when making long-term forecasts, which are useful for making decisions today about investments with long-term returns, is to provide alternative futures accompanied by specified conditions and probabilities of their occurrence to form well considered expectations for the future and to monitor them continuously and revise the forecasts with new information as time passes.

Organizations and people display trends as well as societies and countries. Within the context of a certain social structure, or paradigm, you will see evidence of prevailing cultural patterns, social norms of behavior, operational procedures, routines, and habits. Social structures limit the range of variability in everyday behavior. Some organizations and people are highly predictable, because they repeat the same patterns of behavior in certain circumstances over time. We know from observation that some companies are very flexible when faced with new opportunities while others are not. We also know from experience that some people are quick to panic while others remain remarkably cool under stress. Some people will speak out, while others remain silent. We all have met those rare individuals who appear to be completely unpredictable, which is itself a predictable state (we learn to expect the unexpected). We learn what to expect from the people whom we know best. Yet, even they surprise us from time to time. Like all other trends, organizational and individual behaviors may change over time (and at different ages and life stages) and circumstances may vary. We can never assume behavioral consistency over time with 100% certainty.

I have seen many examples of what I call the opportunity cost of success: because a company had a product or process that worked well in the past, they are highly reluctant to change it. I have frequently heard the expression, "If it isn't broken, don't try to fix it!" This may be true in some cases, but too often a company will stick with a product or process too long and not realize that it is broken relative to changing customer preferences, market conditions, and competitors.

Trend momentum analysis, or just "trend analysis," will likely remain the single most popular futuring method. The futuring manager, however, must know when and how to justifiably use trend analysis rather than just carelessly interpreting trends as simple linear projections of the past to the future.

Cause-and-Effect Relationships and Sequences

As mentioned previously, the 18th century philosopher David Hume warned us that we too often jump to conclusions that may be wrong about effects attributed to causes. Too often things that we witness may appear related but are really only coincidental. We may grow used to certain cause-and-effect relationships and assume that such relationships will always exist in the future because we are accustomed to them in the past. When we assume cause-and-effect relationships, we form expectations for the future, but those expectations may or may not be logically justified. We may see patterns when no patterns can be materially validated and we may attribute causes, or human motivations, when none can be shown to exist. Countless psychological experiments over the last century have validated Hume's observation as a valid observation of typically human perception.[24]

People draw everyday conclusions from assumed cause-and-effect relationships. The ways of "everyday logic," however, may be neither logical nor correct. People make perceptual errors all the time. Causality can be purely coincidental, even accidental. Statistical correlations may appear as causality, but they may be totally unrelated in substance and only appear related within a time frame. Correlations may demonstrate relationships, but not necessarily cause-and-effect phenomena.

However, to recognize Hume's caution does not invalidate the scientific observation that cause-and-effect sequences exist in nature and that we can perceive them accurately when we apply an informed and logical override to our snap judgments. Cause-and-effect relationships have been well established in modern science since Galileo dropped objects from the Tower of Pisa. Newton's laws of physics are based on consistent cause-and-effect relationships within a specified frame of reference. Although philosophers and psychologists have commented on the numerous mistakes that people frequently make in assigning erroneous causes to events, scientific studies have validated that people can accurately perceive and anticipate correctly results coming from demonstrated, not just assumed, causes. The laws of nature are based upon consistent and long-term physical cause-and-effect relationships. If this were not the case, then there would be no foundation for modern physics, chemistry, engineering, dentistry, and medicine.

I have seen some very perceptive people with strong observational skills demonstrate a remarkable ability to anticipate (at least approximately, if not exactly) what others will do or say based on repetitive experiences. The great ice hockey player Wayne Gretzky is frequently quoted as having said that he did not skate to where the puck was but to where he anticipated it would be. He

---

24 Hume, *A Treatise of Human Nature,* especially pp. 188-193, 197-199. Also see Steven Pinker, *The Stuff of Thought. Language As A Window Into Human Nature.* New York: Viking, 2007, pp. 153-158, 210-216; Daniel Gilbert, *Stumbling on Happiness.* New York: Vintage Books, 2006, pp. 98-104, 108-119, 147-161, and-204-210; Philip Zimbardo and John Boyd, *The Time Paradox.* New York: Free Press, 2008, pp. 73-98. It should be noted that Hume emphasized heavily the role of experience in learning and he tended to dismiss the concept of innate knowledge, as either a gift of God or as a result of biological evolution of the human species. Hume may be counted as an opponent of determinism and as a champion of the concept of randomness in our lives.

developed an exceptional ability to read the game on the ice, anticipating both the position of the puck and other players to help him score time after time. There are equally talented athletes in football, soccer, baseball, basketball, and golf who can consistently guess correctly where the ball is going to go and what the next play will be. Great pool players also know how to run the table because they line up a succession of shots. They know how to anticipate where every ball will be on the table and at what time and in what sequence. They develop what we call a keen intuition, almost a "second sight" or "sixth sense." But what they actually have developed is an extraordinary foresight based on very extensive experience of cause-and-effect relationships, within the boundary conditions of the game's rules.

One area in which the state of the art of forecasting has greatly advanced due to technologies and discovered cause-and-effect relationships is weather forecasting. Mark Twain allegedly quipped that everybody complained about the weather but nobody did anything about it. In truth, meteorologists have significantly improved their ability to predict changing weather conditions, although they still cannot control them. During the 19th century, weather forecasters relied on visual observations of clouds, winds, sun, and rain; they added to time-tested visual methods the accurate measurements of temperature, wind speeds, and barometric pressures. They learned about the effects of low and high pressure cells and the movement of weather fronts, typically from west to east in the US. Then in the second half of the 20th century, meteorologists discovered the direct impacts of sun spots and the jet stream on weather conditions near the surface of the earth. High-altitude airplanes and orbiting satellites provided a wealth of information that had not been accessible in the past. Meanwhile, computers provided the ability to construct mathematical models and perform simulations of different weather patterns. While the accuracy of weather forecasts has greatly improved over the last 50 years, to say nothing of the last 100 years, it is still not always perfect. Wind currents can be very unstable and weather conditions can change rapidly, doing unpredictable things. Particularly problematic is the prediction of how great storms will play out.

In addition to forecasting the weather, science and technology have greatly improved our ability to predict failures in industrial machinery and manufacturing processes. Computerized diagnostics are run to check known indicators of potential process deviations and failure. These indicators include (parallel to weather forecasting) temperature, pressure, viscosity, and other operational parameters. We have moved from simple mechanical diagnostics in automobile and airplane gauges to very complex, computerized data collection, modeling, and sequential pattern recognition in very expensive off-the-road vehicles and manufacturing processes. Likewise, physicians rely on the leading signs, or indicators, of potential future health problems, ranging from rather indirect causes like weight and blood pressure to such sophisticated diagnostics as biopsies, MRIs, and CAT Scans. Health care providers are well aware that diseases and disorders take certain patterns and they test for indicators of those patterns, knowing full well the potential mistakes of false positives and false negatives. All of these examples of indicators are based on our expanding knowledge of well documented cause-and-effect relationships. They have greatly improved our ability to detect and predict future problems, but variations and inconsistencies still remain that defy every-time consistency and 100% reliable predictions.

Another aspect of this discussion is the matter of direct versus indirect cause-and-effect relationships. Particularly in modeling, one can confuse direct and indirect impacts. An example of a direct relationship would be trend or element A influences B, which in turn influences C. The direct cause-and-effect relationship is A on B and B on C. The indirect relationship is A on C. Many models require just primary relationships, both impacts and feedbacks, and rely on an algorithm (literally or figuratively) to sort out the secondary and tertiary impacts. Other models may try to explicitly calculate all the relationships, both direct and indirect. An inherent problem, however, is building redundancy into the model. If you model both A on B and A on C as direct cause-and-effect relationships, then you may be exaggerating the impacts of A and underestimating the impacts of B. My experience is that simple, elegant models are more reliable representations of phenomena than very complex models, which run the risk of including too many variables and calculating too many redundancies. Having said this, the building of simple, elegant models that represent the phenomena, which are dynamic rather than static over time, is a very difficult thing to do.

Intuitively visualizing long chains of cause-and-effect relationships is very difficult, if not impossible, to do. Constructing a hypothetical sequence of events leading to a logically consistent result in the future is one definition of the term "scenario" (as opposed to another definition, which is a description of a set of conditions that will plausibly exist by a certain time in the future). Such a sequence of cause-and-effect events is easier to describe than to quantify, although scenario paths and trees and real option analysis can be quantified, at least with judgment probabilities.

It is much easier, and more theoretically sound, in most cases to forecast future conditions as the likely culmination of multiple trends interacting with each other than it is to predict specific events by specified times in the future. The "if... then" proposition can be a type of cause-and-effect relationship. Rather than my telling you what I think will likely happen in the future (and leaving my thinking processes to myself), I should tell you what conditions I think will come to pass and discuss likely outcomes in the context of expected conditions in the future. I should do this with an explanation of what will impact upon what and where the feedback loops are.

My experience has been that it is more valid to interpolate trends hypothetically from a future set of conditions (scenarios) back to the present than it is to project the present to future states. The more popular approach is to project trends forward using the linear momentum of history and current conditions. As we have seen, linear projections can be prescient in some cases (boundary conditions) and can be widely off the mark due to the occurrence of changes (and even mistakes and lack of correct information in the process of making linear projections). The approach that has worked best for me is to begin with generating the scenarios of alternative future states and then work backwards to fill in the gap between the future and the present with hypothetical paths. These paths can provide the basis for strategic plans to reach desired future outcomes (with futuring merging with visioning).

Interpreting leading indicators (such as the inflation rate, unemployment rate, the GDP growth rate, etc.) is like reading the signs of ancient prophecy or fortune telling. One interpretation of the validity of leading indicators is based upon trend momentum. Another interpretation is that leading indicators are states in well-known and high probability cause-and-effect relationships. The logic of the leading indicators is "if x happens, then y will surely follow." This proposition may be based on excellent past evidence or it may be an intuitive hunch, but it must be made explicit and subject to peer review and future validation.

While understanding and documenting cause-and-effect relationships, especially in human affairs, can rarely if ever be achieved with 100% predictability, it remains along with trend momentum one of the best approaches we have to anticipate the future from the past and present.

Closed Systems and Fixed Sets
In a closed system, we know all of the variables and their relationships, which remain stable because they are insulated from outside influences. A fixed set, or a finite area (also called "boundary conditions"), of objects or data is virtually the same as a closed system. In many forecasts, we see assumptions used as boundary conditions. Both closed systems and fixed sets can be highly predictable. A common example is a deck of cards, which numbers 52 cards of known values. As cards are played, and played only once per hand or game, then you can calculate what cards remain to be seen. Solving card probabilities, like billiard chances, is another excellent application for Bayes' theorem, which is exactly why casinos forbid card counting by players. When systems are closed and when sets are finite,

you can predict future performance, which is why many mathematical models make correct predictions. Relatively small numbers of variables, constancy of relationships among them, the lack of externally influenced changes, and relatively short time horizons will lead to high levels of predictability.

It might also be noted that completely closed systems, in nature and in human affairs, are rare. Most remain vulnerable to outside influences. Semi-closed systems, however, are historically common due to factors like geographical isolation, stable social and economic sub-systems, and the lack of invading predators. Any system that experiences a consistently repeating pattern of regular inputs, processes, outputs, and feedback, although not strictly "closed," resembles a closed system and may be predictable with high degrees of certainty. Truly open systems, on the other hand, with many and often changing variables, dynamic rather than constant relationships among the variables, irregular inputs and outputs, and with exposure to periodic shocks from the outside, are virtually unpredictable due to a broad range of variability in performance.

Another way of looking at closed systems and finite sets is to use the framework of social structures, which are effective boundary conditions. Culture determines what behaviors are socially acceptable and what behaviors are not. The restraints of a cultural paradigm, reinforced by customs and laws, limit the total range of behavior and channel it in ways that are predictable to a certain extent. Rules and laws are meant to limit potential human actions, but people do in certain circumstances break them and sometimes even get away with it. By and large, however, culture provides a structure that qualifies, to one extent or another, as a closed system or finite set, thereby providing patterns with some predictability. In fact, the French historian Fernand Braudel subtitled his masterpiece on cultural structures of everyday life in Europe from the 15th to the 18th centuries "The Limits of the Possible."[25]

In theoretical terms, a totalitarian state would be a nearly closed social system. The government would be dominated by an elite, or what the ancient Greeks might call an oligopoly with a monopoly of power. They would highly restrict the flow of information so that they would know just about everything and everybody else would know just about nothing. There would be little or no transparency to government. Elections, if held at all, would be fixed. Freedoms of speech and press would be highly circumscribed. People who spoke out against the regime

---

25 Fernand Braudel, *The Structures of Everyday Life. The Limits of the Possible*. Volume I, *Civilization & Capitalism 15th-18th Century*. Translated from the French and Revised by Sian Reynolds. Berkeley, CA: University of California Press, 1992 (1979). For a psychoanalytic interpretation of how civilization restricts and frustrates natural human behavior, see Sigmund Freud, *Civilization and Its Discontents*. Translated and edited by James Strachey. New York: Norton, 1961 (1930).

would be arrested, typically in the middle of the night, and taken to jail, a penal colony, or an isolated work camp. People would live routinely in fear. The ruling elite might hold periodic purges of its own members just to keep up the authority of the one great ruler.

It appears that the more highly structured and restrictive a socio-economic or political paradigm is, the more predictable the patterns of behavior are likely to be. We have seen regimes in history that were highly regimented. People were punished for certain types of behavior, such as speaking out in criticism of the government, which strongly inhibited what people felt free to do. They naturally avoided the potential threats of wrong behavior and adapted to correct modes of living that made their individual as well as social behaviors less random and more predictable. Cultures, societies, and whole civilizations can be viewed as a spectrum of closed vs. open systems and therefore predicable vs. random behaviors. I must quickly qualify this statement by reminding you that very few if any systems are totally closed, although some can be extensively closed, and there may be some very open systems.[26]

You might also consider the typical bell-shaped distribution curve of statistics as a type of structure. Statisticians are quick to array masses of data into two-dimensional graph shapes that are characteristic of fitting the data to a known pattern.

Stephen Jay Gould, the Harvard paleontologist and popular writer on evolution, wrote a book called *Full House* that was published in 1996. The title is a metaphor for a closed system. The subtitle read *The Spread of Excellence from Plato to Darwin*. His central thesis was that the spread of complexity and excellence is not linear and it cannot objectively be called "progress." In addition, the story of evolution is captured in its entire record, not just in its most advanced state. The spread also has a limit, which he calls the "right wall", as an allusion to the right boundary of a two-dimensional graph. Gould, who popularized the concept of punctuated equilibrium, characterized evolution as a process of long periods of stability with short intervals of great disruption, at which a surviving species might branch out in several evolutionary directions. What we see alive today are the descendents of the survivors; what we find in fossils are the remains of the victims. Gould denounced the metaphor of evolution as any kind of directional

---

26 Professor Harold Lasswell developed the model for the garrison-police state during the early Cold War. By identifying consistent characteristics of a highly structured political order, he was able to anticipate logically consistent modes of behavior. See Harold D. Lasswell, *National Security and Individual Freedom*. New York: McGraw-Hill, 1950, especially pp. 21-49. In the same vein, the argument for a highly tolerant and open system can be found in Karl R. Popper, *The Open Society and Its Enemies*. Princeton, NJ: Princeton University Press, 1950.

progress. In all living systems, he argued, there are theoretical limits to growth, complexity, and excellence – they will eventually hit the right wall.[27]

While Gould may have been very perceptive in the realm of biological evolution, the application of this theory to social systems must be circumscribed. Human systems tend to be extremely complex with many interacting variables, delayed feedback loops, and changing relationships. When we experience periodic crises, such as a war or a recession, how do we know at the time whether we have hit the right wall or not? Maybe we have hit a plateau or the maturation of an era and we are transitioning to another era? When is the system really closed, or when is the "house" really full? Maybe we fill up one house and then move on to another. Social systems appear to grow and survive with much more agility than some biological organisms.

Systems analysis became very popular as a field of study in American universities after World War II. There are several varieties of this discipline. One originated at the Massachusetts Institute of Technology. Having worked extensively on problems of feedback in the control of electronic systems for the military, Jay Forrester in 1956 transferred to the Sloan School of Management at MIT. He applied concepts of electronic systems design and control to industrial and then broader social systems. He called his approach "system dynamics." Forrester demonstrated that the modeling and simulation that came with systems could provide prescient forecasts for the future. One of his most celebrated colleagues was Donella Meadows, who gained fame with the first Club of Rome gloomy forecast of global economics and subsequent updates called *Limits to Growth*. She defined a system as "a set of things – people, cells, molecules, or whatever – interconnected in such a way that they produce their own pattern of behavior over time… The system, to a large extent, causes its own behavior!" The most famous recent MIT champion of systems analysis for solving business problems has been Peter Senge, the author of the extremely successful book,*The Fifth Discipline*.[28]

A system in its basic sense is a relationship among inputs, processes, outputs, and feedback. Its first academic applications emerged from the field of biology before World War II. For example, a plant is a system that requires the inputs of water, carbon dioxide, and nutrients to perform a process called photosynthesis,

---

27   Stephen Jay Gould, *Full House. The Spread of Excellence from Plato to Darwin*. New York: Harmony Books, 1996.

28   Donella H. Meadows, *Thinking in Systems. A Primer*. Edited by Diana Wright. White River Junction, VT: Chelsea Green Publishing, 2008; quotations on p. 2. Also see Donella Meadows, Jorgen Randers, and Dennis Meadows, *Limits to Growth. The 30-Year Update*. White River Junction, VT: Chelsea Green Publishing, 2004. Peter M. Senge, *The Fifth Discipline. The Art & Practice of the Learning Organization*. Revised and Updated. New York: Currency Doubleday, 2006. For Senge, systems analysis was the fifth discipline of management.

that produces oxygen and other outputs. These outputs produce feedback loops that are incorporated in the next round of inputs. A major proponent of what became general systems theory was the Austrian-born biologist and professor Ludwig von Bertalanffy. Interestingly, he advocated the approach that systems are inherently in nature open rather than closed.

Another approach to systems analysis was developed at the University of Pennsylvania. It originated from operations research in World War II, particularly the routing of supply ships across the Atlantic to avoid German submarines. This approach to solving problems in defense contexts was successfully applied to industrial and business problems by a group at the University of Pennsylvania led by C. West Churchman and Russell Ackoff. Their approach included mathematical modeling and simulation, like the MIT approach, but it placed less emphasis on the importance of feedback and more emphasis on the design of desired systems with predictable outcomes. They stressed that the design of a system began with desired goals, which in turn determines the elements and their relationships within a system. The system must be a synthesis of all of its parts to achieve a purpose. They also stressed that systems should be seen as parts of larger systems, so that no system is ever entirely closed. As Ackoff wrote in one of his last works, "Analysis of a system reveals *how it works*; it provides know-how, knowledge, not understanding; that is, explanations of why it works the way it does. This [understanding of why systems work] requires *systems thinking*... Analysis is the way scientists conduct research. Synthetic thinking is exemplified by *design*."[29] Ackoff was emphasizing how many components and subsystems are synthesized into larger systems to achieve a purpose. He was also stressing the importance of designing systems for preferable futures within the context of visioning rather than futuring (as explained further in Chapter 3).

For futurists and planners, understanding *why* is just as important as understanding *how* a system works. Often this understanding comes from trend momentum and cause-and-effect relationships in addition to the characteristics of a closed system or a fixed set.

Yet another approach to systems thinking concerns complex adaptive systems (CAS). Its proponents argue that both the MIT and the University of Pennsylvania

---

29 Russel L. Ackoff and Daniel Greenberg, *Turning Learning Right Side Up. Putting Education Back on Track*. Upper Saddle River, NJ: Wharton School Publishing, 2008, pp. 59-63; quotation on p. 61. The Battelle-originated approach to generating scenarios that I have practiced since 1982 includes the use of cross-impact analysis, which shares many principles with systems dynamics. I learned a great deal about the MIT approach from a client who had received formal training in the discipline and who had used MIT extensively as a consultant. I learned about the Wharton School approach to systems thinking from a former student of Ackoff's who became a close colleague of mine at Battelle. We worked on several projects together using the University of Pennsylvania approach to systems design.

schools of systems analysis and design deal primarily with inanimate objects rather than living organisms. Biological systems can be self-designing and self-controlling. It is much harder to design, control, and predict social systems than industrial processes or naval logistics. The concept of independent agents dates back at least to the 1940s and the mathematics of John von Neumann, one of the creators of the computer. This approach to systems thinking recognizes the potential randomness of living systems that makes prediction of future behavior almost impossible.[30]

Organisms, however, are not totally random and follow their own laws of nature. Biological systems are indeed extremely complex and difficult to predict, but they are not impossible to anticipate, with varying degrees of uncertainty, with an understanding of specific conditions. Organisms have structures and they have requirements to maintain life and they may have hard-wired, evolutionary patterns of behavior consistent with past and future survival.

There is no question that biological systems are typically open systems, subject to all kinds of predators and disruptive events, even the occasional sighting of black swans. They are the most difficult of all systems to model and predict. In general, closed and quasi-closed systems are much easier to model, simulate, and generate predictions from than open systems. Meadows herself made this observation: "Self-organizing, nonlinear, feedback systems are inherently unpredictable. They are not controllable. They are understandable only in the most general way. The goal of foreseeing the future exactly and preparing for it perfectly is unrealizable… Our science itself, from quantum theory to the mathematics of chaos, leads us into irreducible uncertainty."[31]

Even if we cannot use systems thinking, including modeling and simulation of possible futures from a system, for predicting, we can use it for understanding and anticipating potential futures. Like Heisenberg, we can estimate but not literally know what we are seeing. I have seen many examples of models using the systems approach that have opened up insights previously missed. Models are excellent learning tools, even when they are wrong. A model gives you an explicit *a priori* position from which to learn, to expand your knowledge, and to anticipate possible and even likely alternative outcomes in the future.

The inherent danger of systems thinking, of course, is the belief that any model is an exact representation of some reality, either now or later. We cannot literally model the future; we can model only our expectations for the future. Modeling, like every other method and tool for futuring, is the beginning of a learning journey,

---

30 Peter Bishop, "Teaching Systems Thinking," *Futures Research Quarterly*, Vol. 24, Summer 2008, pp. 7-38.

31 Meadows, *Thinking in Systems*, p. 167-168.

not the destination of a prediction. In this regard, I have found simple models to be more helpful than complex models, because they are easier and less expensive to use and give us only gross estimates without any of the false presumptions of accuracy and predictability that come along with complex models. In addition, modeling of a presumed closed system, with a fixed set of trends (variables) and known relationships among them, can give you a baseline forecast of the future as though all known trends were to play out as expected; then you can introduce disruptive events to see how they might change the baseline future.

Scenarios, which have become very popular for both forecasting and planning in both the private and public sectors, are speculative models or structures (closed systems or fixed sets of trends). The term "scenarios" has different and often confusing meanings. One type of scenario, made popular in military planning, is the hypothetical sequence of events toward an expected outcome. To the extent that this approach has predictability, it would fall under cause-and-effect relationships and self-fulfilling prophecy. Another type of scenario analysis, however, focuses on alternative futures independent of any particular path through time leading to them. These are static snapshots of future conditions. As a set of conditions, a scenario is a type of model, but there are alternative models (scenarios), not just one.

The EU scenario case study provided in Chapter 1 is an example of identifying multi-trends, determining their interactions, creating a cross-impact model, and generating alternative scenarios as sets of different outcomes and conditions in the future. The model was a working hypothesis of the future based on a closed system or a fixed set of trends. By the standards of statistical, econometric, and systems analysis, this model was fairly simple. Yet it provided a great learning tool and some prescient expectations. It also provided a laptop software model for baseline forecasts and simulations of possible and actual disruptive events enabling the generation of updated scenarios.

The historian David Staley makes the argument that scenarios are analogous to alternative structures for the future. Scenarios, used in the sense of alternative future conditions rather than hypothetical sequences of events, may be predictive in as much as we can analyze trends, imagine alternative outcomes, and describe different future contexts for a given topic of inquiry. Events are virtually impossible to predict, but structures may be predictable.[32] In this regard, a scenario is a structure that is also a plausible if not probable closed system or fixed set of conditions in the future wherein some behaviors would be logically expected and certain events could happen.

---

32   David J. Staley, *History and Future. Using Historical Thinking to Imagine the Future.* Lanham, MD: Lexington Books, 2007, pp. 71-97.

In the context of economics and business, structures include fixed assets, institutions, corporate cultures, business models, technologies, processes, and distribution channels. In stable conditions, an economic model and a business paradigm act very much like a closed system. The metaphor of a model as representation of a structure as a closed system works. But in moments of crisis and panic, we learn that a system is more open and vulnerable to changes than we previously thought.

The concept of closed systems and fixed sets leads us to employing trend analysis, scenario generation, and modeling and simulation for futuring. You might also view planning as the process of erecting structures (boundary conditions) for future investments, strategies, and actions.

Knowledge of Intentions
One basis of predictability is the foreknowledge of what others intend to do. People's plans reflect their goals and intentions. Some people will publicly announce their goals and even their plans before they do something. If you knew what a person (or organization, company, or country) intends to do, then you could improve your ability to anticipate what they were likely to do in combination with the knowledge of their typical patterns of behavior, their resources, and circumstances. Of course, everybody expresses good intentions that are never carried out, so even knowing others' plans and wishes does not mean you can anticipate the future with certainty.

The knowledge of enemy intentions and plans is a particularly acute challenge for national intelligence. In the case histories of the Japanese surprise attack on Pearl Harbor on December 7, 1941, and the terrorist attacks on the US of September 11, 2001, the intentions of the enemy were not known prior to the attacks, but they became well known after the deeds.

During the Cold War, we could sometimes, but rarely, penetrate Soviet planning. With time, the US learned to better anticipate what the Soviets were and were not likely to do based on their ideological mental models, their actual military resources, and particular conditions. The Strategic Arms Limitation Talks (SALT) were particularly valuable to the US in picking up on patterns of Soviet thinking about deterrence and potential nuclear war. We learned that the Soviets were just as paranoid, if not more so, than the US was about a potential surprise enemy attack upon them. After all, they had suffered a surprise attack from Nazi Germany just six months before the surprise Japanese attack at Pearl Harbor. The Soviet intention in the case of a perceived imminent nuclear attack upon them from the US was apparently (logically deduced from what they would articulate) a preemptive attack of their own, thereby causing the very nuclear war that they

SALT contributed much to the relieving of Soviet fears that in ...es were the cause of so many Soviet military intentions and plans.

Whether in national security or in business, one person's surprise may be another person's intention.

In general, if you know the intentions, plans, and preparations of any person, company, organization, or government, you are in a better position to anticipate correctly what they are likely to do in the future. Planning is a leading indicator of future behavior and understanding the plans of others helps to make likely futures more predictable.

Self-Fulfilling Prophecies

People can make remarkably precise and accurate predictions about the future when they have the motivation, intention, plans, and resources of their own to make them happen. Unlike the prophets of old, they do not warn others to change their ways or else, but rather go about their own business creating the future. The idea of self-fulfilling prophecy is very old, with literary examples remaining from ancient Greece and India. In our own times the concept has been attributed variously to William James, Karl Popper, and Robert K. Merton. It is applied both in positive and negative terms. The positive occurs when a person makes a prediction and then goes out and makes it happen. In a broader sense, a self-fulfilling prophecy may occur when the prediction or forecast itself influences people's thinking or actions toward the predicted outcome. In the negative sense, people can make predictions or experience premonitions based on great fears and those fears can so influence their own behavior (and the behavior of other people responding to them) that they perpetrate the very result that they dreaded.

In the contemporary world of politics and business, the concept of the self-fulfilling prophecy applies primarily to visioning and planning – seeing a desired outcome in the future, acquiring and allocating necessary resources, and working very hard to make it happen. Some self-fulfilling prophecies occur, but many fall short. In a larger sense, the self-fulfilling prophecy can occur only under specified and controlled circumstances, such as a closed system, otherwise intervening variables might frustrate and divert the effort toward the goal. When the self-fulfilling prophecy happens as a form of visioning with little or no reference to futuring, it may amount to little more than wishful thinking and good luck rather than astute futuring, planning, and operations.

Everyday people make everyday plans every day. Many of them are fulfilled, particularly when the person has control over the vital elements of the plan. To the extent that any plan contains elements beyond the person's control, such plans are vulnerable to outside interference, chance, and change. Many plans are intentions that may or may not be realized depending upon varying conditions. A familiar example is when the father of a family says that he will take the whole family to the local amusement park on Saturday. This is a promise and a prediction to the ears of children. It is also an intention, a plan, and an expectation in the minds of adults; it may or may not actually happen depending upon circumstances. There may be a terrible storm on Saturday; the father may have to go into work unexpectedly; a child may come down with the flu; the amusement park may close for the day because of a power failure; etc., etc., etc.

Plans reflect one's self-centered expectations for the future that can be changed for any number of reasons. Knowing this, when any corporate or non-profit plan that I have ever participated in actually produces the fully intended results, I call it "luck" – it may have been a particularly prescient plan, but it got implemented correctly with no outside interference. Most successful plans turn out to be general guidelines for investments and operations, but remain sufficiently flexible to tolerate changes and still remain "directionally correct."

Both personal and corporate planning reminds me of Robert Burns' famous Scottish poem *To A Mouse* (1785). It tells the story of what happened when a common mouse built a home in a field that subsequently got plowed up by the farmer much to the surprise of the mouse. Burns wrote:

> But, Mousie, thou art no thy lane,
> In proving foresight may be vain;
> The best-laid schemes o' mice an' men,
>> Gang aft a-gley,
> An lea'e us nought but grief an pain,
>> For promis'd joy.[33]

My translation into contemporary English goes like this:

> But little mouse, you are not alone
> In proving that foresight may be in vain.
> The best thought out plans of mice and men often go wrong
> And leave us nothing but grief and pain instead of expected happiness.

Despite their potential perils, individuals, organizations, and companies have to formulate plans for the future. No planning would result in no way of controlling resources, actions, or results. An operation without plans would rely on little

---

33 Robert Burns, "To a Mouse," in George Gilfillan, ed., *The National Burns [Complete Works].* London: William Mackenzie, 2 vols., no date [1880?], Vol. I, p. 48.

ial and error and luck. Planning affords us the opportunity of molding
.uture in our own way, giving us the chance to realize the self-fulfilling
prophecy.

A Case Study: Trends in American Consumer Value to 2050

At this point, let me build a mental bridge from the theoretical to the practical
with a case history of my own. It is an excellent example of using the theory of
trend momentum to generate well considered expectations for the future.

Several years ago an Asian corporation approached me with a request to do a
forecast of American consumer value in personal transportation to the year 2050.
At first I suspected that the client was kidding me, but when he showed me the
budget for such a project I said to myself: now that is a serious amount of money,
so I had better give this some serious thought. But upon what basis does one
construct a forecast out 50 years into the future? Based on the corporate culture,
the client required that we use trend analysis for our forecast, so he requested that
we look back at least 50 years in order to project trends 50 years ahead.

So I began to give the mission serious thought. Were there any long-term trends
that would provide foresight that far over the time horizon or would we just
make it all up like a science fiction novel? If we were to use long-term trends,
what trends? After giving the question some critical thought, my associates and
I concluded that, yes, there were such trends: long-term socio-demographics,
especially generational and life-stage trends (combining trend momentum and
cause-and-effect relationships); long-term economic growth since 1945 (trend
momentum, not laws of nature); and five hundred years of American culture and
popular attitudes toward mobility (combining trend momentum and a closed
system or fixed set).

The client was clever enough to request characterizations of American consumer
value in personal transportation decade by decade, not year to year, from 1950
to 2050. The issue was to what extent American consumer values had remained
constant and how they had changed. We discovered that American consumer
values toward transportation had in one sense always been the same: Americans
love the independence of personal transportation, if they can afford it. The US is
a large country in which mobility has always been a challenge. Americans have
developed a national attitude that they enjoy an inalienable right to go wherever
and whenever they like. Americans loved horses, buggies, and wagons. With the
invention of commercial automobiles in the early 20th century, they gravitated
to cars, motorcycles, and trucks. In addition, Americans, like many other people

around the world, love the sensation of speed, the freedom of mobility, and the pride that comes with owning a personal vehicle.

In the 1950s, when deciding what vehicles to purchase, American consumers sought out vehicles with exaggerated styling and lots of power – the "muscle cars." They paid little attention to fuel efficiency and environmental quality and gave barely a nod to safety. By the 1970s, however, consumer value had shifted. The air quality laws of state and Federal governments required reduced air emissions from cars and trucks and the first Energy Crisis of 1973 made people very frightened of potentially unaffordable gasoline prices. Also, safety became an issue with mandated seat belts and the improved quality of vehicles. Therefore, many people shifted to smaller, more fuel efficient and cleaner cars, even when small cars felt less safe on the road than heavier vehicles.

A major shift in consumer value occurred in the 1990s and early 2000s when computer chips became micro-processors in vehicles. Inside the workings of a vehicle, chips improved engine fuel efficiency, automatic transmissions, four-wheel drive (when needed), safety and comfort. The same decade also saw a dramatic change in communications. People became used to being on-line with their friends. They wanted their telephones and Internet connections in their vehicles as well as in their homes. One major trend expected to continue for decades is the further integration of computers into vehicles, perhaps leading eventually to automated "smart" driving. Computers will provide improved diagnostics of vehicle performance and thereby improve safety and avoid repairs. In large, off-the-road vehicles, remote sensing of vehicle performance is already available. People will have on-board GPS and navigation aids, as some have today, in addition to other communication conveniences. With breakthroughs in voice pattern recognition software, the driver will be able to speak directly to the vehicle itself. A car will be "trained" to recognize its owner's voice and start, stop, and lock on command.

It seems likely that styling will be important in the future, but more in terms of interior design than the external extravagances of the 1950s. Safety, comfort, convenience, and reliability will likely remain important up to 2050.

While Americans have a heritage of traveling when they want to, the roads have become so congested at times that nobody can drive anywhere through the gridlock. In this picture, by allowing everybody to travel at will, everybody jeopardizes his or her freedom of mobility in traffic jams. A probable solution to the traffic problem of the future is better road information and automated coordination of drivers. By the 2020s, almost every car on American roads will offer real-time information on the weather, road construction and conditions, accidents, potential travel problems, and traffic tie ups. There will be little need for external Amber Alert signs as all that information will be accessible within each car. At some later time, most probably by 2050, each driver will file his or her driving destination and route into a central computer, which will store the routing information and come back to the driver with further instructions and travel suggestions.

Fuel efficiency and environmental emissions declined in consumer importance during the 1990s, when the price of gasoline dropped to as low as 99.9 cents per gallon. The people who felt safer in larger and heavier vehicles shifted their preference from the small, fuel-efficient vehicle to mini-vans and Sports Utility Vehicles (SUVs). SUVs replaced the earlier generations of station wagons for families, and were especially popular with the "soccer moms" who had to transport their children from one activity to another.

In the 1990s Americans wanted comfort, communications, and safety, both from the car itself and from outside. Cars became more reliable and fewer accidents originated with the vehicle than with the operator. People, however, were afraid of being pushed around the road by big trucks and even of being shot at by drivers with road rage. The SUV increasingly became popular, despite the fact that it did not achieve a high standard of fuel efficiency.

Then came the oil crisis of 2008. I had asserted years before that the gag point of gasoline prices in the US was about $5.00 per gallon. Events proved me only slightly off. In July 2008, the global market price of oil hit about $147 per barrel and gasoline at the pump in the US soared to over $4.00 per gallon. For the first time in American history, people began to cut back on their vehicle driving in order to conserve gas. Previously, Americans had driven more and more miles despite up-and-down gas prices. What we did not know in July 2008 was that the American economy was already sliding into a recession and that a huge financial panic would occur from late September 2008 into March 2009.

Energy for personal vehicles was a major focus of our forecast. Significant technologies for alternative energy sources had already emerged in the 1990s, and we believed that they would become only more important in the future. Previous consumer value in energy efficiency and environmental quality would likely shift to energy systems. We foresaw the growth of hybrid fuel vehicle sales and the eventual proliferation on the road of plug-in, re-chargeable vehicles and vehicles with fuel cells. We expressed the point of view that fuel cells would most likely be introduced as auxiliary power sources for automotive computers and electronics before they became power train systems.

In our forecast to 2050, we provided historical data on American economic growth. Since 1945, the annual GDP of the US has grown steadily despite a few recession years. Compared with the Great Depression, the recessions after World

War II were relatively minor and brief. Since 1980, there had been an almost regular cycle of recessions every 10 years, but they were nothing on the scale of the unexpected Great Recession that began in 2008. We did not see this huge downturn coming. Basically, we asserted that economic growth would continue with periodic ups and downs all the way to 2050. In any event, we asserted that American consumers would generally continue to be able to afford to own their own vehicles across a spectrum of low-priced, basic vehicles to high-end luxury vehicles. In the long term, the global over-capacity in automotive manufacturing would reduce prices for basic vehicles, while new technology would provide higher valued benefits at additional prices. Whether we were right or wrong still depends upon four decades more of trends.

Our client was very sophisticated: he knew that we could not predict the future of American consumer value with precision, but he wanted our well considered expectations to use as a baseline for monitoring trends and events. He also wanted an approximation of future consumer value to help him place priorities on technology investments. Since our futuring study, the client has implemented the following fundamental technological strategies:

- Continuing the emphasis on alternative energy systems for personal vehicles in the US due to consumer value (not just government regulations) in energy efficiency (resulting in lower energy costs) and significantly improved air quality emissions.

- Taking seriously the long-term implications of global climate change and carbon management for industries around the world.

- Shifting management focus to developing technologies that provide more long-term benefits for consumers.

- Placing more importance on the integration of information and communication systems in vehicles.

- Placing more importance on passenger comfort and interior design.

Chapter 3. Futuring and Visioning

Futuring Principle 3: Futuring and visioning are different but complementary perspectives of the future.

Experienced managers and investors know the importance of emerging business opportunities and threats. Executive managers in particular are the stewards of investors and owners, and they have to protect and grow the asset base with which they have been entrusted. To do that, they have to think about and plan for the future. In this sense, futuring and visioning are forms of risk management, or "uncertainty management." No executive can afford to take the cavalier attitude that "whatever will be, will be."

In the words of contemporary futurists, futuring addresses possible and probable futures while visioning concerns preferred futures. The two approaches are different, but complementary. In making decisions and plans for the future, you have to do both and fit them together. But don't make the common error of confusing one with another. Just because you *want* something to happen in the future does not automatically mean that it *will* happen.

Millett's Hourglass

Several years ago when I was still formulating my concept of futuring and visioning, I was exchanging e-mails with a futurist in England. After I expressed my ideas about the different but complementary nature of futuring and visioning and how they should fit together like mirror-image triangles, he came back to me with my ideas visualized as a slide called "Millett's Hourglass." I have modified the slide over time and expanded my theory (see Figure 3.1).

Futuring appears at the top of the "hourglass." It is an approach that moves from the external to the internal environment. In futuring, you have to set aside temporarily your own wishes in order to see the world much as others see it. We all live within a macro-environment of trends and events typically, but not always, beyond our immediate control. Futuring works from the most general macro-environmental trends down to the more specific opportunities.

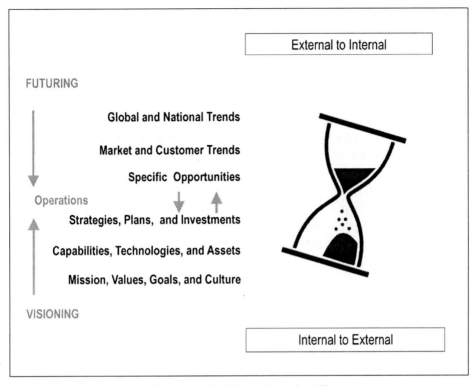

Figure 3.1: "Millett's Hourglass"[34]

I am tempted to say that futuring is "objective" while visioning is "subjective." These popular terms that we use everyday are actually misleading. I see no absolute standard for objectivity when various material self-interests are at stake; what I see is a consensus of people's perceptions that align well with each other and receive positive reinforcement from the external environment. So in a very general sense, futuring is more objective and less subjective, or idiosyncratic, than visioning, which can be highly normative. The focus of futuring is placed on your customers, markets, and their conditions. Think about the trends and issues beyond yourself and your own enterprise and to try to see the world as others do. On the other hand, visioning is all about you – what you want, what you do, and what you expect of yourself.

Visioning is the "internal to external" or "inside-out" or "bottom up" approach to the future. It begins with the foundations of any enterprise: its mission,

---

34 Figure and explanation adapted from Stephen M. Millett, "Futuring and visioning: complementary approaches to strategic decision-making," *Strategy & Leadership*, Vol. 34, No. 3, 2006, pp. 43-50.

values, aspirations (goals, both long-term and short-term), and culture. Every enterprise has an origin and history based on the vision and hopes of its founders and investors. It will have a culture (the proper ways of doing things), mission, and values, typically reflecting the board of directors (or investors) and senior managers. This is the sustaining foundation of any enterprise. Next, the enterprise will have a physical character represented by facilities, plants, offices, equipment, tools, and capabilities, both material and cerebral. This is the intermediate level of visioning. At a more operational and day-to-day and month-to-month basis, an enterprise of whatever sort will have strategies, plans, and investments for the future. The intersection of futuring and visioning most clearly occurs with operations, which is the physical manifestation of strategies as embodied in plans and where the enterprise tries to make a future in the marketplace to its own liking. Operations are where visioning encounters futuring, both the thinking about – and the emerging realities of – the future. It is the point where the internal and external environments of the enterprise intersect.

The Perspective of Futuring

While the more sophisticated managers know that they cannot predict the future with certainty, they realize that they have to anticipate it, or at least salient features of it, in order to recognize potential market changes and opportunities. Many companies and organizations will perform a type of external environmental analysis, trend monitoring, or horizon scanning called PEST: political, economic, social, and technological. Some include the natural environment, business ethics, and other factors of particular importance to the enterprise. The point is that a manager has to be informed about, and prepared to respond to, the prevailing trends and events external to operations.

A very popular business textbook by John F. Steiner and George A. Steiner that first appeared in 1980 and is now in its twelfth edition (2009) identifies six environments external to the enterprise that every manager must recognize and track: the economic, technological, cultural, governmental, legal, and natural environments.[35] I find their nomenclature somewhat confusing, so my list of external (macro-environmental) trends and factors that are generally most relevant to futuring is adapted slightly from theirs:

- Economics (global, national, and market)

- Technologies

---

35 John F. Steiner and George A. Steiner, *Business, Government, and Society. A Managerial Perspective*. Text and Cases. Twelfth edition. New York: McGraw-Hill Irwin, 2009, pp. 34-44.

- Socio-demographics

- International and national politics, policies, laws and regulations

- National history and culture

I strongly agree with Steiner and Steiner that these external environments have profound impacts on the internal, corporate culture of any company or organization.

If you did not believe this before 2009, then the Great Recession should have taught you to mind at least the macro-environmental trends. But even the ones who were watching then did not believe in what they were seeing.

Back in April 2002, I was in Tokyo giving a presentation on American economic trends and I made the statement that the future of the US economy depends almost entirely upon the continued heavy spending of American consumers. My mind was very much on the spectacular economic surge of the 1990s caused largely by the digital and dotcom gold rush. A young Japanese business analyst corrected me only to the extent that he added that the whole global economy depended upon the strength of American consumer spending. In the post-war years, the impressive growth of the Japanese economy was largely fueled by automotive, consumer electronics, and industrial goods sold into the American market. The Japanese were quickly followed by the Koreans and the Chinese. Today, the rapid economic growth of both China and India rely heavily on American consumer spending and corporate investments.

Arguably the vigor of the American consumer market is the single most important trend for the entire global economy. Prior to the Great Recession that began in late 2007, the US economy experienced a virtual marathon of sustained growth with but a few momentary recessions to catch its breath. Going back to the end of World War II, the GDP of the US was $212 billion in current (1945) dollars. In the next 15 years, it grew to more than $500 billion. In those same years, there were only two years (1946 and 1949) when the annual GDP dropped relative to the year before, and the declines were relatively minor. Of course, much of the growth in terms of current dollars has been due to inflation, but the real growth, calculated in constant dollars, has still been very impressive. For example, by 1970, the GDP amounted to a little more than $1 trillion in current dollars (closer to $4 trillion in constant 2000 dollars). By the end of the 20th century, just 30 years later, it had expanded to nearly $10 trillion in 2000 dollars. Even in 2009, a year of recession, the American GDP exceeded $14 trillion in current dollars. Although there have been "soft" years with little or no growth, the general trend has shown strong, steady expansion of the American economy, of which roughly 70% is consumer spending.[36]

Many futurists, with formal economics training or not, have viewed American consumer spending and GDP growth as linear and likely to continue so into the extended future. One of the all-time great financial axioms says that while the Wall Street stock market may go up and down from day to day it will always go up over the long term. This reasoning has been the foundation of long-term investing, especially the appeal of such investments as 401(k) accounts for eventual retirement. This line of thinking, an excellent example of "time's arrow," prevailed in countless companies. The inevitable long-term growth of stock market prices, making investments a "sure thing" with enough time, was the self-serving hook of many investment firms. The US would never see a repetition of the Great Depression with collapsing stock prices, failing banks, foreclosing home mortgages, and rising unemployment... or would we?

Both the importance and inadequacies of economic forecasting hit Americans right in their faces in September 2008. Most Americans never foresaw the economic left jab to the nose that bloodied many home owners and investors eagerly waiting for a comfortable retirement. As early as March 2008, I became aware of the slow decline in American economic growth, but I did not see the crash coming. I rarely consulted with banks and financial institutions, so I was not watching what was going on in this sector. Partly because of my lack of knowledge about the financial market, I monitored other trends and so missed those that proved to be most important for our economic future. In addition, while I had a casual awareness of real estate trends, I was not monitoring residential loan and sales data. As my case illustrates well the potential importance of knowing and not knowing about certain trends, I will go into more detail.

In the early spring of 2008 I was being asked whether or not the US had slipped into a recession. The ubiquitous TV pundits were saying that we were. My answer to the question was typically, "I don't know, but it sure feels like one." The data on economic performance typically lags behind the phenomena by as much as three months. Even preliminary numbers may not be accurate; GDP growth rates are being continuously adjusted up or down over time. We rarely have real-time information on many economic trends, except for sudden events, which get immediate exposure in the global media. I was following the usual

---

36 US Department of Commerce, Bureau of the Census, *Historical Statistics of the United States, Colonial Times to 1970*. Bicentennial Edition. Washington: US Government Printing Office, 1976, Part 1, p. 224; US Census Bureau, *Statistical Abstract of the United States: 2007. The National Data Book*. 126th edition. Washington: US Government Printing Office, 2006), p. 429; www.census.gov/compendia/statab/; Central Intelligence Agency, *The World Factbook*, www.cia.gov/library/publications/the-world-factbook/

"leading indicators:" the GDP growth rates as reported quarterly by the Bureau of Economic Analysis, consumer confidence as reported by the Conference Board and the University of Michigan, unemployment rates, interest rates, inflation rates, and the Dow Jones Industrial Average on the New York Stock Exchange. These sources of information showed a gradual downward trend, but we still did not have adequate information in the early spring of 2008 that would indicate a forthcoming panic in the banking and financial sector. In the meantime, while I was waiting on the data, I was using my senses to observe economics in action, or what anthropologists call "ethnography." I witnessed the behavior of caution if not outright fear.

At this same time, I was watching closely another trend, which at the time I thought was very important: the sudden increases in the global market price for oil. For this indicator, we had daily market information. I was concerned that oil prices would trigger another economic downturn in the US like the energy crises of 1973 and 1979. As a consumer of gasoline, I felt very much touched personally by oil prices. I watched in horror as oil prices went above $100 per barrel and retail gasoline prices soared above $3.00 and then went directly to $4.00 a gallon. People were also asking me what I thought the price of gasoline would go to and at what point would consumers cut back. I knew that the trend indicated that in the past people continued to drive just as many if not more miles even as gasoline prices rose. As long as people had jobs and incomes, they spent money, including more money for personal vehicles and their fuels. Knowing the past behavior of American consumers, I expected that the gag point (the level at which people would gag at prices and turn away) for gasoline would be $5.00 per gallon. I was proved wrong, or only 80% correct depending upon the point of view. Consumers gagged at about $4.00 per gallon. In the summer of 2008, for the first time in recent history, consumer miles driven began to decline as pump prices rose. Consumers also began to cut back on other expenditures, too, even their monthly home mortgage payments.

The dramatic rise of oil prices in 2008 was apparently due to at least three factors: increases in American energy demand, increases in oil demand in the rapidly developing countries of China and India, and market speculation. I undervalued and so underestimated the importance of speculation. The TV "talking heads" blamed much of the oil increase on investors, including venerable American pension funds, playing margins on the global markets for oil and various metals. As an historian, I knew about past "bubbles," and I knew that they almost always burst at some, and often apparently arbitrary, point. On this score, I was correct. The global price of oil hit a peak of about $147 per barrel on July 11, 2008. Then speculators turned elsewhere while consumer demand was gradually declining. But, at the same time, I did not know about the bursting of the real estate bubble, which turned out to be far more significant than that of oil prices, and the panic that was about to come. Some analysts still maintain that there was no connection between high energy prices and the bursting of the real estate and financial speculation bubbles, but I think there was.

The long-term ramification of the oil bubble of 2008 was that energy prices got so high that consumers started to cut back on their spending in general. They tried to drive fewer miles and conserve their fuel when prices exceeded $4.00 per gallon. They also cut back on trips to the stores and their spending for other things while they were trying to balance their monthly budgets. If more went to gasoline, then less had to go to other things – or consumer debt, which was already high, would go in the same direction as gasoline prices (through the roof). American consumer confidence and spending buckled in the summer of 2008. Consumers also turned away from the highly popular SUVs and mini-vans, the so-called "gas guzzlers." Car sales went soft, too, in the summer of 2008, and the auto companies could not shift production quickly enough from SUVs to smaller cars and hybrids. Consumers were also over-extended in car loans. The recession in the auto industry began before the financial bust and only exacerbated the multi-sector decline of the American economy.

Gasoline prices also impacted commercial transportation costs, especially for trucks running goods across the country. Higher distribution costs were being felt in higher retail costs for many consumer products. In addition, food prices went up along with rising gasoline prices. That is to be expected, since food is an energy-intensive industry at virtually every stage of the value-added chain. Corn prices in particular rose rapidly, since the high gasoline prices were stimulating the emerging ethanol fuel industry, which in turn drove up corn prices. It also drove up meat prices, since many livestock are fed with corn. The consumer was taking a beating in the summer of 2008 from rising fuel, food, and consumer product prices.

Meanwhile, as I was monitoring energy prices, I was not following residential construction, real estate, and financial industry trends. I was well aware that the US had gone into a prolonged period of residential construction and escalating home prices in the 1990s. The strong real estate market in part balanced out the dotcom bubble burst of 2000, so that the recession of 2001 was not as severe as the recessions of 1981-82 and 1991-92. When one or two sectors of the economy decline, then other sectors have to grow to balance out the trend in economic growth. Since I was not monitoring as many trends as I should have been and I did not understand the inner workings of home debt financing (I had only the vaguest idea of what a derivative was), I did not anticipate the cumulative impacts of these multiple trends all going "south" at the same time.

As late as 2007 we were still enjoying a period of economic growth with no end in sight. My wife and I often asked ourselves as we drove past new neighborhoods of "starter castles" and "McMansions" in exurbia how people could afford such large and expensive new homes. Sadly, the answer for many was "they couldn't." Interest rates were very low, credit was easy to get, even at variable rates initially below the prime interest rate, and people expected home values to rise fast enough to acquire paper equity to outpace any future increases in mortgage payments. In addition to the built-in amenities of new homes, people bought new furniture, computers, and home entertainment centers, typically on some kind of extended payment schedule. They also bought large, gas-guzzling SUVs and other types of vehicle (parked in their new three-car garages) that they might not have been able to afford under less generous lending conditions. Life was good; the American Dream was being realized.

After the home construction, real estate, banking and financial, and automotive bubble burst in 2008, much of the blame for bad residential debts was laid at the doorstep of working and lower middle class families that had bought houses, digital gadgets, and vehicles that they could not afford. Home ownership had risen to about two-thirds of all households in the country. This was considered a good thing: the belief was that democracy is strongest when people own their own properties and feel vested in the general state of the economy. In retrospect, the financial experts claimed that too many people bought homes on flimsy credit who never should have tried to own their own homes. Maybe so, but plenty of upper middle class and wealthy families bought homes that they could not afford either. Toward one end of the socio-economic spectrum, there were buyers who could not comfortably afford a new house at $190,000; and at the other end of the spectrum, there were buyers who could not really afford a new $1,900,000 mansion, but they got the loans just the same.

The Federal income tax reforms of the Reagan Administration eliminated the long-time tax deduction for interest paid on consumer purchases, such as the taxes and interest on car loans and home furnishings. The only major tax deductions left to most American consumers were the write-offs for home mortgage loans and property taxes. During the economic boom of the 1990s, people took out home equity loans, not just for home improvements, but also for cars, furniture, trips, and everyday consumer purchases. It was like giving yourself a raise so that you could achieve a higher standard of living with no additional work. Toward the end of the booming 1990s, Alan Greenspan, the chairman of the Federal Reserve, warned Congress of the potential bad effects of increased consumer debt, especially leveraged from personal wealth as manifested in home equity. Even though he saw a trend that he did not like, Greenspan's main concern remained inflation, which was the professional obsession of his economic youth.

I knew that real estate prices had hit an historical high in 2006-2007 and were generally declining. I knew that there were many more homes on the market than there were buyers, even in my home city of Columbus, Ohio, which had enjoyed a long period of prosperity in residential expansion. I was also aware that the number of home foreclosures and personal bankruptcies was rising in Ohio, which had one of the highest rates of such disasters in the country. But I had no idea of the size of the national real estate bubble, the extent of sub-prime mortgages, and the derivative trading crisis until the collapse of Lehman Brothers. I had been watching the Dow Jones average gradually fall from a high of 14,165.02 on October 10, 2007, to below 11,000 by mid-September 2008. I was buying stocks then because I thought there were some good buys available with dividends paying more than I could get through low interest rates on savings.

Wow! I had no idea what was coming in just a few more weeks. With the collapse of Lehman Brothers came a cascading implosion of commercial banks, investment houses, and insurance companies that looked like a repeat, but on an even larger scale, of the financial disaster of 1929-1932. The unthinkable was about to happen: another great depression. Panic quickly replaced previous optimism. The Dow Jones Industrial Average fell by about 768 in just one day, September 30, 2008. By the end of the year, it had fallen to about 8666. In addition to all the bad news from Wall Street came the pleas for a Federal life line from the Big Three automakers in Detroit. The Federal Reserve and the US Treasury Department came to the rescue of banks, insurance companies, and financial enterprises. Congress passed the Troubled Asset Relief Program (TARP) bailout of the financial industry, and the Obama Administration saved the car industry. Some skeptics observed that the meaning of GM changed from General Motors to Government Motors. The bottom (we hope) was reached on March 10, 2009, with the closing Dow Jones Industrial Average at 6547.01.

So I made the mistake of buying stocks in the summer of 2008 thinking that the stock market was already low and was going to go back up by the end of 2008 or early 2009 to its heights of October 2007. I had no basis for that expectation except faulty trend analysis and wishful thinking. Then when the stock market cascaded downward from late September 2008 to February 2009, I held on to my stocks rather than sell them. After all, I was still receiving more dividends on my stock (although it had lost value on paper) than I was receiving interest on savings. My savings looked relatively secure, so when the stock market went down, I bought a few more shares based on optimism tempered by fear, as a relatively small bet on a potentially modest return. We are told to "buy low, sell high," but the emotions of the situation are exactly the opposite: we buy when markets are rising in expectation that they will continue to rise and we sell when the prices are falling in fear that they will fall even further. There were people who hit the panic button and sold their stocks, mutual funds, 401(k)s, and other liquid assets to minimize their losses. (They may have also sold them for the cash if they lost their jobs in the recession.) They will have compromised their future gains if markets go up in price in the future. In personal investment, courage goes a long way, along with rational thinking and well considered expectations for the future.

The purpose of this narrative is to illustrate how important it is to identify the right trends and to monitor them closely, especially in turbulent times. Saying this, of course, is easier than doing it. I just showed you what I got wrong, and I have been doing this for four decades. But identifying trends is always a working hypothesis about what will be important in the future. You have to have a basis to work and learn from. Your learning is one thing, but when you get the story right, you still have the job of convincing others to see conditions and trends as you do.

I was working on a scenarios project through the summer and autumn of 2008 with a global market leader in consumer products. We anticipated the "Great Recession," even on a global level, not based on a banking and financial crisis but because of long-term high energy prices. The trend analysis and cross-impact analysis showed that if we had continuous high energy prices then consumer spending on other things would contract. If the American consumer pulled back spending, then there would likely be recessions in countries that sold goods in the US, especially China. We held an analytical scenarios workshop using trend outcomes with Bayesian probabilities and cross-impact analysis with a software modeling program. The prevailing scenario, the one with the highest probability of occurring, portrayed a long-term global market in which general standards of living did not continue to rise over the next decade as they had over the last decade and in which lower everyday prices would emerge as more important to consumers than additional product features.

The clients did not believe this scenario. They believed that their product brands were so powerful that consumers would still prefer the quality that they were used to having rather than lower prices. They gravitated to another, but less likely, scenario of continued strong global economic growth, more product differentiation, and consumer willingness to pay more for additional product attributes (functional, stylistic, and environmentally green). I made a case for the prevailing scenario, while they made a case for the scenario that they preferred. We ran many simulations, but their favored scenario, although it might occur, always fell rather low in the probabilities of occurrence. We also ran a simulation with a disruptive event, a global recession. The resulting black swan recession scenario was almost identical to the prevailing baseline scenario. The clients were still highly skeptical, but they started to ask questions among themselves about what they would have to do if the recession scenario were to occur. It was a good day's work.

In early January 2009, I held another analytical scenarios workshop for a group of industrial clients. Many of them were telling me at that time that the recession was a fluke and would not last long. They were expecting consumer confidence and spending to be back to "normal" by the summer of 2009. I was not nearly as optimistic as they were given the data that we were getting on economic performance. I was reading the events of late 2008 with gravity that others did not yet share with me. I knew that Christmas spending, which is so important to American retailers, had been way down. I also watched the unemployment rates rise. While I, too, believed in an eventual recovery, I thought it would take at least two years and even then there might be structural changes to the economy and consumer behavior based on the traumas of 2008-2009.

By 2010 I was being asked a different question: when will the Great Recession end? The GDP data at that time showed growth, but these data are often incomplete and revised at later dates. In September 2010 the economic statisticians claimed that the recession was officially over. But unemployment was still high (nationally near 10%). A more meaningful question for the future would have been, and remains today, what the post-recession economy will probably look like. Has the Great Recession inflicted important and long-term changes upon the structure of the American economy and the behavior of American consumers? I worry that the US may be going through a major economic transition during which we may experience structural unemployment of 6-8% rather than 3-5%, which would cause potentially significant challenges for society in maintaining those people who will be chronically out of work and so consuming far less. From where will come the new jobs and how well are they likely to pay? I expect the value of manufacturing in the US to increase, but the number of manufacturing jobs to go down. I expect that digital automation will replace a lot of jobs in both the manufacturing and service sectors. People will appreciate their jobs in the future more than they did before the recession because well-paying jobs with benefits will become harder to find and harder to keep. I also expect that the same people who experienced consumer pain in 2008-2010 will become more cautious in their spending and investing habits to avoid further pain in the future.

Perhaps we are in one of those long-term business cycles explained by Joseph Schumpeter. With current economic knowledge and government regulations, perhaps the long-term growth trend can be extended for a period longer than 63 years. But maybe the economic growth trend since World War II is losing momentum and coming to an end. In this same line of reasoning, consumer spending in the last few decades has been largely driven by the Boomer generation, which was born between 1946 and 1964 and which entered its peak earning and spending years in the period of 1991-2009. The youngest Boomers, who are in their mid-40s today, could continue the generational trend of earning and spending for another 10-15 years, but the older Boomers (like my wife and me) will reach retirement years, when incomes and spending typically decline. One of the major uncertainties of the future of the American economy is how long Boomers will continue their pattern of consuming behavior and when the consumer spending of the US will decline due to the aging Boomer population. This is a question that virtually every company, organization, and government agency has to consider in their long-term planning and investments.

Perhaps the spending habits of the younger Boomers and the X Generation, who are entering their peak earning and spending years, will propel American economic growth in the future. We shall see.

From the point of view of futuring, I believe we can learn at least five lessons from the tracking and forecasting of American economic trends since 2008:

1. The most important trends require the closest monitoring; but the trick is knowing what the most important trends will be in the future, not just presently and in the past. Selecting the most important trends is a continual exercise in expert judgment.

2. A wide variety of trends have to be tracked, because so many trends may emerge to shape the future. This activity is known as "environmental scanning" or "trend scanning," which typically goes to more breadth but less depth than trend monitoring (see Chapter 5 for further discussion of trend scanning and trend monitoring).

3. While multiple trends must be watched, they rarely play out in isolation from each other. There must be a way to think about the future as multiple combinations of trends that interact with each other. Some trends provide positive while others give negative reinforcement to other trends. The ways to do this include cross-impact analysis, systems analysis, and modeling and simulation.

4. Because of uncertainty and the spectrum of possible outcomes in the future, it is more helpful to think in terms of multiple outcomes, or scenarios, with varying Bayesian probabilities of occurrence than trying to imagine a single outcome in the future.

5. Thinking about the future is one thing, but doing something about it is another. Often in the face of great uncertainty we tend to wait too long and commit the sin of omission. We may or may not be able to influence the course of trends and events, but we can think about alternative futures and prepare for them the best we can.

In the context of futuring, the general point to be made here is that trends and changes in the American economy affect, directly or indirectly, every American company, organization, and household. These trends and changes occur regardless of what plans people have made – the general economy might have benefited some plans while it compromised others. The economy runs on the patterns of human behavior in a market economy, not individual plans. The plans that companies and people make have to take into account, if not anticipate, potentially unstable trends in national, even global, economics. Just because a financial institution, for example, predicts that the US annual GDP will grow by 4% does not mean that it actually will, despite what assumptions and strategies have been made based on such a projection. This is exactly why futuring has to be done before visioning and why trends have to be tracked but discounted for potential changes.

In addition to general economic trends, we also need to track demographic trends as part of futuring. This includes population growth and the reasons behind it, such as a rising birth rate and immigration. While today's birth rate in the US is 14 per 1,000 population, compared to 25 per 1,000 in 1955, it has begun to increase since 2004 and at the current rate it is projected that we will add 40 million to our population in this decade. The changes in birth rate over time affect the overall age of the population and so of the people who are both the producers and the consumers of goods and services. Changes to immigration numbers and countries of origin also affect the creative and consumer environments within which businesses operate. Going on figures from between 1991 and 2005, it is easy to estimate official figures might show 10-12 million legal immigrants during the first decade of the 21st century. The greater numbers of immigrants from Hispanic regions like Mexico, the Caribbean and Central and South America since 1985 has led to more cultural diversity. Today, many products offer labels in Spanish as well as English; the US is moving toward a multi-cultural and bi-lingual population. This trend has profound impacts on virtually every sector of the national economy, and every product and service.

Other social or demographic factors important for futuring are the aging population, the ratio of women to men and changing working patterns for women. While in elementary schools there are more boys (19 million) than girls (17.2 million), there are more women (9.8 million) than men (7.6 million) in higher education across the country. Because women tend to live longer than men, the proportion of women in American society will increase as the population continues to age. Both women and the elderly have emerged in the marketplace as significant purchasers and consumers, whereas in the past the most powerful consumers were considered to be younger and male.

Technology trends are very important to anybody's macro-environment. From the point of view of people familiar with technology developments, innovations in technology appear as progressions toward more sophistication, a pattern that constitutes a trend. From the point of view of people not familiar with technology developments, the apparently sudden introduction of new technologies manifested in new products and services may appear as a disruptive event.

Two great economic thinkers in the 20th century recognized the profound importance of technology to our economic system. John Maynard Keynes asserted as early as 1930, at the beginning of the worldwide Great Depression, that technologies were cumulative, resulting in increasingly improved productivity. Technological advances were linear, perhaps exponential, but not cyclical. By 2030, looking ahead 100 years, Keynes speculated that sustained economic growth would be maintained by public policy and highly productive technologies would virtually eradicate depressions and provide sufficient resources to all elements of society. Technology, he argued, would contribute to the end of periodic economic booms and busts. Meanwhile, Schumpeter, Keynes' less known but perhaps equally farsighted contemporary, developed an elaborate theory of how technology and other types of innovation, championed by disruptive entrepreneurs, change economies forever. He predicted that in the future a politically democratic type of socialist economy would emerge with sustained performance without the troublesome disruptions (including creative destruction) of capitalism.[37] Some political pundits in 2009 asserted that the US had already gone over to a new type of socialism in reaction to the potential financial meltdown and the Great Recession.

I have made a career providing technology forecasts to clients around the world. These clients were looking for new business opportunities in the future; they were often most interested in the apparent disruptive technologies that were beyond their own experiences. The most interesting technologies typically involved information and communication technologies (ICT), the revolution in human genome knowledge and manipulation that is leading to a virtual revolution in health care, innovative materials, nanotechnologies, and energy. Beginning in 1995, I managed a series of "top 10" technology forecasts for Battelle that received global media coverage.[38] These were exercises in expert judgment. In addition, I managed trend analysis and scenario projects that provided a futuring context for clients to make long-term investments and business strategies.

---

37   Robert L. Heilbroner, *The Worldly Philosophers*. New York: Touchstone Book, 1999, pp. 288-310.

38   The top 10 technology forecasts since 1995 appear at the Battelle website under "News" and "Technology Forecast Archive": www.battelle.org/SPOTLIGHT/tech_forecast/index.aspx

Arguably the most significant worldwide technological developments in the second half of the 20th century were the computer, the laptop, the Internet, and the mobile phone. They all required years to develop into commercial and personal products, but when they were introduced they were novel and revolutionary in their implications. In 1943, the President of IBM allegedly estimated that there was a global market for about five computers. Developed primarily for defense applications, computers became very popular in all kinds of industries and government agencies in the late 1950s and during the 1960s. They were able to contain huge quantities of data and perform difficult calculations within seconds. It is very difficult to imagine today how agencies such as Social Security and the Internal Revenue Service in the US government or how the airlines or banking industry operated in the "good old days" with just paper records and mechanical adding machines. The mainframe computer industry was dominated by just a few corporations until the introduction of the transistor led to the development of digital chips. Innovators, exactly the type of disruptive entrepreneurs described by Schumpeter, disrupted the mainframe industry with the introduction of micro- or personal computers (PCs). The PC market grew slowly at first, then exploded in the late 1980s and during the 1990s. Information technologies (chips, computers, peripherals, and software) merged with communication technologies. In parallel with digital computers and all kinds of digital electronics came the mobile phone. The Internet was launched as a complete surprise to most people in 1995. By the early 21st century, the ICT industries were beginning to replace automotives as the engine of national economic growth.

When looked upon from inside the ICT industry, these technology developments appear as stages of a general trend toward smaller sizes, converging devices, and lower prices. There has been a steady progression in combining computers with cell phones, hand-held portal devices, and printed and verbal communications. When looked upon from outside the ICT industry, however, new products and services based on unfamiliar technologies constituted major changes in consumer behavior and value and in the management of supply chains. ICT literally revolutionized manufacturing in the US, providing quality control and productivity never dreamed possible by many people. ICT certainly created whole new product and service categories with demand growing quickly behind the rapidity of technological changes, at least until the digital boom went temporarily bust in the early years of the 21st century.

The Internet allowed everybody with a computer and access to the World Wide Web to express an opinion or sell goods and services around the world. It contributed to the globalization of business competition.

Another extremely important cluster of technologies will impact the future of alternative energy. Energy trends in general have captured much attention since the sudden increases in the price of oil and gasoline in 1973. The subsequent energy crises of the 1970s demonstrated how disruptive volatile energy markets could be for all kinds of industries and businesses. For decades we have been expecting major breakthroughs in alternatives to oil, such as wind power, solar panels, batteries, bio-mass, synthetic fuels, and fuel cells. The commercialization of these technologies, however, has been slower than expected. The technological advances in energy have been slow and gradual rather than spectacular. For example, batteries are more powerful today than they were just 20 years ago, yet electricity storage remains a major challenge. The technologies of mobile energy storage were pulled by the increased demands for portable electronics, laptops, Internet portals, and cell phones. Wind power grew in popularity in the early 2000s due to government support. Solar has become widely used for small power demands, but is still not sufficient to provide large amounts of electricity. Bio-fuels also grew in popularity, but DNA-engineered crops on "gasoline farms" are still an expectation on the horizon.

Many forecasts of future technology emphasize gee-whiz factors, which are entertaining but not necessarily predictive. It is often difficult to separate the science from the science fiction, especially when science fiction sells well. Forecasts of technologies, at least those from which products and services are derived, cannot be performed in a vacuum, concentrating only on the scientific and technological variables. Technology forecasts have to include market factors, financing, government policy and support, consumer value and behavior, distribution, competition and substitutions, etc.

The macro-trends just mentioned above provide the top, or most general, level of futuring. These are the trends that are most general to the overall business environment and the hardest to control and to anticipate. Consumer and market trends comprise the intermediate level of Millett's Hourglass. Consumers change over time, just as other things do. Even though some commodities are essential, product content and packaging and consumer tastes shift. An obvious change in consumer behavior resulted from the advent of on-line shopping over the Internet. We were asked by several clients whether the Internet would put stores, especially department stores, out of business in the US. Some people thought that the Internet would also kill product catalogs and telephone orders. We learned that when given more choices, consumers just exercise more options. While Internet sales continue to grow every year, shoppers still go to stores, including department stores (which have had to adapt to changing times), to see, test, and buy products. Shopping is a social as well as an economic activity. One recent trend is that consumers will look at catalogs and then go to the website to place their orders. Or, they will look at products in catalogs and on websites and then go to stores to purchase the same products. Consumers still like to touch and try products before they commit to purchasing them. They will also phone in their orders. As long as consumers have different cognitive styles and preferences, there will always be different ways that they can spend their money.

Finally, the third level of the hourglass consists of specific opportunities within specific industries, in selected markets, and for targeted customers. Understanding the larger context, thought through from the general to the specific, provides the identification of potential new products and services providing greater value for customers.

Competitive intelligence falls into both the second and third levels of futuring in Millett's Hourglass. In the context of broad market segments and entire industries, it is necessary to know who the competitors are and how they position themselves in their value propositions in the eyes of customers, consumers, and clients. At the third level, when considering specific products and services for targeted customers, you have to consider who the competitors will be and what alternatives they are likely to offer to the same customers.

One example of futuring from the top to the bottom was a scenarios project that I managed in the 1990s for an American consumer product company. The company was at least a century old and was famous for one particular household commodity. It had diversified in many ways, but its flagship brand had become so common that consumer value depended upon ever lower prices. All the value-added benefits of the product and its brand had been spent. Were there new opportunities for similar products that would be exciting and sell at premium prices?

After studying numerous economic, demographic, consumer behavior, and technology trends, we identified the most important trends and integrated them through the mechanics of a cross-impact matrix. Using alternative trend outcomes with *a priori* probabilities and cross-impact values, we were able to generate alternative futures (scenarios) with the use of a scenarios software program. The matrix was a type of model and we could run any number of simulations. We examined numerous scenarios and deduced several common themes from them. One theme was that the rise of consumer anxiety about bacteria and viruses in the house, especially in bathrooms and kitchens, demanded a product that gave consumers confidence that they could disinfect household surfaces. But the demands of two-wage earner families with children over-scheduled with activities provided less time for cleaning. Consumers would want a cleaner house with less time and effort given to it. They would also want convenience. From these themes, combining the implications of several different scenarios, the project team generated specific product concepts to meet the emerging needs of consumers.

One concept was a highly effective sterilizing wipe, like a cleaning cloth with a cleaning agent already in it that could be used once and then thrown away. The idea seemed so obvious after the analysis that we wondered why nobody had introduced such a product yet. The company went to work, and within about three years they had the new product on supermarket shelves. It caught on immediately and soon became a new, multi-million dollar product category.

I will have more to say about the methods and mechanics of futuring in later chapters. Let us now turn to an overview of visioning.

The Perspective of Visioning

Visioning, unlike futuring, stems from internal factors, such as corporate mission, values, goals, and culture. As mentioned previously, every enterprise has a reason for existing. It has a mission, which provides the direction for both thinking and acting. The long-term mission sets the context for short-term goals. Typical mission and goals include:

- Enhanced brand image and corporate reputation
- Fulfilling an empty market niche or social need
- Superior customer satisfaction
- Increased market share
- Sales growth
- Profit growth
- Improved returns on investments (ROI) and returns on assets (ROA)

Values, obviously, must be consistent with the goals of the organization. They come through in such things as annual reports, press releases, corporate announcements and e-mails, operations guides and manuals, and the day-to-day culture. They are the signposts of behavior according to what is "right" and what is "wrong" to believe, say, and do. Values are typically learned through both instruction and example; often they become internalized so that managers and employees feel them without necessarily being able to articulate them. In order to keep their jobs, people learn what the company rewards and punishes.

Culture, in companies and organizations as well as in societies, provides physical and psychological security through established expectations and norms of behavior for each individual. Incentives, rewards, and punishments become well-known and highly predictable. Culture provides continuity. For some companies, culture becomes the vehicle to sustain success over time. Therefore, by its very nature, culture resists change. Oddly, the corporate culture that sustains operations also stifles innovation. In this sense, we often hear the employees and lower-level managers say, "If it isn't broken, don't try to fix it." Innovations might be distractions and deviations. As many executives have discovered, changing a company's culture is no trivial undertaking.

One of the most developed corporate cultures that I have ever seen exists at the Honda Motor Company, especially as manifested at the automobile manufacturing plant northwest of Columbus, Ohio. The Honda culture began with Soichiro Honda himself as he created his company in 1948 from the ruins of Japan after World War II. He insisted that each employee be treated respectfully and equally. All employees to this day wear white uniforms with just their first names appearing on them. The Honda culture emphasizes the Three Joys: the Joy of Buying, the Joy of Selling, and the Joy of Creating. The corporate philosophy is that workers will take pride in their work, as reflected in the quality of their products; that they will work together to solve problems without blaming any individual; and that they believe in their products to the extent that they would recommend them to their friends and buy them themselves. Honda feels very much like an extended family. Like other families, Honda has its own internal tensions, but Honda's success cannot be denied. It has emerged as a global motor company long respected for its product quality, fuel economy, and affordable prices.[39]

As in the case of Honda, business cultures typically begin with the personality, values, and behaviors of the founders. They create the working environment that they want. They institute procedures and they hire the types of people whom they can work with, and let go those who do not fit with the company culture. People must adapt to the corporate culture in order to keep their jobs. Over time, the values and behavioral norms of the founders spread to all parts of the company through manuals, policy, promotions, and incentives (and punishments). Corporate cultures can be relatively informal, or they can be highly structured, like Honda's, but they always exist to sustain operations with consistent quality.

A fundamental foundation of any enterprise's existence is the visionary leadership of its founders and executive managers. Some corporations, for example, have famous leaders who pronounce and pursue their vision for what the company should do. They are their own futurists in as much as they understand the market conditions, see trends, and visualize opportunities that others did not.

Many of us are dreamers, but few are visionary. We have fantasies about wonderful experiences in the future, but they are mostly flights of fancy: we will make a lot

---

39 www.world.honda.com/profile/philosophy/ ; "Honda Philosophy," booklet published by the Honda Motor Company in English and Japanese, 1998; personal company briefing and plant tour, Marysville, Ohio, on Friday, February 15, 2007.

of money and live free and well; we might have spontaneous erotic encounters with beautiful partners; we might travel to exotic places beyond the ordinary. But most of these dreams are the stuff of our imagination unbounded by everyday reality. Making our dreams come true often ends up requiring too much time, effort, and money beyond our mundane everyday lives. Very, very few of us, on the other hand are visionaries to the extent that we can imagine a highly desired future and actually make it happen.

What makes visionaries so rare and different from the rest of us? I wish I knew. They certainly have active imaginations – but they have the ability to go far beyond just wishful thinking. They seem to have the capability of seeing many trends, recognizing patterns, understanding cause and effect relationships, and anticipating important changes. They have bold goals and they know how to achieve them. Visionary leaders may do either explicit or intuitive futuring. They are futurists in their own ways. They are very well informed about economic, demographic, social, consumer, and technological trends. But they also see opportunities that others miss. They not only have a vision of a desired and possible state in the future, they have specific ideas about how to achieve it.

When we think of visionary leadership in American business history, we immediately think of inventors and corporate empire-builders such as Eli Whitney, Cornelius Vanderbilt, John D. Rockefeller, Andrew Carnegie, Thomas Edison, Alexander Graham Bell, Howard Hughes, Ted Turner, Steve Jobs, and Bill Gates. Many less famous visionary leaders on more modest terms have also appeared in thousands of companies, organizations, and non-profits. They have achieved wondrous results to the awe of their contemporaries.

The key to visionary leadership is the combination of extraordinary intuition and ingenious practicality. Intuition along with imagination provides the mental images of what could be emerging opportunities in the external environments; practicality, based on education and experience, provides the guidance as to how to gather and use resources for achieving aspired goals in the future. Visionary leaders and managers see the trends around them and they act in surprisingly effective ways to achieve their dreams.

Before leaving this discussion on visionary leadership, an important point needs to be made in order to keep our perspective in balance. A corporate vision is a two-edged sword. On the one side, it provides a strong sense of identity and purpose to the work of managers and employees. It generates enthusiasm, but it also resists changes. The dangerous side of vision is inflexibility. A strong vision and mission can discourage innovation, which is viewed as deviation from the norm even in the face of changing circumstances. A set of expectations for the future can easily be wrong, but people continue to hold on to them despite changing conditions. Visionary leaders can be very reluctant to modify their dreams for the future. They can hold on to unmodified goals too long. Not all visionary leaders or companies produce fairy-tale endings – many implode into nightmares. The trick, of course, is knowing when to be persistent in the face of adversity and when to make adjustments to keep the spirit, if not the letter, of the dream alive.

Another foundation of company life is its asset base. It ranks in the intermediate range of visioning. Enterprises make investments in the present in order to make more money in the future; their investments become the engine for their continued existence. In the industrial age, mills and factories were enormously expensive to build, but after they were erected they were also an effective barrier to competition. Andrew Carnegie, for example, built an industrial empire on steel mills that were so expensive that few could compete with him. His strategic competencies included making big deals, putting together large financing, and organizing enterprises into a cohesive business system. His steel empire, in the hands of J. P. Morgan and his associates, became US Steel, the first American billion-dollar corporation. E. H. Harriman pursued a parallel strategy with railroads and John D. Rockefeller with oil refineries. In addition to infrastructures, they invested heavily in distribution networks, which also afford competition protection – at least until certain industries appeared so strong that they were assailed as monopolies by the Federal government.

With contemporary computers, the Internet, e-mail, and websites, there are much lower barriers to competition today than in the past. Virtual stores can be created with virtual manufacturing and virtual distribution chains. A new enterprise can enter the world markets of goods and services with as little as $5,000 initial investment, with all other costs becoming operational rather than fixed. In the world of ICT, competition is wide open. It has been observed that Bill Gates began Microsoft and a personal fortune once estimated to have been as high as $100 billion with an initial investment not much larger than pocket change.

Once a company makes major investments in plants and distribution networks, it seeks to maximize its returns on them. The larger the capital investment, the longer financial managers seek to receive returns from them. Substantial assets provide both capabilities and limitations to change, so they can be just as stabilizing as corporate culture for sustaining success. And like corporate culture, protecting the asset bases often means resisting threats and changes to it, including changes that others might call "innovations."

Strategic competencies and strategic technologies also fit into the middle rung of visioning. The concept goes beyond just core competencies, which are too often interpreted to mean what one company or organization can do better than any others. It is entirely possible that a company might provide a "best in show" product or service but nobody buys it. A more complex definition was offered in 1995 by management consulting gurus Gary Hamel and C.K. Prahalad: "A core competency is a bundle of skills and technologies that enables a company to provide a particular benefit to customers." They went further to describe three attributes of a core competency:

1. It provides customer-perceived value (or cost savings through innovative processes).

2. It provides competitor differentiation.

3. It provides a basis for new products and services.[40]

In the early 1990s, my colleagues and I developed a different approach, which we called "strategic technologies." We gave "technology" a broad definition so that it would include hardware, software, systems, and technical knowledge and skills. It could be applied to all kinds of processes and systems as well as to products and services. Our definition allowed us to include what managers and employees know as well as what they do, with knowledge often being a highly under-leveraged resource. While applying our definition in projects with clients, we learned that most people related easier to the words "strategic competencies and technologies." To round out our method, we developed categories for "enabling technologies" and "commodities" in addition to "strategic technologies."[41]

A strategic technology has to meet all of three criteria:

1. It directly provides benefits and value, through packaged products and services, to customers as seen and paid for by customers.

2. It enjoys some kind of competitive protection through patents, copyrights, or proprietary information.

3. It fits squarely with the company's business definition, mission, and value propositions.

An enabling technology fits any one of three criteria:

1. It is not seen by or necessarily valued by customers.

2. It enjoys no particular or sustainable competitive production.

---

40 Gary Hamel and C.K. Prahalad, *Competing for the Future*. Boston: Harvard Business School Press, 1994, pp. 199, 202-207; quotation on p. 199.

41 The visioning method developed by Battelle in 1992 was called STEP-UP. It was inspired by Andrew M. Messina, "Technology Management for the 1990s," *Manufacturing Engineering*, June 1989, pp. 49-51.

3. It could be outsourced to other firms that could claim it as a strategic technology to them.

Finally, a commodity technology meets either of two criteria:

1. It is rarely differentiated by quality, but usually by the lowest price.

2. It is readily available on the open market

A strategic technology, or a strategic competency for those who continue to think of technology as the tools but not the systems or know-how behind them, has to be more than just able to do something better than anyone else can. It must, first and foremost, provide benefits and value to customers that customers can see, appreciate, and respond to.

In many cases, customers may have a difficult time distinguishing among technologies, products, and services. In a very literal sense, customers buy benefits from products and services, not technologies *per se*. For example, I have an HP Photosmart C7280 All-in-One printer, fax, copier, and scanner. At one level, I own a product that performs multiple functions with very high quality (to my eyes). But I have also bought technologies that are strategic to HP. I may have also, in the same package, bought enabling and commodity technologies that I do not notice – maybe the wires and mechanics inside are commodities, maybe the plastic is a commodity; I don't know and I don't care. But if I worked with HP as a consultant I could go through a process in which we could identify the strategic, enabling, and commodity technologies; the income from the technologies packaged into specific products and services; and the leverage that strategic technologies could gain through product and service diversification.

Generally, a strategic technology can provide three types of value to customers. The first is superior benefits through quality, utility, and design at "reasonable" prices, which can be wholly subjective to customers, although prices must be affordable given customer resources. A traditional core competency of superior capability, manifested in product and service quality, may indeed be the key to customer value. Or, secondly, a strategic technology, and its resulting products and services, might be virtually unique, such as an exciting new product to hit the market ("the best thing since sliced bread"), and highly desired by customers. Customers may be willing to pay premium prices. Or, thirdly, a strategic technology leads directly to lower production costs that are passed on to customers in the form of lower prices.[42]

---

42 The analysis here is leveraged from the concepts of competitive advantages and business strategies presented by Michael E. Porter, *Competitive Strategy. Techniques for Analyzing Industries and Competitors*. New York: Free Press, 1980.

In addition, strategic technologies must enjoy some kind of competitive advantage. We have previously mentioned that large capital investments provide one type of barrier to potential competitors. To say it again, investments provided a huge barrier in the early days of the steel industry; they provide little or no barriers in the information and communication technologies today. Another form of competitive advantage is a monopoly, which was much favored in the past but illegal today. Companies now seek dominating market share. Legal forms of competitive protection include patents, copyrights, trademarks, and proprietary knowledge. In the US, we have seen many types of technology and resulting products and services protected by patents. Many types of software program are protected by copyrights. They are also protected by the fact that software companies typically sell the object code but not the source code to customers. (This paradigm, however, could change if there were a general shift to open source rather than proprietary software.) The general rule of thumb is that if a product can be reverse engineered, it needs to be protected by patents or copyrights, and if it cannot be reverse engineered, then it is virtually protected by proprietary knowledge. This is why we see many more product than process patents – many strategic technologies in manufacturing are protected by proprietary knowledge manifested in exclusive service and non-disclosure contracts with employees, limited access facilities, and locked-up factories.

Finally, a strategic technology has to be one that contributes directly to the corporate mission, goals, and business strategies. There must be a close fit among strategic technologies, corporate culture, and assets.

Over time, strategic technologies (and their packaged products and services) will erode. They will degrade to enabling technologies when better technologies appear and when others can provide more value and protection. Given enough time, all technologies become commodities. For example, Henry Bessemer's technology to produce steel revolutionized the global steel industry in the second half of the 19th century. The quality of Bessemer steel was clearly differentiated and affordable prices were realized through huge vertically integrated and mass-producing mills. Through a strategic technology combined with enormous investments and dedicated distribution channels, Andrew Carnegie engineered the first industrial conglomerate in the US. Yet, over time the Bessemer technology declined to an enabling technology, and later into a commodity. US steel, for example, became a commodity driven by lower prices rather than differentiated quality. Eventually, old steel processes and inefficient production facilities resulted in the decline of the American steel industry in the face of intensive competition from the Japanese, who adopted new technologies and new mini-mills.

Another strategic technology can be a distribution system, whereby a company enjoys the benefits of retail exclusivity in others' stores (including store brands, like Kenmore at Sears) or a network of retail outlets of their own.

I have facilitated or participated in hundreds of new product and innovation workshops with various corporate clients around the world. Some of these workshops were very exciting, but too many were disappointing. The inertia of continuing business as usual, especially if the business had been particularly successful in the past, is very strong. I eventually learned that there are three principal barriers to new product and service development: corporate culture, assets, and distribution. Companies are very reluctant to go into a new business that "just does not feel right." This means that the corporate culture preserves stability and resists change. If a new opportunity fits the existing culture, it is much more likely to be pursued, and be successful, than something that goes against the grain of corporate culture. The second barrier is the existence of capital assets that executive managers, particularly Chief Financial Officers, are highly resistant to abandoning. Once large investments have been made, managers want to get the most out of them and not have to make new investments. So, a new product or service concept has to fit the existing asset base or it is highly unlikely to be approved. Unless the business case is very compelling, companies resist making large new capital investments and under-utilizing existing assets to support new products and services. Finally, I have seen many attractive new product and service concepts shot down by people who say "I don't know how to get this product to market." Companies like to use their existing distribution channels and do not lightly venture into new channels that may be expensive, unfamiliar, and risky. The distribution barrier, however, should become less of a problem in the future with the Internet and courier services like FedEx, UPS, DHL, and the US Postal Service.

So assets and strategic competencies and technologies, including distribution systems, act to reinforce both the positive and negative attributes of corporate culture.

The final rung of the visioning ladder consists of strategies, plans, and investments. Historically, "strategic plans" have referred to specified goals (from the mission) and ways to achieve them. "Strategic" has meant "big picture" and "at the corporate level." Of course, there are all kinds of plans, with some strategic plans being not very "strategic" and some operational plans ending up quite "strategic." Strategy in the historical military sense was the general means to achieve a goal; it was the moving of armies into position to capture a fort or town or to confront the enemy on the most favorable terms. Some military strategies are so decisive that they achieve their objectives without even having to fight the enemy. (Tactics, on the other hand, meant the movement and engagement of forces on the field of battle.) Strategic plans tend to be general in nature, with much of the detail left up to lesser commanders in the field (depending upon the willingness of the commanding general to delegate the details).

Operations mark the intersection of futuring and visioning. It is the doing of everyday work and business. It is to the market what tactics are to the battlefield. It engages the customer with transactions in the setting of business customs and regulations in the face of competition. An individual or an enterprise might take one day at a time and act totally spontaneously. Transactions for the day could be left up to chance (fate). Few business people or enterprises are willing to run such risks today. They plan ahead to have the right items for the right customers at the right price, at the right place, and at the right time. When a person or an enterprise has expectations for daily (monthly or yearly) transactions and those transactions meet or exceed expectations, then the person or enterprise has in fact influenced the external business environment and realized an internally desired result. This is the moment of the well considered expectations for the future being met by futuring and visioning.

Futuring is typically incorporated into the planning stage of visioning that precedes operations. Operations can put into action the mental functions of strategy and planning; they can also make desired futures happen to the extent that any company or organization can effectively apply its resources to achieve its desired results (a phenomenon that we call the self-fulfilling prophecy). Operations can impact external environments, and thereby influence futuring.

Theoretically, in the planning process it should make little difference whether you start with futuring or visioning – you need to do both. But in practical terms, it does make a difference. Futuring generally should be done first. It provides an external and customer-focused orientation for visioning. Many companies will do the visioning without even doing the futuring. The result may be only wishful thinking. Having said this, the relationship between futuring and visioning is not linear, but rather iterative. Elements of visioning (the mission, business definition, and goals) will show up in the expert judgment of which trends to research and forecast in the futuring.

When formulating strategies and making plans, you can evaluate options according to seven criteria, three from futuring and four from visioning:

1. *Market conditions and business opportunities*, or the total environment within which customers live, work, play, and spend (from futuring).

2. *Customers,* their behavior, and their value proposition are clearly identified and present attractive business opportunities (from futuring).

3. *Competitors and their likely responses* (from futuring).

4. *Corporate culture*, business mission, values, and goals (from visioning).

5. *Corporate assets and strategic competencies and technologies* (from visioning).

6. *Distribution networks* (from visioning).

7. *Risk and potential returns on investments* (ROI) (from visioning).

These criteria may be evaluated across a spectrum from very good (maybe five points) to poor (one point).

I have told clients that I can think strategically and I can think operationally, but I can't think strategically and operationally at the same time. They can't either. We get so wrapped up in the practical work of daily operations that we put aside abstract thinking, which is the nature of strategy. We are so busy fulfilling orders and meeting deadlines that we suspend watching trends outside the walls of our own offices and plants. Recognizing this fact of contemporary business life, I recommend that every company and organization do futuring on a routine basis (once every three years, unless rapidly changing business environments call for more frequent futuring), but do visioning at least once, maybe twice, a year at a strategic retreat. Although it should be open to many participants, futuring will likely be done by relatively few people. They will continuously track and report on trends. The reporting takes the forms of periodic briefings to senior management and regular newsletters to both managers and staff through e-mails and paper copies. The people doing the futuring should prepare background materials and briefings for the more numerous participants of visioning retreats. My experience is that most people do not enjoy doing futuring and are not particularly good at it without proper training. But they have lots to say about the nature of the company or organization, especially corporate politics.

The Tilting Hourglass

You may have noticed that Millett's Hourglass tilts at the top to the right. This is not a graphic mistake. It represents an important point: external environments change faster than internal environments, creating a misalignment of the two. The demographics of customers change over time. In the US, they are increasingly diverse, older, and more female than male. Economic conditions change, just as we discussed in connection with the Great Recession. Technologies can unexpectedly explode in benefits and cost savings to customers. Competitors and business modes change over time, too. A strategic issue for every company and organization is to keep up with external changes and stay as well aligned as possible with external business conditions. To do so requires well considered expectations, current information, and the courage to adapt to new situations.

Internal environments for companies and organizations are grounded by corporate culture and assets. People become comfortable with routines, which provide stability and sustainability through the ups and downs of business. Values are deeply held and resist change. Interestingly, the values of quality management in manufacturing actually work against change and innovations, which are viewed as deviations from the norm. Also, as mentioned earlier, large assets provide barriers to change when new investments are required to replace old capital. Especially in companies that use return on assets (ROA) as a metric of performance, there is a strong incentive to get more leverage out of existing assets and not invest in new ones. This is why some companies do not want to own assets if they can lease everything they need to do business. Such a strategy not only greatly improves ROA, or makes that metric meaningless, but also allows the company much more flexibility to innovate and quickly change products and services in response to changing customer demand.

So, corporate culture and assets provide stability and resist change. This works well when customers remain stable, too – but they usually don't. Macroscopic trends change customers, who will shift their demand to different products and services with different value propositions. Economic trends can change consumer behavior and value. I have observed that people are more willing to spend their dollars when they feel confident that they can replace those dollars with new dollars in the future from their jobs or investments. People with good jobs and investments are not only able to spend more, they are also *willing* to spend more. But people become very reluctant to spend dollars when they are unsure where the next dollars will come from. This happens with people who are in fear of losing their jobs, or have already lost their jobs and don't know where the next jobs will come from. They become afraid to spend what money they have today for fear of being worse off in the future. When the worth of a dollar goes up in people's minds because they think that money will be worth more to them in the future than today, then they will demand more value (more benefits and/or lower prices) from their purchases. This puts the value squeeze on retailers, producers, and service providers. This is an example of a change in the external environment that, if not anticipated and prepared for, could bust a business.

Technology breakthroughs always pose potential disruptions in macroscopic trends. Schumpeter argued that profit in capitalism does not stem just from the value of capital or from the value of labor but rather from new value for customers and profits for enterprises created by new technologies and innovations.

Capitalism will always be an economic system in flux, always subject to change by entrepreneurs and never sustained by prior investments. Capitalism loves change – it thrives on it. From one point of view, technologies create new business opportunities by increasing consumer value. But from another point of view, technologies can be highly disruptive, even ruinous. In part, Schumpeter asserted the concept of creative destruction by recognizing that technologies and innovations, especially in the hands of entrepreneurs, had to eliminate old assets and ways of doing business just to clean out the old and make room for the new. He also concluded near the end of his life that vision more than analysis drives entrepreneurs to change the present with innovations and technologies that best benefit them at the expense of established interests.[43]

Those "established interests" are the enterprises already in existence with corporate cultures and assets to sustain them. But every enterprise must be flexible and willing to make changes in order to respond to both new opportunities, as though they were entrepreneurs themselves, or to respond to the potential threats of "man-eating" entrepreneurial "sharks."

As a futuring manager, you must continuously watch market and customer trends, be alert to their changes, and track business successes and disappointments. You may have to make adjustments in internal operations and culture in order to keep up with changes in the external environment. When you realize that internal changes must be made to realign your enterprise with the external world, you have to show people how those changes can be implemented and convince them that doing so will make them winners rather than losers. My experience is that employees do not oppose change itself; they oppose loss – the threats of losing their jobs, promotions, benefits, and friends. So any change in culture has to be framed as innovations, reforms, and improvements that will likely fulfill everybody's needs.

A Case Study: Trends with Opportunities But No Strategic Technologies

I will close this chapter on the differences between futuring and visioning with an experience that I had in the mid-1990s. A very large international consumer products corporation invited me to present my ideas on technology forecasting. From this successful engagement, the senior company managers asked me further

---

43 Thomas K. McCraw, *Prophet of Innovation. Joseph Schumpeter and Creative Destruction.* Cambridge, MA: the Belknap Press of Harvard University Press, 2007, pp. 254-258. Also see Robert L. Heilbroner, *The Worldly Philosophers.* Touchstone/Simon & Schuster, 1999, pp. 291-310.

to undertake a scenario analysis of future strategic technologies in a particular food category.[44]

The corporate clients dominated global markets in several categories, but they worried that one of the oldest products in their food and beverages portfolio was losing rather than gaining market share around the world. As mentioned in the discussion of strategic technologies, a company may have a strategic technology and a market-leading product for years but, unless it reinvests in new technologies and product improvements, old products erode. In this case, the product continued to enjoy a strong brand reputation and presence with food retailers; the real problem was the continuous erosion in prices, so that the product in question had fallen to the status of a commodity – most households had it, they just didn't want to pay much for it. Meanwhile, competitors were introducing similar products that looked new, fresh, and exciting while my clients' products looked old and common.

My clients started with the premise that their product was excellent, but that market trends that favored other products were working against them. My associates and I worked closely with a client team that included technologists, consumer behavior researchers, and marketers. We generated five baseline scenarios and then performed numerous simulations with possible disruptive events. The prevailing scenario foretold of a future in which there would be strong market growth in this food category, but only with strong industry leadership. While the product was traditional, it was enjoying new respect due to emerging scientific research in nutrition. The product could legitimately claim health benefits, but such claims would have to be vigorously asserted by industry leaders.

After numerous frustrating discussions, I realized that the basic reason why this food product was tired was due primarily to the fact that the company was tired of it. I saw little enthusiasm for it compared with the almost wild excitement that I encountered with other products that were being aggressively pushed as world market leaders. The product in question was organized with diverse subsidiary companies that had more profitable products to offer local consumers. One conclusion that we drew was that the company would have to make a major reinvestment in this product line and push it hard or sell it off and be done with it.

Another problem that we encountered was that the client claimed strategic technologies in this product when none was apparent. The ingredients had not

---

44 An earlier version of this case history appears as Stephen M. Millett, "Futuring Consumer Products: An Illustrative Example of Scenario Analysis," in Liam Fahey and Robert M. Randall, *Learning from the Future. Competitive Foresight Scenarios*. New York: John Wiley & Sons, 1998, pp. 285-295.

basically changed for decades; manufacturing processes had certainly improved, but the homemaker could make the same product at home. Packaging had not changed significantly in years. The company offered one basic product with one market position. I saw no particular benefits to the product that the consumer seemed to regard highly; it certainly was not protected by any competitive barriers; and it was not achieving the sales, market share, and profitability demanded by the corporate mission and goals. At most, I saw a product with enabling technologies.

The ending, however, turned out happily for the clients. The corporation did not sell off the product in question, but rather affected a global reorganization of it that grouped it with other products like it. They found managers who were willing to champion the product. The most significant strategic asset, if not technology, was the company's exceptionally powerful distribution system, and the company successfully leveraged it for increased worldwide sales. Finally, the company adopted a strategy of viewing their basic product as a product platform, or as a line of products, from which they could spin out numerous product iterations, each offering something special to the consumer. The new managers repositioned the product line with both price-value products in large packages and differentiated products in new packages. They realized that if consumers want more variations on a common theme, then they had to adjust their manufacturing and business processes to accommodate consumer changes.

While the prevailing scenario was not what the managers wanted or expected, it forced everybody to verbalize their values, biases, and self-interests. The discussions that we had in closed conference rooms were less painful than the excuses for product sales disappointments that had to be presented to executive managers. Senior managers decided to reinvent the whole product category, and the strategy proved effective. Meanwhile, the R&D agenda was revitalized to more actively pursue strategic technologies for the future.

Chapter 4. Well Considered Expectations – Potential Errors and Remedies

Futuring Principle 4: The best forecasts and plans are methodically generated and provide well considered expectations for the future.

In Chapter 2 we reviewed the theoretical basis for predictability. To coin a term that would be more precise, I might have said "anticipability," because predictability is an ideal that can rarely be achieved. The best that we can do in futuring and visioning is to employ best practices from theory and experience to generate well considered expectations for the future. This chapter will explore in more detail those best practices based on common errors and omissions and the elements of predictability in futuring and visioning. A discussion of best practices in managing futuring projects will appear in a later chapter.

Forecasts from futuring and plans from visioning processes disappoint for many reasons. One obvious reason is that you cannot predict "the future" with certainty, only with degrees of uncertainty, and therefore too many forecasts assert too much. Forecasts and plans contain the same kinds of common errors found in many forms of scholarship, such as failing to define terms adequately, not accessing appropriate information or acknowledging sources, committing the sins of omission, failing explicitly to state our assumptions and trains of logic, being too precise when precision is lacking, being too vague when more specificity could have been provided, failing to describe the conditions that bound future outcomes, and failing to admit appropriate shadows of doubt.

By examining the reasons why most forecasts and plans fall short, I can recommend ways to form well considered expectations for the future.

Predispositions

People's predispositions include firmly held beliefs, convictions, biases, optimism and pessimism, values, preconceived ideas, and mental models. I have often admitted that I hold some strong convictions, although my associates suffer from biases. I remember as a young man being told that every story has three versions: yours, mine, and the truth. The reality is that we all have biases of one kind or another and they color our entire perception of the world and of time, including the ways we manage the present and the uncertainties of the future. Biases come in all shapes and sizes; they are often implicit and deeply rooted in our logical assumptions, so much so that we hardly recognize them ourselves and rarely make them explicit to others. They are based on our past experiences, good and bad, and they stem from the emotional structure behind seemingly objective rationalizations. We have developed over time preferences and predilections to help us cope with uncertainty and the fears of the future, which may hide very scary monsters.

A very common bias in thinking about the future is the attitudinal inclination toward being either too optimistic or too pessimistic. The most commonly observed type of optimism in both every day and professional lives is the view that the future will be better than the past and that we just need to get through today. I saw an upward spiraling of optimism during the boom of the 1990s – some futurists were calling for an extended boom that would last another 20 years or so. Then, after the crash of 2008-2009, some of the same optimists switched to excessive pessimism that the Great Recession might last another 20 years or so.

When most people venture to tell you what they *think* the future will be, they are really telling you what they either *hope* or *fear* the future will be. Their views are often more emotional than logical.

Some people are called "eternal optimists," because they always see the proverbial silver lining in every dark cloud. By the nature of their personalities and their personal experiences, they see the future as being more wonderful than it is today. We enjoy plays, movies, works of fiction, and forecasts that have happy endings. Of course, in our own lives, we sadly learn that not every situation has a good ending.

The opposite is the persistent pessimist. This type of person sees disaster in every situation and can make only gloomy predictions for the future: "Things are bad now and will only get worse." No amount of information or arguments will sway them from their bias toward negative expectations for the future. The ultimate pessimists, of course, are the ones who predict the imminent collapse of the stock market, the fall of Western civilization, or the end of the world itself.

Many famous forecasts have been excessively negative. The most famous example was an anonymously authored tract entitled *An Essay on the Principle of Population As It Affects the Future Improvement of Society* that appeared in England in 1798. The author proved to be the Rev. Thomas Robert Malthus, a friend of David Hume. Malthus calculated that population would grow faster than the resources of society to feed, house, and employ them. The result would be poverty and famine until populations were reduced back into balance with resources. Malthus may have been influenced by the catastrophic famine in Scotland in 1699, and he had no inkling of the potato famine that would devastate Ireland during the 1840s. His work prompted one English intellectual to characterize economics as "the dismal science." Joining with Malthus in his pessimistic view of the future was the economist David Ricardo, who rejected the optimistic attitude of Adam Smith toward the continued economic growth of the Industrial Revolution. Ricardo saw a growing scarcity of resources resulting in social tensions and even upheavals. Of course, in this same vein, no one was more pessimistic about the future of the industrial order than Karl Marx, although Marx swung from being overly pessimistic about the future of the economic conditions that he observed in his day (and condemned as "capitalism") to being overly optimistic in predicting the triumph of the working class and the achievement of a classless (communist) social order in which all people would have their needs met while contributing as they could to the overall well-being of a global society.[45]

Malthus was overly pessimistic because he saw the trends in rapid population growth and concluded that the social and economic paradigm that he knew could never support it. But the social and economic paradigm changed with the population growth. New technologies led to improved productivity in both manufacturing and agriculture. Since Malthus's theory appeared, forecasters, futurists, and the "prophets of doom" have repeatedly warned that the Earth's resources cannot sustain continued population growth and economic development. Their attitude appears to be "enough is enough," which too often means that other people have to give up what they want.

The errors of overly pessimistic demographic and economic forecasts originate in making linear extrapolations of trends judged as "bad" without acknowledging the possibilities of trend variations (such as cycles), countervailing trends, or good disruptive events (good luck or "white swans" as opposed to black swans). The "good luck" that Malthus, for example, failed to consider was the rapid increase in both agricultural and industrial productivity due to innovations in technology. Likewise, Marx failed to consider adequately the ramifications of the fact that in a free market system workers are also consumers: people have to earn enough money to buy the goods produced in their factories, or factories cannot continue to produce the goods for which there are no consumers.

Further, the pessimists see closed systems with fixed elements and defined limitations. A scientific variation on the negative bias toward the future was offered by the Harvard zoologist and geologist Stephen Jay Gould, whose writing I discussed in Chapter 2. He rejected the idea of "progress" or any particular directionality in biological evolution. In the tradition of Darwin, who saw chance as the primary force behind evolution, Gould was just as opposed to linear determinism in biological evolution as Karl Popper was in philosophical

---

45   Robert L. Heilbroner, *The Worldly Philosophers*. Revised Seventh Edition. New York: Touchstone Books/Simon & Schuster, 1999, pp. 75-104, 136-169.

historicism. He observed that, in general, species vary *from* smaller but not necessarily *toward* larger sizes. Gould characterized a complete, or closed, system as a "full house" and argued that the limits of nature in such a system constituted a "right wall," a metaphor for the right side of a two dimensional graph (which is a representation of a closed system). He argued that genetic variation in species could occur in any number of possible directions within the system, but could not cross over the "right wall."[46] Such would be the biological equivalent of exceeding the speed of light in Einstein's relativity. Gould would have agreed with those economic and environmental pessimists who would say "this is the limit" or "this is just as good as it gets."

But how do we know that we are in a "complete system" and that the "right wall" is fixed rather than adjustable? The bias of pessimists is that the "right wall" is rapidly approaching; the bias of the optimist, on the other hand, is that we are nowhere near the right wall.

An historical example of Gould's "right wall" concept as applied to economics and politics is the New Deal of President Franklin D. Roosevelt. In 1931-1932, with the US falling into the despair of the Great Depression, Roosevelt, the then governor of New York state, convened evening seminars in his home with leading economists and other academics who would later be called the President's "Brain Trust." These experts laid the foundation for the strategy of the New Deal following Roosevelt's election to the Presidency in 1932. They argued that, although economic recovery was important in the short term, economic systemic reforms were more important in the long term. Their prevailing view was that the Depression had been caused by gross overproduction, wasteful competition, and an excessive concentration of wealth in the hands of too few large corporations and businessmen. While factories produced too many goods, too few consumers could afford to buy them. The Brain Trust came to the conclusion that the American economy had hit its capacity and that in the future the annual GNP would be in the range of $90-$100 billion, or just about the same as it had been before the crash of 1929! The great corporations of history had been formed and the technologies of the modern era had all been discovered. Having reached a theoretical limit of growth, most people were not likely to realize higher wages from unregulated industry in the future. In an economy driven largely by consumer spending, the wealth of the nation had to be somewhat redistributed to give more spending power to consumers in order to sustain manufacturing. From here developed the concept of "demand side economics" as practiced by the Roosevelt administration and rationalized by the British economist John Maynard Keynes. The Brain Trust behind the President, therefore, placed more importance on reforming society and

---

46   Stephen Jay Gould, *Full House. The Spread of Excellence from Plato to Darwin*. New York: Harmony Books, 1996.

the economic order than in stimulating economic growth, which they dismissed as having long-term marginal prospects.[47]

The New Deal economists thought that the Depression was caused by the economy smashing into a natural "right wall" of systemic limitation. Based on their interpretation of history and the recent hardships of economic catastrophe, the experts framed excessively pessimistic expectations for the future. They could not imagine how large the American economy could grow beyond the paradigm that was familiar to them. They failed to anticipate World War II, jet engines, the atomic bomb, the computer, the transistor and digital technologies, plastics, and DNA. Yet many of them lived to see the American annual GNP exceed $300 billion as soon as 1951. The belief in the idea that the Depression marked the limits of growth led many economists to predict that the US would fall back into the Depression after World War II (or after the Korean War or after the Cold War, etc.) The same economists would be stupefied if they knew that over the next 75 years, from 1933 to 2008, at the brink of the Great Recession, the US annual GDP (Gross Domestic Product, as we now calculate what used to be called the Gross National Product, or GNP) would expand beyond $14 trillion. In the year 2000 or so, Bill Gates, the world's richest man as a result of founding the world's largest digital computer software company, was estimated to have had a personal fortune of about $100 billion, or approximately the same size, at least in current dollars, as the entire American GNP in 1929.

We relearned the lessons of the Great Depression some 80 years later. In the 1920s and 1990s, periods of strong economic growth stimulated excessive optimism about the future. People felt that what they were experiencing was "normal" and would continue for years to come. Then came the financial "earthquakes" of 1929 and 2008 with successive market after shocks. People shifted from over-optimism to over-pessimism virtually overnight. Good times and good feelings tend to reinforce themselves in an upward spiral of optimism. Likewise, bad times and bad feelings also reinforce themselves in a downward spiral. Eventually calm people regain their sense of balance, but the eternal pessimist is persistently negative and gloomy about the future.

A very similar example of a pessimistic forecast, but in an entirely different context, was the report from the Club of Rome in 1972, which I discussed in Chapter 2. It was called *Limits to Growth*, and the title precisely captures its central thesis. Published as a book, it sold some 30 million copies around the world. Using the World3 computer-based model employing the systems dynamics method of Jay Forrester at MIT, the authors of the study generated projections for selected

---

47   David M. Kennedy, *Freedom From Fear. The American People in Depression and War, 1929-1945.* New York: Oxford University Press, 1999, pp. 117- 124, 372-375.

trends and concluded that the global population would hit a high of 10 billion in the year 2050 and then drop by 40% during the following 5 decades. Food production was very unlikely to keep pace with the global population explosion following World War II. They also predicted that the global oil supply, given known consumption patterns and oil reserves at that time, would run out in the year 1992. *Limits to Growth* was updated and re-released in 1992 and 2004. Even though later simulations modified the initial forecasts, concluding that oil would not run out until the year 2070, the major themes remained the same: that in a world constrained by limited resources, the only solution to eventual catastrophe on a Malthusian level was the curtailment of consumption and the adaptation of simpler, less exploitive life styles.[48]

A parallel global forecasting project was commissioned by President Jimmy Carter in the 1970s. Its three-volume report *Global 2000* that was released in 1980 contained many of the same types of predictions found in *Limits to Growth*. It sounded a warning on the potential future degradation of the Earth's environment. It was immediately attacked by futurist Herman Kahn and University of Illinois economist Julian Simon, who offered a counter-balancing, over-optimistic view of the world's future. Kahn denounced modeling in general in favor of trend extrapolations (and virtually ignored his own scenarios methodology for generating alternative futures that had been adapted by the *Global 2000* team). Relying heavily on projections of technology progress, Kahn and Simon framed expectations for a future with alternative energy sources, improved personal vehicles and homes, agricultural abundance, population control, generally lower prices, and strong economic growth.[49]

Many of the same themes expressed in *Limits to Growth* and *Global 2000* were heard again in the first decade of the 21st century, although packaged somewhat differently. While the impending global population crisis appears to have fallen off people's lists of worries, there is still much anxiety about the future of energy and the planet's macro-environment. Some people have predicted that we have hit or will soon hit the mid-point of total global oil extraction; that as the world's reserves of oil decline, oil can only become scarcer and more expensive. When the global market for a barrel of oil reached about $147/barrel, many felt as though the day of reckoning had finally arrived. Then the price fell continuously

---

48   Donella Meadows, Jorgen Randers, and Dennis Meadows, *Limits to Growth. The 30-Year Update*. White River Junction, VT: Chelsea Green Publishing Co., 2004. Also see William A. Sherden, *The Fortune Sellers. The Big Business of Buying and Selling Predictions*. New York: John Wiley & Sons, Inc., 1998, pp. 152-154;"Club of Rome," "Limits to Growth," and "Donella Meadows" on www.wikipedia.com

49   Constance Holden, "Simon and Kahn versus *Global 2000*," *Science*, Vol. 221, 22 July 1983, pp. 341-343.

to about $40/barrel. Another major fear for the future is global climate change due to increasing concentrations of greenhouse gases in the atmosphere directly attributed to human activities on Earth. Some dire predictions (some would say excessively negative) have been made about future shifts in agricultural zones and seasons, the melting of the ice cap at the North Pole, the rising of the oceans, and the more frequent occurrences of violent storms around the world.

The principal problem, from a futuring perspective, with the overly pessimistic forecasts mentioned above was an excessively negative bias on the part of the forecasters. The forecasts contained an underlying distrust, if not contempt, for modern ways of life – especially the social and economic ways of the industrial and post-industrial era. Malthus, for example, could not, or was unwilling to, picture in his mind the possibilities of the agricultural revolution, whereby innovative ways and technological advances greatly increased productivity. A major problem in the early 21st century is how to get an abundance of foodstuffs from areas of excessive production through our distribution channels and at acceptable prices to the undernourished people of the world. Malthus also had no appreciation for the future of family planning. Likewise, the forecasters of *Limits to Growth* were excessively pessimistic because of their own convictions (biases).

Oddly, the predispositions of optimism and pessimism can take on the predictive characteristics of self-fulfilling prophecies. In some extreme cases, very optimistic people may have such faith in themselves and such strong confidence in what they are doing that they make their own happy futures. Their energy, endurance, and example for others contribute directly to achieving the very result that they have so much faith in. At the other extreme, very pessimistic people can also make their own dreaded futures happen. Their negative behavior and their rejection of positive counter-trends as well as their sense of doom and self-defeating behavior may alienate other people and may contribute to, if not cause, the occurrence of the very future that they fear the most.

Closely related to biases of optimism and pessimism are the biases of values – both religious and ideological. Futurists are human, too, and they share all the attributes of the human condition. Some futurists have strong religious beliefs that color their expectations for the future; some others may hold strong deterministic views based on motion, molecules, and DNA. There are futurists in the public sector who embrace public values (what is good for the people), and there are futurists in the private sector who embrace private values (what is good for the company). Likewise, political biases can skew forecasts.

I recall a futuring project that I managed during the Reagan Administration for a major aerospace and defense company. They had experienced huge growth in business volume due to the major military buildup at that time and they projected more growth throughout the 1980s and 1990s. They were making their own significant investments in future strategic weapon systems for the US Air Force. I concluded from our scenario project that the client had unrealistic expectations. They were seeing the trends that supported their biases and ignoring those that did not. At the end of the project, which had generated a lot of contentious debates, the client smiled and said to me, "Thank you for not bringing any biases in our forecast." I had to laugh and confess, "Oh, I have plenty of biases – they're just not the same as yours." For this very reason, well considered expectations for the future need to explicitly identify underlying assumptions (mental models), present evidence and compelling logic, and then be subjected to expert peer review and validated and modified by continuous trend monitoring.

Convictions, biases, and values are all wrapped up into the larger context of mental models, or what the Germans call *Weltanschauung*, "world view." The term refers to an orientation based on personal experiences, attitudes, beliefs, and culture. It may be highly individual or it may be shared among a large group, even a nation. Some might argue that there may be a genetic predisposition to a particular way of thinking (or, at least, the processing of information). Professor Peter Senge of MIT called patterns of behavior "nature's templates" and emphasized the importance of mental models in the contexts of both systems analysis and management.[50] Regardless of their origins (inherited, learned, or both), mental models provide filters for both intellectual and emotional expectations for the future.

In short, predispositions such as personality orientations, religious or secular beliefs, convictions, biases, preconceived ideas and mental models compromise most forecasts and plans because they lead people to skew expert judgment, exaggerate trend momentum, misinterpret cause-and-effect relationships, and omit information that does not fit their mental models. Even more egregious than errors in forming well considered expectations, biases contribute to the inflexibility of some managers and leaders in making adjustments (also called deviations) in their plans in response to unexpected changes.

I recall an incident that occurred just a few years ago when representatives from the US Department of Energy (DOE) were visiting a major electric utility. I was there as a consultant to the utility, but many of my colleagues were also doing business with DOE, so I just sat and listened so that I would not say anything offensive to either side. Good thing. The conversation was on the topic of distributed power generation. The DOE representatives advocated that the utility should invest more in distributed generation closer to its customers, but they offered no Federal incentives to do so. They were advocating more choices for

---

50 Peter M. Senge, *The Fifth Discipline. The Art & Practice of the Learning Organization*. New York: Currency/Doubleday, 2006 (1990), especially pp. 91-112 and 163-190.

customers and championing public values. Of course, the utility had the opposite point of view. They were a publicly traded corporation with stockholders who demanded both quarterly dividends and stock appreciation. The utility people viewed distributed generation as a threat to their investments in central station power generation (the huge coal-burning power plants). So the DOE and utility participants in the discussion went back and forth with their conflicting values and interests, reaching no common ground at that time.

I mention this episode because it shows how biases (in this case, those of the public versus private sectors) converge with self-interests. The two are so closely related that I want to talk about self-interests and then give you my recommendations for how to manage both.

Self-Interest and Wishful Thinking

The predispositions and biases discussed above may be conscious or subconscious, but they are largely ways of processing data within a pre-existing mental framework. They are largely psychological. Self-interest, on the other hand, is very material. It is more about the pocketbook than the head. Self-interest leads some people to listen to and believe those expectations for the future that make them look or feel good now. Their wishful thinking is that the future will inevitably unfold just as they want it to. Futurists and managers are subject to tremendous temptations to tell their customers and superiors what they want to hear rather than what they need to hear. In ancient cultures, the king might kill a messenger who brought ill tidings.

I admit that the line between abstract predispositions and material self-interests is very vague. People like both: they feel most comfortable when their abstract ideas and expectations for the future align well with their self-interests. Their mindset for thinking about the future is highly influenced by wishful thinking. Given the historical faith in the generous prospects of the American Dream, the notion of self-interest as an article of faith, both religious and secular, is especially strong in American culture.

I have experienced many awkward moments when managing futuring projects that produced forecasts that were not to the liking of the client – more precisely, when I presented scenarios that warned them that the future that they wanted and expected had a low probability of occurrence due to circumstances beyond their control. The challenge is not to change the scenarios to suit the client's wishes, but to present the scenarios as options that may occur under different sets of circumstances. Potentially unwelcomed views of the future have to be packaged particularly well to persuade the skeptical client to consider them.

There are many historical cases of someone giving a forecast designed purely to please an executive. I will share with you my favorite story of a prediction that served well the self-interests and wishful thinking of both the forecaster and the patron. During the Jewish uprising against the Romans that began in 69 CE, the Roman legions systematically besieged and massacred rebel strongholds in and around Judea. Masada was the most famous of these. When the rebels saw that they could not win, they committed suicide rather than fall into the brutal hands of the conquerors. But at Jotapata in Galilee events took a different turn. After a long and bloody siege, the few survivors of the Jewish garrison killed each other, leaving only one alive, the commander, Josephus. According to his own account in *The Jewish War*, Josephus did not commit suicide but allowed himself to be taken prisoner. As was the custom, he was presented to the Roman commander for the sentence of death. Rather than humbling himself and begging for mercy, Josephus announced to the Roman general: "You suppose, sir, that in capturing me you have merely secured a prisoner, but I come as a messenger of the greatness that awaits you… You, Vespasian, are Caesar and Emperor, you and your son here. So load me with your heaviest chains and keep me for yourself; for you are master not only of me, Caesar, but of land and sea and all the human race…" Vespasian, being a traditional Roman who embraced the customs of Fate and fortunetelling, decided to keep Josephus alive. True to the prophecy, Vespasian was proclaimed the Roman emperor in that same year, 69, founding the Flavian Dynasty. When he died ten years later, he was succeeded by his son Titus, a great Roman general in his own right who had stood at his father's side in Galilee when Josephus had made his prediction about their destiny. Josephus became a Roman citizen, an advisor to the emperors, a scholar, and the historian of the Jewish people.[51]

We often see a convergence of convictions, biases, values, and self-interest. People find it emotionally very difficult to reconcile their values with self-interests if they are not in harmony. In general, people like to enjoy harmonious emotional states in which their values and their self-interests are well aligned. This alignment very much influences their views of the future as well as the present. To generate well considered expectations for the future that are relatively if not absolutely free of convictions, biases, values and self-interest is theoretically possible but very difficult. It would require a great deal of latitude for emotional detachment, a strong sense of security, and much hard analysis and logic. In addition, there may be no absolute standard for "objectivity," which may only be a consensus of perceptions among people who share the same belief system or experiences. This observation suggests that effective forecasts are not so much those that please

---

51   Josephus, *The Jewish War*. Translated by G. A. Williamson. Revised with a new introduction, notes and appendices by E. Mary Smallwood. London: Penguin Books, 1981, p. 221.

the self-interests and biases of executives but rather those that emerge through participation in the process of futuring and broad agreement over their results.

I have seen many forecasts and plans fail because they were too ambitious given existing and changing conditions. Especially in planning, high goals can be set that are substantially misaligned with opportunities. As I have repeatedly said, planning based on visioning with little or no futuring to temper it can amount to little more than wishful thinking. It is not enough to want to achieve a goal in the future – you must also know how to achieve it within the context of external circumstances and your own resources.

Yet, it must be admitted that sometimes wishful thinking works. It works everyday in many small ways, but it is hard to achieve with the big things in life. Certainly goals provide motivation and direction. I suppose that if you had no goals you would not need plans; but if you have goals, you have to have plans. Without sound planning, adequate resources, and hard work, wishful thinking depends too heavily upon luck.

To counteract the potential errors of predispositions, biases, and self-interest in futuring, I recommend the following measures:

- Identify and admit to yourself your own predispositions, biases, and self-interest. Guard against implicitly imposing them upon your forecasts and plans.

- Do sufficient research and prepare evidence and logic to back up your conclusions; it will give your work more credibility to others who may not see or share your own convictions.

- Frame your forecasts and plans as "if...then" propositions and make explicit the conditions surrounding your expectations. You may wish to present multiple possible outcomes (scenarios) expressed as stories with a point to them rather than as quantitative, and potentially misleading, forecasts for the future.

- If you are going to be an advocate of any particular point of view or course of action for the future, do so *after* rather than *before* thorough analysis of the trends and issues that lead to well considered expectations for the future.

- Submit your forecasts to outside experts and peer review – the strength of your forecasts emerge with the strength of your ability to defend them explicitly and rationally.

- When disagreements about the future emerge, make the strongest possible case for your point of view and then ease off – agree to disagree and then monitor events to see whose point of view appears to be emerging. The resolution of disagreements about the future can only be resolved by the future.

- Be prepared to be humble and to be proven wrong by future events. Often being intellectually honest in the face of uncertainty will count for more in the long run than being right. I have never known a futurist who was right all the time, including myself.

- Having made a forecast, monitor trends and be prepared to modify a forecast based on new information – be flexible and adaptive to new information and be prepared to revise previous forecasts and prepare new ones.

The Recency Effect

People are more influenced by the present than they typically realize. Trend analysis is inherently limited by information from the past and the present, and the more you rely on trend analysis alone the more you will be confined to the proposition that the future will look a lot like the past and the present. Beyond the potentially hypnotic power of trend analysis, managers often fall into the trap of assuming (setting parameters and boundary conditions) that the most important trends and issues of the present will also be the most important ones in the future.

We call the influence of the present on our thinking about the future the "recency effect." It is one of the major causes of errors in both futuring and visioning. It leads to both errors of commission (including factors and relationships that seem important today but will prove not to be so important in the future) and errors of omission (failing to see emerging trends and issues that appear to be minor today but will prove to be major in the future).

As we explored in Chapter 2, the Scottish Enlightenment philosopher David Hume concluded as early as 1739 that people's perceptions of cause-and-effect relationships are based on their past experiences, habits, and expectations. While people can recognize valid chains of causes and effect, they also make frequent errors simply because the future is not going to be exactly like the past. Anticipating Bayes' theory of conditional probabilities, Hume observed that "probability is founded on the presumption of a resemblance betwixt those objects, of which we have had experience, and those, of which we have had none…" More than two centuries later, countless psychological experiments have demonstrated that people's perception of the present frames both their memories of the past and their expectations for the future. How people *feel* about the past and the present typically colors how they *think* about the future. Harvard psychology professor Daniel Gilbert concluded that "Because predictions about the future are made *in* the present, they are inevitably influenced *by* the present….[W]e tend to imagine the future as the present with a twist…." Curiously, the theologian (Saint) Augustine of Hippo made a very similar observation in the fourth century: "…[T]here are three times, a present of things past, a present of things present, a present of things to come….The present considering the past is the memory [or history], the present considering the present is immediate awareness, the present considering the future is expectation."[52]

While people can often correctly identify relatively short-term and limited causes and effects, they typically cannot easily recognize long-term and extended chains of cause-and-effect relationships. Hume correctly observed that people often make mistakes in attributing effects to causes that may reflect more accurately the state of mind of the witness rather than the phenomena. Yet, as mentioned before, time itself may be a very long chain of cause-and-effect sequences. Because they are so hard to trace, cause-and-effect relationships are much easier to identify when isolated and when judged from the immediate present, hence giving a cognitive bias to expecting the future to emerge from the most recent effects.

Stanford University psychologists Philip Zimbardo and John Boyd agreed with the concept of the future of the present. From their own experiments, they concluded that one's memory of the past and one's expectations for the future are highly colored by one's feelings about the present. Both "the past" and "the future" are psychologically constructed mental states based primarily on the present. They identified six different psychological types of time perspectives:

- The past-negative: memories of the past that emphasize hurt and disappointment that can be influenced by one's negative feelings in the present.

- The past-positive: memories of the past that emphasize happiness and achievement, likewise influenced by one's positive feelings in the present.

- Present-fatalistic: perceptions that one is reactive to forces beyond one's control.

- Present-hedonistic: feelings of joy and pleasure in the awareness of the present.

---

52 David Hume, *A Treatise of Human Nature*. Edited by Ernest C. Mossner. London: Penguin Books, 1985, p. 138 (also see pp. 179, 183-184, 188-189, 194, and 197-199); Gilbert, *Stumbling on Happiness*, p. 162 (also 121-162, 171, and 215-257); Saint Augustine, *Confessions*. Translated by Henry Chadwick. New York: Oxford University Press, 1998, p. 235.

- Future: expectations as plans to do and achieve certain goals and states of being in the future based on both individual ambitions and cultural influences.

- Transcendental future: expectations of reaching paradise, Heaven, or perfection in the afterlife.

They concluded that the healthiest mental state of the present is a blend of past-positive, present-hedonistic, and future. As for considerations of the past, they asserted that one cannot change what happened in the past, but one can embrace a positive attitude about it. They also advised that positive feelings about the present can lead to more proactive and less reactive approaches to the future. The past is important to mental health, they found, because it provides a sense of identity and continuity. From their psychological perspective, "The past is also our best predictor of the future. It's notoriously imperfect, but it is all that we have."[53]

We tend to think that the issues that we are wrestling with today will be the same ones that will dominate our thinking in the future. Using this line of reasoning, we might expect that the big issues for another decade or more will be renewed economic growth, financial stability in world markets, terrorism, the war in Afghanistan, health care, energy, and global climate change (in other words, the things that obsess us today). But the big issues in the future might be very different, such as:

- Political unrest and domestic violence in China leading to the collapse of political domination by the Communist Party (somewhat but not exactly the same as what occurred in the Soviet Union in the 1990s).

- Cuba becomes a democratic and free-market country closely allied with the US.

- The dissolution of the current country of Canada into smaller countries.

- The addition of new states to the United States (perhaps Puerto Rico, Cuba, Haiti, other struggling Caribbean nations, former western provinces of Canada, etc.).

- A new energy crisis caused by inadequate supplies and soaring prices of electricity in the US.

- US military intervention to restore political, social, and economic stability in Mexico.

---

53 Philip Zimbardo and John Boyd, *The Time Paradox. The New Psychology of Time That Will Change Your Life*. New York, Free Press, 2008, pp. 52, 61-68, 80, 86, 91, 94, 137, and 318; quote on p.95.

- Shift in security focus from potential acts of terrorism by Muslim extremists to acts of domestic violence by drug cartels and political and social fringe elements (survivalists, extreme libertarians, anarchists, eco-terrorists, etc.).

- Social, economic, and political conflicts between aging Boomers and younger generations in the US over government spending priorities (health vs. education), employment (Boomers staying in jobs too long to the detriment of younger employees), taxes (especially for Social Security and Medicare), and interest rates (with the aging Boomers demanding higher interest rates).

- Reduced size of the European Union with countries gravitating to other economic blocs (such as a trans-Atlantic trading group and an energy-rich economic bloc including Russia and central Eurasia).

- Al Qaeda takeover of Saudi Arabia.

- The middle class revolution brings a democratic and pro-Western government to power in Iran.

- Taliban takeover of Pakistan and its nuclear arsenal.

- Re-emergence of Russian power in Eastern Europe and Central Asia.

- The collapse of Pakistan and its reunion with the rest of the Indian subcontinent.

- A cartel of oil-buying countries that will set the global price of oil rather than the free market or the oil-producing countries.

To summarize, the futuring manager can easily fall into the trap of identifying and projecting trends that seem very important at the moment that the futuring project begins. Perhaps this is another variation on bias – the bias to study the known rather than the unknown. I am still working on the problem of how to think about trends and events that do not even occur to me now.

To counter the recency effect, you should follow these best practices:

- Understand trends and present circumstances, as they provide the continuity aspect of futuring, but never assume that they will automatically play out in the future as they have in the past.

- Resist the temptation of assuming that what exists today will automatically continue in the future.

- Always consider possible trend changes and black swans.

- Think in terms of alternative futures, or scenarios, rather than a single future. Only one future will occur, but we have limited certainty in the present about which possible future will play out. Seemingly random events and black swans do occur.

- Never prepare a forecast alone and in isolation – always conduct a futuring project, no matter what methods are used, with participating experts drawn from many different specialties and points of view. All forecasts should be peer reviewed and subject to constructive criticism to uncover elements of the recency effect.

- Monitor trends and events and revise your forecasts according to new information.

False Starting Points and Assumptions

Like any other train of logic, the point of departure often determines the destination for well considered expectations for the future. I have seen many peculiar assumptions made at the very beginning of a forecast that were excused by the disclaimer, "Well, we had to start some place." Assumptions in futuring are essentially setting 100% *a priori* probabilities on certain conditions, or arbitrarily setting variables to parameters. It is also, to one extent or another, an arbitrary (and possibly biased) definition of a closed system or a fixed set for purposes of predictability. Many assumptions are based on little more than predispositions and wishful thinking, as discussed above.

One place to start a futuring project is with the present. This is a valid but limiting starting point because it fails to consider history and risks the bias of the recency effect. Another place to start is with the past. Economists have told me that in their forecasting they prefer to go back twice as far in time as they will go forward in the future; a forecast, therefore, of GDP in the US, for example, from 2010 to 2020 would require trend analysis back to at least 1990. However, in the case of consumer value in personal transportation discussed earlier, the time frame was 50 years in the past as a run up to 50 years in the future. If you believe in long waves, you might need to go back at least 60 years in time just to forecast economic performance 10 years into the future.

False assumptions include incorrect estimates of what trends, issues, and factors will be important in the future (reflecting the recency effect and potential errors of omission); linear extrapolations of trends without due consideration of potential changes to them; inconstant relationships among trends, issues, and factors; cause-and-effect relationships that may be neither valid nor predictable; the belief that the environment, or paradigm, under consideration is more or less a closed system unaffected by random events or exogenous variables.[54]

To combat the potential problems of false starts and assumptions, you should:

- Ask yourself what assumptions, even philosophical premises, theories, and models underlie your work and why you assert them.

- Explicitly identify and justify the starting points and assumptions at the beginning; citing respected if not authoritative sources for them adds to their credibility.

- Submit your work for peer review, which may catch underlying assumptions.

Omissions and Unexpected Events

Parallel to the recency effect, by which current conditions and issues dominate a forecast, another common cause of the failure of forecasts and plans is the omission of trends and issues that do not seem important at the moment but emerge as major themes in the future. In addition, there will always be the potential for unexpected and disruptive events to occur that may be impossible to anticipate. In everyday life, we make plans and then we may have to change them because something unexpectedly interferes with them. Or, we hear people say "Now, all things being equal, then…." But "all things" do not always remain "equal," which is another way of saying "all things remaining the same." Lots of variables can change, producing unintended and unexpected circumstances. Common examples of how plans can go awry include changes in the weather, accidents, illness, and other people doing unexpected things that impact you.

Another kind of omission is the failure to anticipate Taleb's black swans, or those highly disruptive events that seem from the point of view of the present to have very low probabilities of occurrence but potentially very great consequences if they do happen. Such disruptive events are also called "outliers" by statisticians and "exogenous variables" by economists. As Taleb argues, in many if not most cases they are impossible to anticipate or even detect at an early stage. So the strategy is to be aware of the possibility of an approaching black swan and be prepared to deal with it when it lands. In this situation, the mental attitude of awareness of the possibility of change and the willingness to be flexible are more useful than trying to see a black swan in the dark.

---

54 Adam Gordon, *Future Savvy*. New York: American Management Association, 2009, pp. 93-103 and 276-277.

Be that as it may, you can still watch for emerging trends, or what are called "weak signals." The problem is that too often they are so weak that nobody sees them as signals. Here is where the distinction between monitoring and scanning is helpful. You should know what the most important trends are and you should monitor them carefully. Monitoring is the continuous review of information on known trends; it is the deep-dive approach. On the other hand, scanning is broad and shallow: it is based on the realization that you do not know exactly what you are looking for, but you are staying alert to anything that looks unusual. In a more or less stable market environment, you would spend 80% of your resources for such activities on monitoring and 20% on scanning. In highly volatile environments, however, you would spend more on scanning than monitoring.

Yet another challenge is how to imagine events that today seem unimaginable but nonetheless come to pass. This is the very riddle "how to think about the unknown that is totally unknown," or the space called "the unknown unknowns." I have not figured out any better approach to this dilemma than the processes of continuous learning and exercising the imagination.

In the case history of the future cohesion of the European Union that appeared in Chapter 1, the client and I missed the fall of the Berlin Wall and the collapse of the entire Soviet Union and its sphere of influence. To us and millions of others, the events of 1989-1991 from Berlin to Moscow came as complete surprises. We would never have believed as late as 1988 that it was remotely possible that Soviet power was on the verge of collapse. The closest that we came to anticipating such a stupendous black swan was the trend of détente in Soviet-Western relations. The prevailing scenario said that Western relations with the Soviet bloc would continue to be "friendly," yet we had no idea of how friendly. We initially concluded that the Cold War would have little or no direct impact on the EU reaching its 1992 unification goals, and we were correct up to a point.

What we failed to foresee in the beginning of our futuring project we did recognize fairly quickly with further information and simulations of disruptive events on the baseline scenarios. We feared that the collapse of East Germany might threaten EU cohesion because it could distract the West Germans from achieving the EU goals due to their own national unification goals. Further events proved, however, that the challenge of integrating East Germany into West Germany stiffened rather than diminished the resolve of the EU cohesion champions to see their goals through to completion. An even larger potential distraction from the focus of EU unity arose when several countries of the former Soviet bloc applied for membership in the EU, further increasing potential diversity and lack of cohesion among an even larger set of EU members. What we omitted from consideration was that the EU might grow stronger both in depth (cohesion among its members) and breadth (number of member countries). Even so, while we missed some major developments of the future for the EU, our business implications for our client's strategic growth remained entirely valid.

The following advice is offered to futurists and planners to cope with potential omissions and unexpected events:

- Begin by admitting that no forecast or plan is ever complete – recognize that unknown and unexpected events can and may occur. Do not be too quick to dismiss potential black swans that currently appear outlandish, fantastic, or utterly impossible.

- Use expert imagination to identify potential changes and black swans (the outliers to a futuring model and forecast) and simulate their potential impacts on baseline forecasts and plans.

- Monitor real-time data to see whether there are emerging changes to forecasts and plans; also do random scanning to pick up on any possible "weak signals" of emerging trends or potential disruptive events.

- Think in terms of multiple possible future conditions (scenarios) and multiple variations in plans to cover any number of contingencies.

- Learn to be more flexible and willing to adapt when circumstances are known to justify changes in forecasts and plans.

Lack of Information

Similar to the sins of omission is the lack of information about past and present circumstances that compromise well considered expectations for the future. In the case of the lack of information, you may be aware of the most important trends, issues, and factors and even correctly appraise their potential importance, but you may not have adequate information to form an educated guess about the future. You may have no factual basis for a probability, so that any *a priori* probability will be simply guess work, which is OK as a starting point. The lack of information can be caused by the absolute absence of any information (secrecy of existing information or the total absence of any evidence of any phenomenon) or by the inadequacy of time, effort, and drive on the part of the forecaster or planner to acquire information that is available but obscure.

Lack of information plays a very important role in trying to anticipate what will occur in the stock market and in all kinds of wagers. Since the Great Depression, the Security and Exchange Commission (SEC) has tried to police buyers and sellers so that they have more or less equal access to critical information. They crack down on "insider trading," when parties have privileged information upon which to act that other investors do not. This kind of insider trading has been attributed as a source of the fortunes of the super-rich, such as Joseph Kennedy. In fact, when President Roosevelt appointed Kennedy as the first chairman of the SEC in 1934, critics cried that the President had "let the fox in the chicken coop." Kennedy was an expert in insider trading, so he knew what needed regulating to prevent abuses by others in the future. Today, stock prices go up and down on shared expectations of what stock values should be according to information sources *and* rumors of unexpected changes in company performances and government actions. A company's stock price can go up when it reports corporate losses when such losses were less than what traders expected; likewise, a company's stock price can plummet when there are rumors of a merger or a business failure that were not expected. Lacking critical pieces of information, investors and traders can become highly emotional, driven by bouts of greed and fear of exaggerated expectations. By restricting the flow of information to create a "fair" market environment, the stock market can actually become more volatile due to rumors and sudden changes.

Expressed in the terms of Bayesian logic, the probability that you place on the outcome of a forecast or a plan increases with information gained; as you get closer to the outcome, your information becomes more complete and your expectations more on the mark. This is why short-term forecasts are more likely to be accurate than long-term forecasts: the system is closer to becoming closed, the set is closer to becoming fixed, your information gets more complete, and the time for disruptive events to occur is reduced, although not entirely eliminated.

An example of the lack of information resulting in ill considered expectations for the future is the slow reporting of data on US GDP. I have mentioned before that I was being asked in March 2008 whether the American economy had slipped into a recession. We did not have the data at that moment, but I said that from what I was seeing it certainly felt like a recession. It was not until early 2009 that the data were published showing that the Great Recession had begun as early as December 2007. The time lag for GDP figures is typically in the range of three to six months, with figures being adjusted even as long as a year later. We had data for the downturn in real estate prices and residential construction activity. But virtually all of us (including such experts as Federal Reserve Chairman Ben Bernanke, New York Federal Reserve bank CEO Timothy Geithner, and super-investor Warren Buffett) did not foresee the global financial meltdown caused by the boom, bubble, and bust in the international trading of sub-prime mortgages, derivatives, hedge funds, and high risk debts. In March 2008 the financial giant Bear Sterns virtually collapsed, but was rescued by JP Morgan Chase under the watchful eye of Geithner. It was widely believed at the time that a major financial crisis had been averted. Then the collapse of Lehman Brothers on September 15, 2008 shocked most people. We had no idea how extensive the exposed debts of sub-prime mortgages and derivatives actually were, not just in the US but also worldwide. We did not see the crisis coming because so few people knew about the abuses of the mortgage, debt, and derivative markets and even fewer were talking about it. New York Stock Exchange prices, which had been slipping through the year, plummeted in late September and fell into a pit of raging bears through early 2009.

When tracking trends for clues of what may be coming with time, we rely on "leading indicators" as prophetic signs of the future. These leading indicators are taken as "signs," not from God, but from trend momentum, cause-and-effect chains of events (both those that are firmly established and those that are hypothetical sequential scenarios), and possibly the laws of physics. Sometimes the leading indicators are prescient and many times they are false leads. Some indicators are well proven and stable, while others are assumed and highly vulnerable to the impacts of other trends and events. The high oil price of the first half of 2008 turned out to be a weak rather than a strong leading indicator: it anticipated the rapid demise of General Motors and Chrysler, but not directly the financial crisis of Bear Sterns and Lehman Brothers. On the other hand, with perfect hindsight, the decline in housing prices and the exceptionally high volume of sub-prime mortgages leading to borrower defaults proved to be foreshadowing of the financial crisis that began in mid-September 2008. We are becoming more sophisticated with the enormous amounts of information accessible today and with well-documented experiences, but our ability to read leading indicators is just as much an art today as the reading of "the writing on the wall" by ancient prophets.

My experience has taught me to use trends for the information that they provide and to use experts for opinions as a placeholder for future information. Expert knowledge of trends (and their leading indicators) and informed imagination for potential disruptions provide more guidance for the future than just guessing or wishful thinking. Yet, the experts, of course, can be wrong, and they frequently are, because expert judgment suffers from at least two great disadvantages. Contrary to what the experts may think, no expert knows everything. In fact, the more the expert knows about one thing the less he or she is likely to know about many other things. Experience tells us that generalists often prove to be more prescient than specialists. Likewise, using many experts across many areas of expertise provides a richness that rarely comes from just one expert. In addition, all experts suffer from biases, so again using many experts spreads the biases out and provides more diversity of thinking.

In economic, political, and technological futuring we continue to make mistakes in our judgments because we are too certain of trend momentum and assumed cause-and-effect relationships and respect too little the potential disruptions of sudden changes. While some black swans may be theoretically impossible to anticipate, other changes could be anticipated if more of us had information about trend outliers. The lack of information on current conditions often contributes to our surprise when something occurs unexpectedly, but which in retrospect might have been predictable if we had only had sufficient and proper information. Surprise is often a point of view depending upon the position and knowledge of the observer.

For most people the lack of information is one of the most serious problems in anticipating the future. In so many cases, using 20/20 hindsight, we realize that we framed incorrect expectations and made faulty forecasts and plans when we finally see information that was not available to us when we were forming our expectations. This is why some managers and futurists "learn" from the future in the sense that their well considered expectations for the future provide a framework for absorbing and using future information as it becomes available to them.

To address the challenges of gaps in information:

- Be as thorough as you can be in your research and monitoring of trends given time and resource constraints.

- Learn from experience to sort out the most important pieces of information required to frame well considered expectations for the future.

- Rely on the expert judgments of many experts, not just a few, and do not rely too much on "genius" forecasts and predictions by highly esteemed authorities (specialists).

- Face the future with due humility and respect the potential for sudden dramatic changes.

Too Much and Incorrect Information

In addition to the above challenge of too little information is the problem of having too much useless and incorrect information. Analysts can get carried away, especially with the distractions of the Internet, and make the investigation of trends an endless process. It is easier now more than ever to gather too much information, much of which may be outdated or just plain wrong. The trick is finding and selecting the best information available – best in terms of currency, accuracy, and relevance to the futuring or visioning project at hand.

Having worked with many scientific and technical organizations, I have frequently witnessed analysts who were reluctant to draw conclusions because they demanded more data. At some point in time for every project, enough information is enough – more data past a certain point will have a decreasing marginal value. But the quality of information is always important. As many managers and futurists know from experience, it is better to have just the right amount of the right information as an input to a conclusion or a decision than to have either too little or too much information.

Managers, futurists, and planners, just like everybody else, make mistakes in using bad information and then misinterpreting it. Even if no biases or self-interests were involved, they would still make mistakes based on bad information. A major mistake is the misinterpretation of leading (or early) indicators and erroneous expectations for cause-and-effect relationships. Similar errors can also be made in the interpretation of trend momentum. It is very easy to jump to unjustified conclusions – and unjustified expectations – based on too little or just plain wrong information. It is also possible to make mistakes because of too much information; that is, too much bad or irrelevant information taking the place of too little good information.

To guard against the potential use of wrong information and errors of interpretation, the following measures can be taken:

- Exercise critical judgment about the inherent quality and reliability of information being used for a forecast or a plan. What should you believe or doubt and why?

- Allow your peers to review and critique your work. It is better to have your forecasts and plans criticized by respected colleagues and friends early in the process than to have them attacked by others later.

- Continuously challenge your own beliefs about cause-and-effect relationships and do not rush to conclusions, especially concerning whether or not emerging Type III patterns are repetitions of Type I patterns.

Vagueness

The common trick of oracles, soothsayers, astrologers, and fortunetellers through history has been to be dramatically vague, which allowed them to claim that they were right after the fact. "Yes, that is exactly what I meant," they would say later. Or they would claim that others misinterpreted what they really meant. They relied on the tricks of their trade, including mysterious rhymes and riddles full of alleged allegories, metaphors, and symbolism.

The traditions of shamans and medicine men who claimed to see the future predate the earliest civilizations. Beliefs in prophets and so called "wise men" were common in ancient Egypt, Mesopotamia, Greece, and Rome. The most famous sibyl in ancient Greece was the priestess Pythia, or Oracle of Delphi from the 8th century BCE to the 4th century CE. Her prophecies were attributed to the god Apollo, although there is evidence that she sat in a spot exposed to intoxicating gases rising from under the ground. She was notoriously vague and mysterious. The interpretation of the Oracle was left up to the supplicant, allowing people to get their money's worth by hearing what they wanted to hear. After events occurred, people could give a retroactive interpretation of the Oracle that made her look very prophetic. In addition, given the high authority attributed to the predictions of the Oracle of Delphi, her most famous customers took the appropriate actions that fulfilled the Oracle's prophecy, making it appear correct in hindsight.

There is a famous story, possibly true, that when Alexander the Great sought her out for a prophecy before his Persian campaign in 336 BCE, the Delphi Oracle refused to receive him. The young Macedonian king was so frustrated that he hunted her down in her private chambers and dragged her by her hair to the place where she would give her prophecies. She then allegedly cried out with unaccustomed clarity, "Let go of me, you are invincible!" Alexander certainly had his winning ways.

The ancient Roman astrologers, seers, and soothsayers were equally vague. They had to be. The Romans placed great stock in auspices. If the fortunetellers gave unwelcome let alone wrong predictions to powerful men, they were likely to be held accountable with their lives. Again, the vagueness of the predictions allowed a wide berth of interpretations and *ex post facto* validation.

Arguably the most famous seer since ancient times was the 16th century Frenchman Michel de Nostredame, or Nostradamus in Latin. He was what was called an apothecary in his day. He dealt in medicinal chemistry. Maybe he also dabbled in alchemy and mind-altering drugs. In any event, he combined advanced skills in medicines with progressive views about hygiene and healing during epidemics of the plague. His local fame became national when he began making his predictions in his almanacs, which sold widely. His admirers included Catherine de Medici, the Queen of France, who brought him to the French court as both an apothecary and fortuneteller. In 1555 his *Les Propheties* were published. He made numerous predictions presented in French quatrains. They are all extremely obscure in meaning and subject to all kinds of interpretations. The most accurate predictions were those that were declared to have proven correct *after* events occurred so that the known events could fit the quatrains.

In our own times, as sophisticated as we think we are today, we still indulge ourselves in horoscopes, palm readings, Tarot cards, and other forms of fortunetelling. We want to believe that there are special people who know how to read "the signs" and tell us what we want to know about the future. Remember the joke of the gypsy fortuneteller predicting with a flourish "a tall, dark, handsome man will come into your life"? What does that mean? It means whatever the person paying for the fortune wants it to mean. Fortune telling, like professional wrestling, is a form of entertainment. The fortune teller, of course, is reading us, not the cards or whatever. The person whose fortune is being read is mystified, thrilled, enchanted, and excited by willing in desired details from the ambiguous "fortune."

Unfortunately, too often managers and futurists who should know better get too vague in their forecasts and plans. As an illustration, some will predict that the American economy will grow, but then they will not give a GDP number or even a range. Nor will they give a date. When they do give a GDP rate, they do not further specify whether the rate is an annual average over a period of time and whether the dollars are current or constant (the difference of inflation). They are not only vague about the numbers, but they waffle on the circumstances and the timing of their predictions.

Other forms of vagueness that are very regrettable but avoidable in so many forecasts are the use of terms without sufficient definition and the use of underlying, implicit assumptions. Too many implicit assumptions are presented as "given." Because all forecasts are conditional, they should take the form of "If...then." Too many forecasts present the "then" and do not sufficiently explain the "if." The lack of conditionality as a form of vagueness has been a problem particularly in econometrics and modeling and simulation. The formula authors and model designers make numerous assumptions that they do not make explicit to others. They make assumptions and value judgments in the very selection of variables to include and not to include in their formulas and models; they make assumptions, too often implicitly, about the relationships among the variables; they fail to adequately define their terms; they are reluctant to reveal hidden algorithms; and they tend to present their forecasts in a vacuum without explaining the conditions required to occur for the forecast to happen.

An odd twist on vagueness is excessive complexity. We often think that highly detailed and complex forecasts have to be more credible, when in reality they are more likely to be off. This is particularly true for forecasts based on very complex formulas and models. You often cannot tell what the forecast means, let alone how it was generated. Models can be so complicated that they are just big "black boxes." Executives and investors are particularly frustrated by complexity of models and excessive numbers because what they want to hear is "the story," which they can understand and use in their decisions and plans for the future.

In one sense, vagueness might be an attribute of humility – the futurist admits that he or she cannot make precise forecasts, so they speak in terms of ranges of possibilities or in general descriptions. This type of vagueness is intellectually honest; it admits that the forecaster has doubts about the future. On the other hand, vagueness might also be a manifestation of arrogance if not charlatanism. The ambiguous futurist might be hiding rather than admitting the limitations of futuring. The key here is that the futurist admits limitations and does not claim more than can be reasonably delivered.

To guard against the errors of vagueness, you should do the following:

- Define carefully the topic for the forecast and make it as specific as needed by the client. Start every futuring project with a clear topic question with enough specificity to satisfy your needs to learn and to make decisions.

- Define your terms.

- Try to be as precise as possible, but express the future as ranges of likelihood rather than very specific numbers and in terms of *a priori* probabilities.

- Be explicit about assumptions, methods, and the conditionalities of your forecast.

- Be honest and humble – don't get carried away with your own enthusiasms and pretensions.

Misapproximations

Sometimes managers and futurists are "directionally correct" when they anticipate a major issue, but they miscalculate numbers or ranges of numbers. They may partially, but not completely, identify trends and their outcomes. They may get the basic story right, even though many of the specifics will be wrong. This is the problem of misapproximation. It is annoying, but hardly a fatal mistake. In many forecasts, like playing horseshoes, being close counts. Of course, you want to get both the details and the conclusions right, but getting the right story with the right business implications is far more important to a manager than a spot-on forecast. I found that in my career, clients and colleagues often assumed that my forecasts would be wrong, so they remembered me for the things that I got more or less right rather than the expectations that I got wrong.

A very common example of misapproximation occurs when you correctly anticipate a trend outcome, but get the date wrong. This has been a chronic shortcoming of technology forecasters: they often get the future parameter right, but they get the timing wrong – typically technologists tend to be overly optimistic and predict technology breakthroughs before they actually occur. This is because they overestimate their own abilities to achieve technology developments and they underestimate the difficulties of integrating new with old technologies and the tremendous barriers to successful commercialization.

The most important way to counter the problems of misapproximation, like vagueness, is to define terms and make forecasts with appropriate levels of uncertainty relative to the topic question and the needs of the customer. The topic question provides the level of detail required for forecasts and plans. Very broadly stated topic questions allow for more flexibility and vagueness in details, while very specifically worded topic questions require more tightly defined terms and more precision in forecasts.

Poor Packaging

In ancient days, the king might kill the messenger of bad news. Today, many managers face the similar dilemma of delivering unwelcome forecasts to powerful people. The death may not be literal – it might only take the forms of losing face, a job, and future opportunities. The trick is in presenting forecasts in attractive packages, so that even unwanted contents can be useful and appreciated. The presentation of a forecast is just as important as the presentation of excellent food; packaging is just as important to a view of the future as it is for a consumer product beckoning to be bought.

To avoid the problems of poor packaging, consider these options:

- Assess the corporate culture and the cognitive styles of executives to learn how to package futuring and planning results so that they will be both understood and appreciated.

- Make reports easy to read and presentations easy to understand with combinations of words (as few as possible) with graphics and illustrations. Focus on the story rather than the details of method. Executives typically need to hear just enough about method to give credibility to the results, but they are much more interested in business implications and potential actions than in the methods of futuring and visioning.

- Rehearse presentations to executives with staff and others who know the executives and their sensitivities.

- Find gentle words to communicate potentially unwelcome results.

Lack of Ownership

A particular problem with both forecasts and plans is that others may not feel any sense of ownership in them and therefore no obligation to work for their fulfillment. The attitude often seen has been "If I didn't make the strategy or plans myself, then I can't be held accountable for them." This is a manifestation of the dreaded NIH (not invented here) syndrome. This was the basic problem of corporate planning staffs that did planning for corporate executives and division managers. As long as the executives and managers did not directly participate in the planning functions, they often felt no commitment to the plans drawn by others. Central planning worked only when they drafted up the directives of senior corporate commanders according to the model of the US Army in World War II. This type of centralized corporate planning was largely abandoned as unnecessary overhead in the troubled days of the 1980s. Division managers and product line managers were expected to generate their own business plans along with their budgets. In time, managers had to become their own futurists as well as their own planners.

Somebody has to have a strong sense of ownership and responsibility for plans in order to feel fully committed to achieving them. As the responsible manager, that somebody is you, but you need to share the process with those who will help you achieve your goals.

To correct the potential problems created by lack of ownership:

- Identify the end-use client or customer (yourself, your senior executives, or external customers) for the forecast and plan and learn what they need to make their decisions and plans for the future.

- Involve various stakeholders, including customers, in the futuring process so that they appreciate the validity of methods and the veracity of results. Let them make inputs so that they feel that they contributed to the results and assume some degree of responsibility for them.

Inadequate Resources, Personnel, and Budgets

Finally, a major problem for both futuring and visioning is the lack of sufficient resources, personnel, and budgets to perform them. Projects may receive too small a budget to produce expected and needed results, and plans may have too few resources allocated to reach their targets.

Futuring projects can be scaled from the very simple to the very elaborate. A "genius" forecaster could generate a forecast, even alternative scenarios, in just an hour. You could hold a two-hour expert focus group on a futuring topic and come up with a forecast of a sort with a prioritized list. I have managed futuring projects from as little as $2,500 to more than $200,000. What is important is truth in packaging: the sophistication of the forecast typically is commensurate with the amount of effort that went into it.

Of course, you always want the most qualified people working on your forecasts, plans, and their execution. Problems arise when inexperienced people generate forecasts and strategic plans. They may make too many errors discussed above and miss important nuances that might prove of great value to leaders and managers, who tend to see finer shades of gray better than many futurists and analysts do.

My experience with both strategic and operational planning has shown that most plans fail because they did not provide for sufficient resources, time, money, material, and personnel to achieve their objectives. It is the opposite phenomenon of the self-fulfilling prophecy; it occurs when people cannot or will not do what is necessary to make their own plans come true. Sometimes this occurs because the plans did not foresee disruptive events, such as delays in receiving raw materials, mistakes made in operations, poor cooperation from other people, surprising moves by competitors, and changes in consumer behavior and marketplace conditions. Planners may not be able to anticipate everything that could go wrong with their plans, but they should anticipate that something will go wrong somewhere along the plan's path.

In order to manage the potential problems of inadequate resources, personnel, and budgets:

- Be aware of the qualifications and strengths and weaknesses of the people who work on your forecasts and plans. Guide individuals toward their strengths and away from their weaknesses. Spread the strengths and weaknesses among various team members so that they complement each other. Have a mixture of specialists and generalists on your project teams.

- In drawing up plans, be very careful and explicit in identifying what resources will be necessary to reach what goals with what level of confidence. Like so many other activities, hold back reserves just in case your project needs more resources than originally thought (and they so typically do).

In summary, I do not expect "perfect" forecasts or plans. No ideal project has ever occurred with ideal results and I expect that none will ever happen in the future. Knowing all the things that can go wrong, both within and outside of my control, I am delighted when my forecasts or plans work out reasonably well relative to my expectations. I strongly believe, however, that well-proven best practices are likely to improve the content and usefulness of both forecasts and plans as well considered expectations for the future.

Given the above warnings of how easily forecasts can go wrong, I offer you the following five key words to keep in mind as managers who are responsible for generating or using futuring and visioning: *thoroughness, honesty, specificity, participation*, and *review*. Using slightly different words, methodical futuring and visioning provide well-considered expectations for the future when you follow these best practices:

1. Given sufficient time and resources, *thoroughly* research the trends for continuities and seek the inputs of many experts to identify potential discontinuities. You may want to frame a forecast as alternative futures (scenarios) predicated on different conditions rather than as a single future.

2. Be intellectually *honest*: don't claim to know or predict more than you can. Also, be aware of your own biases and self-interests and guard against letting them contaminate forecasts and plans. Be prepared to question your own assumptions as well as the assumptions of others. When you are wrong, admit it, but also learn from your mistakes.

3. Define your terms so that you can be as *specific* as possible to avoid the potential pitfalls of vagueness. The specificity of the forecast or plan should be well aligned with the needs of managers.

4. Allow a mixture of various functional managers and staff to *participate* in the process so that they will be better informed and feel a sense of ownership and commitment to the implementation of forecasts and plans.

5. Finally, let the forecasts and plans be critically *reviewed* by others, both insiders and outside consultants, to identify possible errors and to fill potential omissions. Be prepared to monitor new information and events and revise your forecasts and plans accordingly to keep them current as "living documents."

A Case Study: Prospects for Long-Term Economic Growth in India

In 2001 a Japanese manufacturer asked me and my associates to prepare a forecast of economic growth in India over the first decade of the 21st century. At that time China had captured the attention of corporations around the world: companies rushed into China to establish local presence through inexpensive manufacturing and building relationships that would lead eventually to substantial retail sales. Companies found it relatively easy to place manufacturing in China and they could export products to the US and Europe; but penetrating the Chinese retail market proved to be much more difficult. They also downplayed the potential risks of political and social turmoil that might develop in the future based on the present economic expansion. In the meantime, global manufacturers were just becoming aware of a similar economic boom in India, which, to many eyes, did not present the same exciting business opportunities that could be found in China.

My Japanese clients already had some facilities in India, so I wondered why they would commission me to do a forecast for a market with which they were already familiar. I asked them several times why they wanted this project and what they would do with the results. Was there a business decision that needed to be made that required a 10-year forecast? I got several answers to my question, but none seemed to ring exactly true. It is very characteristic of Japanese clients not to reveal the true reasons for their questions to outsiders. The best answer I received to my question was that my clients were uncomfortable in India and wanted my judgment whether the economic "revolution" in India was "for real" and how long it was likely to last. I knew that my clients routinely studied national cultures as context for market research, so that explanation was consistent with my expectations, and I proceeded as directed.

What I discovered in the course of my futuring project was that my clients did have problems that they wanted to solve. As many clients typically do, they were asking the wrong questions and seeking solutions in the wrong direction. Being a world-class manufacturer, they had a predisposition to think that their problem was manufacturing. When I visited their facility in India, however, I saw a fine, world-class operation – what I did not see was a full-capacity plant. They were making fine products, but they just were not selling them. Their throughput was sub-optimized and their inventories too large. The core problem was pricing, marketing, and retailing, not manufacturing.

Like all corporations and virtually all people for that matter, my clients strongly held several cultural and business assumptions. They believed that they knew the Chinese well and that they held no false assumption about that market, but they felt that they did not sufficiently understand the Indian market. I did not feel that they suffered from any negative biases about the Indians, but they worried that the Indians held biases against them based on the experiences of World War II. From extensive research about Indian culture and history and interviews with thought leaders in India, we found no particular biases in India against the Japanese. On the contrary we found that the Indians generally respected Japanese culture and the quality of Japanese products. We found, not to our surprise, some lingering Indian biases against the British, but much to our surprise we uncovered strong pro-American attitudes and sympathies. My clients found that insight very interesting, as they had made extensive investments in the US. We found no reason to expect that these biases would change substantially over the next 10 years.

My clients, however, held some strange (to me) preconceived ideas of Indian culture based on their inadequate understanding of Hinduism. There was an apprehension that all Hindus were highly spiritual and anti-materialistic and that late 20th century consumerism would not take hold in India while it thrived in China. We certainly had our work cut out for us trying as Americans and Indian-Americans to explain the extreme complexities of Hinduism to non-religious, corporate-loyal Japanese. We found some excellent studies on the emerging consumer class in India that provided sufficient examples and data to convince our clients that their concerns about Hinduism were unfounded. There are almost as many variations within Hinduism as there are Hindus, but commonly shared beliefs in the stages of life and the responsibilities of householders argued strongly for the concerns of life in the present. There is plenty of materialism in India, so the cultural basis for long-term economic growth seemed secure.

There was a fear that the caste system in India would adversely affect the capacity of Indians to work together in factories and constrain their behavior as consumers. We found no evidence for these concerns. Ample historical evidence exists to show that the castes are very old and had in the past been quite rigid. The history of India in the 20th century, however, showed significant changes in, but not the elimination of, caste attitudes and prejudices. For example, it is illegal to discriminate on the basis of caste in political and business affairs, but people become aware of caste status and many are sensitive to it in highly personal and subtle social ways. It is still more socially acceptable for a couple to marry one caste lower or higher than to jump several levels; and very rarely would a Brahmin marry a Dalit (many of whom used to be called "untouchables"). There are still occasional incidents of violence in rural areas when couples try to marry out of caste or when Dalits convert to Christianity to escape the social confines of Hinduism. But in general the importance of caste is declining sharply in Indian cities, which are becoming increasingly diverse on many dimensions, but still prevails in many tradition-bound regions of eastern and southern India and in isolated, rural areas. We visited several working facilities, both the clients' and others, and saw no evidence that caste interfered with work. I did detect, however, that Indians may have caste-driven preferences for where they eat lunch, and with whom, and what bathrooms they would or would not use. We saw evidence of socio-economic segregation in Western-style shopping malls and traditional open-air markets, but we could not see evidence of actual caste discrimination in buying behavior, although it might have existed below the social surface. We certainly saw caste as being irrelevant to our clients' products, as all castes would find them useful and desirable.

There were also questions about the future of women in making purchasing decisions. My clients had the stereotypical view of Indian society that women make few if any decisions outside of the home. The view of the traditional role of women in society is often heard all over the world, especially in less-developed countries. We found that women in India for hundreds if not thousands of years have dominated the internal workings of households and have typically participated in major financial decisions, although the decisions appeared to have been made by the male head of the house. We examined trends in the shifting roles of women in Indian society, especially in cities, where many traditional Indian ways were giving ground to increasing adaptation of Western, especially American, tastes. We projected the trends forward and concluded that most likely women would make more major purchasing decisions both for themselves and for their families in the public eye. They should be counted as a target market in the future.

My clients already had their own quantitative market research and financial forecasts for India over the next 10 years. They were aware of, and wanted to guard against, the recency effect of thinking that the Indian economic boom of the 1990s would continue for another decade or more. They also feared that they did not have sufficient information about Indian history, trends, and culture. What they wanted from us was a qualitative forecast based on the analysis of multiple cultural, social, demographic, economic, and political trends in India. They did not want, however, the alternative futures of scenarios. Oddly, I could never get my Japanese clients interested in doing scenario analysis; there was something about the Japanese culture that resisted the uncertainties of such futuring. But they did embrace business stories beyond examining the numbers. So I did my own scenario analysis with simulations in the background to test our expectations. I benefited from the scenario analysis, even though we presented to our clients only the most likely outcomes of trends. The scenarios raised my confidence in the results, and my confidence increased that of the clients.

When we did field work in India, we took our clients with us. We wanted them to see and hear what we were seeing and hearing so that they could benefit from the learning experience, too. We also encouraged them to participate in the structure of the final presentation and to submit their own slides. Their personal involvement in the research and the presentation gave them a sense of ownership and commitment to the results and recommendations.

The high point of this futuring project for me was our final report and presentation to my clients' president and CEO in his personal conference room at corporate headquarters. Having lived in the US, he spoke excellent English and understood our comparisons of contemporary Indian with American cultures. He was very polite and reserved in his manners. He asked excellent questions and assured me that he got what he wanted: our expectation that the Indian economic boom was indeed "real" and likely to last for several decades – that in our judgment, while economic growth in India would likely be slower it would also be more stable than the boom in China. We also offered him our point of view that the company had generally excellent prospects in India, but needed to adjust further to local peculiarities in a vastly complex and highly diverse country. Looking back on this experience, I think we got the story right.

Chapter 5. Updating Forecasts with Trend Tracking

Futuring Principle 5: There is no such thing as an immutable forecast or plan for an immutable future. Forecasts and plans must be continuously monitored, evaluated, and revised according to new data and conditions in order to improve real-time frameworks for making long-term decisions and strategies.

I periodically run into the naïve view that a forecast is a fixed expectation for a fixed future and that we have to wait to see whether it comes true or not. I hear the same about plans as though they were contracts. Nonsense!

A forecast should present its well considered expectations based on best practices, as covered in the previous chapter, as a working hypothesis subject to further revisions based on new information. At the very least, it should identify what is already known about trends, cause-and-effect relationships, and disciplined speculations from informed intuition. In addition, a forecast should identify the most important trends, issues, and factors relating to a forecasting topic of particular interest. These are the same trends, issues, and factors that will require monitoring into the future.

Futuring is a learning process – it's a journey, not a destination. The interim destination is the target date of a forecast, but even when that arrives, and all is revealed up to that moment, there will be a future after that. Until the end of days, the future continues. Therefore, no forecast is ever finished. It represents only a milestone in the path of well considered expectations for the future. The same observation holds for visioning, especially planning. Both forecasts and plans are living documents that must change according to circumstances to keep them fresh and relevant for the ever-moving present.

In 1973, Don Michael, a former defense planner and professor at the University of Michigan, published a little-known book with the revealing title *On Learning to Plan – and Planning to Learn*. The basic argument in his book and subsequent articles and papers was that you have to do planning in order to smartly allocate scarce resources to achieve objectives, but you should think of plans as guidelines that will probably have to change with circumstances over time. In 1989, one year before Senge's *The Fifth Discipline*, Michael characterized planning as "the pedagogy of social learning" for the "learning organization."[55]

The monitoring of trends, forecasts, and scenarios after a forecast or plan has been made provides many opportunities for learning. New information should be captured and shared. It should be used to update forecasts and plans. The effective manager must keep in mind that futuring and visioning are continuous processes of expecting, acting, monitoring, and reacting according to changing conditions. In futuring, this step is often called "trend monitoring" or "trend tracking."

In most cases, we use the terms "trend monitoring" and "trend scanning" interchangeably, but there is a subtle distinction between them that may or may not make a difference depending upon circumstances. Using a narrow sense of "monitoring," you know what the most important trends are and you periodically gather information on them. The focus is narrow and the dive into the subject is deep. Therefore, with a forecast or a plan in hand, we speak of "monitoring" the elements contained in them. On the other hand, scanning is the process of looking for interesting things of apparent marginal value now that may prove to be important later. In contrast to monitoring, scanning is very broad and not very deep. I advise my clients given their resources for monitoring or scanning to do at least 20% scanning and 80% monitoring. If you did only monitoring, you would likely miss the surprises that come from unexpected places. Typically, the term "trend tracking" covers both trend monitoring and scanning.

In some companies, the process of trend tracking is called "environmental scanning," in which the "environmental" refers to the external conditions beyond the company. In this sense of the word, the environment includes many trends and factors, including but not limited to the natural environment. These trends and factors include economic, social and demographic, political and regulatory, natural environmental, and technological conditions, as mentioned previously in Chapter 3. Some companies call the same process "horizon scanning," meaning the horizon of time, or the approaching future. "Trend monitoring" and "trend tracking" are also frequently used terms.

Trend tracking in companies, organizations, and institutions is very similar, although far less elaborate, than surveillance methods used by the intelligence community. You, of course, are monitoring trends, not spying; you are watching for market signals of opportunities and threats. Yet the similarities are such that

---

55 Donald N. Michael, *On Learning to Plan – and Planning to Learn*. San Francisco: Jossey-Bass, 1973; Donald N. Michael, "Forecasting and Planning in An Incoherent Context" (1989), reprinted in Graham Leicester, *In Search of the Missing Elephant. Selected Essays by Donald N. Michael*. Axminster, UK: Triarchy Press, pp. 48-64, quotes on pp. 61-62. The concept of the learning organization was made popular by Peter M. Senge, *The Fifth Discipline. The Art & Practice of the Learning Organization*. New York: Currency Doubleday, 2006 (1990).

we can think of trend analysis and trend monitoring and scanning as forms of pattern recognition.[56]

As discussed previously, trends are patterns in both individual and societal behavior repeated over time. In trend analysis and monitoring (which we can view as continuous analysis and re-analysis), we research these patterns in relation to a futuring topic in order to understand what has occurred in the past and what is happening today. We use trend analysis and monitoring to identify trend momentum that may be predictive in the future. Some trends are strong and resist changes, while others are weak and are easily changed. Some trends experience occasional changes and then return to a familiar pattern; and other trends can be totally diverted, even eliminated, by changes. We have to monitor these patterns and the possible changes to them in order to continuously learn and benefit from them in our decision-making for the future.

Some of the trends that many of us are most interested in today and require routine monitoring include the following:

- GDP growth rates
- Inflation rates
- Prices of energy, especially oil
- Unemployment rates
- Population growth, both in terms of absolute numbers and social composition
- Immigration (both legal and illegal)
- Incidents of terrorism
- Political and social stability in China
- Technological development of DNA maps, diagnostics, and treatments
- Nanotechnologies
- Computer-based automation of processes, including services as well as manufacturing

---

56   Earlier versions of trend analysis as pattern recognition appeared in Stephen M. Millett, "Trend Analysis as Pattern Recognition," *World Future Review*, Vol. 1, No. 4 (August-September 2009), pp. 5-16 (copyright 2009 by the World Future Society/used with permission); Stephen M. Millett, "Trend Analysis as Pattern Recognition," paper presented at the Third Annual Proteus Futures Academic Workshop, Center for Strategic Leadership, US Army War College, Carlisle Barracks, PA, September 18, 2008; and Stephen M. Millett, "Futuring: Anticipating the Emerging Voice of the Customer," in Deborah L. Owens and Douglas R. Hausknecht, Volume Editors, *Integrated Marketing Communication.* Vol. 4, pp. 62-81, in Bruce D. Keillor, General Editor, *Marketing in the 21st Century.* 4 vols. Westport, Connecticut: Praeger Perspectives, 2007.

- Internet commerce

- Internet security

- Sustainable energy technologies

- Global climate change and shifting weather patterns.

Pattern recognition, like trend monitoring and scanning, is very generally defined as the sensing, storing, and classification of data toward achieving an objective. The objective might be general learning – to become more knowledgeable on a topic of present or potential interest to the enterprise. Or it might be the search for new business opportunities. Or it might be intelligence on competitors. Or the goal of pattern recognition might be the making of a decision that may involve millions of dollars over many years. Pattern recognition involves the use of many kinds of sensors, data collection and storage, and data classifications to provide useful information. In contemporary terms, it is typically manifested as "machine learning," or the use of computer software programs to compare large amounts of new information and patterns with existing data sets and proven patterns. The state of the art is advancing quickly since the commercial development of digital optical scanning and pattern recognition software programs. We use digital pattern recognition every day for digital optical scanning and storing of documents, automatic medical diagnostics, data mining, and surveillance and other types of security system. Digital voice recognition is now developing rapidly to supplement visual pattern recognition. Furthermore, we are seeing increasing use of sales data and customer service calls to see patterns in consumer behavior, a trend of great interest to companies around the world.[57]

As useful as pattern recognition has proven, it also has its drawbacks. In some cases, the enormous amounts of data are unintelligible. We cannot find the pattern through all the random data (or what intelligence analysts call "noise"). In other situations we have to deal with both ambiguous and incomplete information in pattern recognition and trend tracking. We lack sufficient "good" or important information while gaining too much apparently useless data. We frequently have to use expert judgment to weigh the evidence and employ educated speculation to fill in the gaps in our information to form a complete mental picture. This intuitive "filling in the gaps" happens all the time: in explaining how and why things happened in the past, what is going on today, and what is likely to occur in

---

57 I thank my former colleagues at the resident School of Engineering, Air Force Institute of Technology (AFIT) and the Battelle Memorial Institute for instructing me in the technical basics of pattern recognition. Much has been published in this field. For example, see Richard O. Duda, Peter E. Hart, and David G. Stock, *Pattern Classification*. Second edition. New York: John Wiley & Sons, 2001. Also check out the website of the International Association for Pattern Recognition, www.iapr.org

the future.[58] While some patterns are very familiar and repetitive, other patterns can be confusing, leading us to make incorrect inferences about trends and events that appear to be similar in many respects but are actually distinctly different when we gain more data to complete the pattern.

The effective futuring manager in business as well as in non-profits and government agencies will learn what trends are most important for his or her operations. The trick is to differentiate the types of pattern for both the trend analysis that goes into forecasts and the trend monitoring that updates them. The danger is confusing one type of pattern (especially Type III) with another type (especially Type I). There are three basic pattern types with slightly different meanings in the contexts of intelligence (trend analysis for national security), trend analysis in the study of history, and trend analysis for business futuring and visioning, as shown below:

Type	Intelligence	Trend Analysis (History)	Business Contexts
Type I	Background, normal conditions	Long-term conditions, trends; everyday life, culture, traditions etc.	Long-term customers, market conditions, corporate culture
Type II	Signals, signatures of known threats	Monumental events, wars, deaths of great leaders, new governments and policies	Economic growth and recession; disruptive technologies; new competitors
Type III	Data arrays, raw data analysis	Fitting data to old or new patterns (Type I patterns)	Understanding and responding to new opportunities and challenges

Each type will now be discussed in more detail.

Type I Pattern Recognition (Background)

Type I, or Background, is a pattern of a place and time with everyday, normal conditions. This type of pattern provides a background for any system or society against which we can detect both continuities and changes to them. By

---

58 Gerd Gigerenzer, *Gut Feelings. The Intelligence of the Unconscious*. New York: Penguin Books, 2007, pp. 16-19, 36-39, 40-53, 112-116; Daniel Gilbert, *Stumbling on Happiness*. New York: Vintage Books, 2007, pp. 90-92, 98-104, 123-129.

understanding the background we can use a variety of monitoring techniques to recognize changes, although we may not know what kinds of changes might occur. In the realm of intelligence, we use such Type I pattern recognition technologies as cameras, audio and infrared sensors; airplanes, dirigibles, and satellites; and radar, sonar, sound detectors, and motion detectors. In trend analysis, we employ the monitoring and scanning of long- and mid-range trends in culture, economics, politics, and technology to explain a baseline condition that may remain more or less stable over decades, even centuries.

Type I pattern recognition entails the study of long-term trends that are documented in histories and recalled by memories. The patterns come to us through documents, narratives, memos, word-of-mouth stories, data tables, and graphs. In addition, we have today extensive archives of photographs and digital imaging. Type I patterns also come to us as physical structures, like buildings, bridges, and roads. Trend analysis and tracking, as methods of futuring, are examples of Type I pattern recognition, with or without the presumption that things in the future will be pretty much the same as things are today or were in the past.

Backgrounds are stable, but that does not mean that they are static. Changes, or deviations and perturbations to normal conditions, may occur. Some changes are relatively small and temporary, while others may be major. We can detect and interpret changes and anticipate them from the perspective of normal conditions of the background. In some circumstances, by monitoring Type I patterns we may detect Type II patterns, which can be significant changes that send Type I patterns into new configurations or create Type III patterns (which in turn may become the new Type I patterns of the future).

Type I pattern recognition is frequently used in generating forecasts and in the follow-up monitoring of trends. A forecast giving baseline expectations for the future represents a Type I pattern. You have identified, analyzed, and projected the most important trends relative to a forecasting topic. Now you are monitoring trends, events, and potential changes that may occur relative to the forecast. You are not looking for any particular change, but rather for any changes that may impact your forecast. You are monitoring in the sense that you are looking primarily at the trends already in the forecast; so you would have to do some random scanning, too, to supplement the trend monitoring. In any event, you are looking for new information that may change your expectations for the future in the context of a Type I pattern.

Over the centuries, historians as chroniclers have shown little scholarly interest in Type I patterns, which were dismissed as commonplace and uninteresting. Yet, in the 20th century, led by a French school of thought, historians discovered that they could say much about ordinary people in the past from unconventional sources of information (for historians), including material culture, archeology, and anthropology. Fernand Braudel talked about the "structures of everyday life." His view was that "In every period, a certain view of the world, a collective mentality, dominates the whole mass of society….A society's reactions to the events of the day, to the pressure upon it, to the decisions it must face, are less a matter of logic or even self-interest than the response to an unexpressed and often inexpressible compulsion arising from the collective unconscious." Braudel may have been referring to the Jungian concept of psychological archetypes and the human collective unconscious. He may have been referring to "world views," or what we today would call paradigms or mental models. In addition to basic psychology, Braudel added geography, social hierarchy, religious beliefs, economic needs, work, and common habits and pleasures as conditions of life's structure. He certainly argued that fundamental values are based on psychological and social structures that were created by people over long periods of time and resist, or at least adapt to, all but the most catastrophic changes.[59]

Braudel employed, without using the same terms, Type I pattern recognition as historical trend analysis and monitoring. These long-range trends were continuities and indicators, although not perfect predictors, of the future. Today, virtually every futurist begins with an understanding of the trends judged most important to the topic question. To understand trends and current issues in the US, in order to anticipate future outcomes, you should consider at least the following patterns:

- Increasing life expectancy and the rapid growth of the elderly population (also seen in Western Europe and Japan) with impacts on many social, economic, and political trends.

- Immigration into the US, especially from Latin America and Asia.

- The persistent lifestyle, habits, and consumer behavior of some 78 million Baby Boomers in the US (born in the period of 1946-1964) and the extent to which such behavior will be changed by retirement and old age.

- Continued advancements and profound social and economic implications of the information and communication technologies (ICT), especially personal computers, e-mail, the Internet, mobile phones, and hand-held computer portals.

---

59 Fernand Braudel, *The Structures of Everyday Life. The Limits of the Possible. Civilization and Capitalism, 15th – 18th Century*, Vol. I. Translated and revised by Sian Reynolds. Berkeley, CA: University of California Press, 1992 (1979); Fernand Braudel, *A History of Civilizations*. Translated by Richard Mayne. New York: Penguin Books, 1995 (1963), p. 22 (the quotation) and pp 27-28.

- Steady increases in the uses and prices of energy, especially gasoline, natural gas, and electricity.

- Technology improvements in alternative energy sources.

- The effectiveness, efficiency, availability, and cost of health care.

- Growing competition to the manufacturing and service industries of the US from less developed countries (including Brazil, Russia, India, China, Japan, and Mexico), and a potential shift of global economic power from the West to Asia.

- Increasing worldwide concerns about general environmental quality with a shift from a focus on air quality near the surface of the Earth to global climate change and greenhouse gas concentrations in the atmosphere.

- Shift to more environmentally "green" and sustainable products and processes.

- International terrorism and potential further attacks upon the US.

- Illegal drug use and drug-related crimes and violence.

The extent to which the Great Recession will change long-term patterns in global economic growth and rising standards of living around the world remains to be seen.

We commonly see the use of Type I pattern recognition in the case histories of medicine and law. Medicine relies heavily on patient and family health histories, which are forms of Type I patterns. The laws in the US and other English-derived countries rely on the use of legal precedents to help decide cases. Legal precedents and legal history are also forms of Type I patterns.

We use all kinds of Type I pattern recognition to perform routine security surveillance, such as the use of cameras at stores, malls, banks, airports, street intersections, etc. We are also using digitized, "smart" surveillance systems in manufacturing to guarantee quality, which is also a Type I pattern.

In the context of business, Type I pattern recognition consists of knowing the long-term behavior of customers, market conditions, and corporate culture. Type I patterns provide consistency in operations and business growth. It represents the "world," as seen by any corporation, "as it should be." This is why so many strategic plans and annual budgets conform to Type I patterns with a heavy emphasis on historical performance and current conditions, reflecting the recency effect.

In the last decade or so, with the enormous amounts of data that are stored, a new kind of Type I pattern recognition has emerged called "predictive analytics." It is a general term that covers many different kinds of techniques, but basically it is data mining. Patterns emerge from the data that can be predictive as long as specific behavior and circumstances continue. We see examples of it with credit card companies that track the buying habits of individual customers in order to detect fraud and identity theft. Of course, mistakes are made, but the errors are on the side of caution and the protection of both the credit card company and the legitimate card owner.

A Type I pattern is a model of continuity. As a model, it is predictive to the extent that it includes correctly (meaning, to the degree that they are well aligned with recurring phenomena and data) trend momentum, cause-and-effect relationships, and the proven laws of nature and that they constitute a (quasi-)closed system or fixed set of variables and data. A Type I pattern should also identify the most important variables: changes which may provide the strongest indications of future changes. If the model is valid, then you do not need to know all possible information; you can infer the details based on the most important aspects of the pattern. But beware! To rely heavily on a Type I pattern is to assume a great deal about both the present and the future. In some cases, you will have little time to gather information and you must act immediately upon what you know now and what you reasonably expect for the future.

Type I pattern recognition, to summarize, is absolutely vital for all forecasts. It is the stuff of trend analysis. The danger of using Type I patterns, however, lies in the misguided expectation that new data, such as the information gathered in trend monitoring, will automatically fit previous Type I patterns. It is very easy to force fit new data into pre-existing Type I patterns (including analytical and mental models in addition to previous trend analysis) rather than recognize that a new Type III pattern is emerging. An over-reliance on Type I patterns will over-emphasize continuity and under-estimate the importance of changes in the context of the first futuring principle.

Type II Pattern Recognition (Signals)

Type II pattern recognition occurs when we are looking for something in particular: signals, or signatures, that we already know constitute potential threats to our security and we want to recognize as soon as they come up on our screens. In Type II pattern recognition, we are not interested in the background, only particular signals; backgrounds are only so much "noise" in which we may lose the definition of the signal. In the field of intelligence, the signal might be a Soviet nuclear missile, a Chinese submarine, or a terrorist on his way to a disaster. We know and fear the signal, which, in the context of trend analysis and monitoring, is a significant and potential change that threatens our comfort and security.

In our everyday lives, the news media pay more attention to Type II than Type I stories. The term "news" comes directly from Type II pattern recognition. The news dwells on changes of known interest to readers and audiences: crimes, scandals, disasters, and storms. The news also reports daily changes in markets, like the Dow Jones Industrial Average and the price of gold; results of elections; battles; outcomes of sporting events; etc. On slow news days, the media resort to "human interest stories" or investigative journalism, which may be forms of Type I backgrounds or trend tracking, to fill time and space. Using the historian Braudel again as a perspective, Type II history focuses on events or "the news" that seem exceptional and important departures from the usual. Since the earliest civilizations, histories consisted largely of records and chronologies made by scribes under the authority of the ruler. Historians retold the extraordinary stories of wars, plagues, famines, and the lives of rulers. The role of scribe shifted to the role of the scholar. The emphasis was placed on changes rather than continuities. It was exactly this genre of official state history that Braudel and his French colleagues renounced in favor of histories of common people and everyday lives.

In fairness to academic history, many scholarly historians for at least 200 years have practiced both Type I and Type II pattern recognition in their works. In biography the genre is called "life and times," in which the biographer recounts the events in the lives of individuals in the context of historical circumstances. Great men affect great times, but great times also make great men. It would seem stilted to write a biography of Abraham Lincoln, for example, without discussing the Western movement of people in the US, the background of American slavery, the economic growth of the country, the importance of the emerging railroad system, the tensions between urban, industrial and rural, agricultural sub-cultures, and the emergence of the Republican Party, among other trends of the times. The event of greatest importance in the life of Lincoln was the Civil War, a stupendous Type II period of American history.

There are overlaps between Type I and Type II pattern recognition. In Type I, we are looking for any changes, but against a specific background. Type I emphasizes the background, but Type II stresses the change, or the signal, rather than the background. Type II pattern recognition is searching for specific changes. Obviously, in many if not most cases, both Type I and Type II pattern recognition styles must be used in trend analysis, monitoring, and scanning. Type I patterns tell us about continuities, while Type II patterns (or events) tell us about changes. There are some intelligence analysts, historians, futurists, and managers who over-emphasize Type II patterns at the expense of Type I patterns. They may produce explanations and forecasts of future events without adequate context. At the opposite extreme, there are others who over-emphasize Type I patterns. The traditional manager is typically trained to be a Type I (everyday) manager. He or she may have to manage daily routines and processes. Preserving the corporate culture and maintaining smooth work performance may be the most important objectives. But the futuring manager may have to learn from experience how to make the transition from a Type I to a Type II (change) manager. The futuring skills and knowledge base of a manager would have particular value in managing Type II and Type III patterns.

People particularly concerned about black swans could use either Type I or Type II pattern recognition, but they would probably rely on Type II more heavily than on Type I. As I continue to assert, futuring must include both trends and disruptive events because the future will be a mixture of both continuities and changes. It is impossible to predict the precise nature and timing of disruptive events, but there are some events that can be imagined if not anticipated, such as:

- Aliens from Outer Space reach Earth (the subject of many science fiction stories).

- Volcanic eruptions, earthquakes, and violent storms with both local economic implications and global climate ramifications.

- A panic in world markets that sets off a global economic depression (which nearly happened in 2008-2009 and certainly could happen again).

- A pandemic that kills tens if not hundreds of millions of people around the world (such as the great flu epidemic of 1918-1919 that killed some 25 million people around the world, except on an even larger scale in the future).

- A nuclear war, accidental or intentional.

- Assassination of a group of top world leaders rather than a single individual, resulting in political chaos in one or more countries.

- A sudden and unexpected peace between Israel and the Palestinians that includes a mutually satisfactory solution to the governance and accessibility of Jerusalem and its holy sites.

- A technological breakthrough in the development and subsequent commercialization of a fuel to replace gasoline.

Whether a pattern is Type I or Type II is often a point of view: it depends very much upon what you are looking at, from what angle, and why. Your mindset, values, interests, and fears strongly affect your perspective. Type II historical events may or may not evolve into new Type I patterns over time. When a Type II event occurs, it may seem at the moment like a very important event indicating a dramatic departure from old patterns and a change toward new trends, but it might be only a temporary shock. Type II patterns can, however, radically change some trends and create new trends according to further information.

In trend tracking, a forecast might be considered as a Type I pattern: things as they are and are expected to be in the future. You might use trend monitoring to identify any deviation from the norm, or changes in the context of a background (Type I). You can also use monitoring and scanning to pick up on potential threats and trend-diverting changes in consumer behavior, market conditions, competitors, technologies, etc. If you were looking for just any changes to the norm, you would be pursuing Type I pattern monitoring; if you were looking for particular changes or for the really large and important changes, you would be pursuing Type II pattern recognition.

Type III Pattern Recognition (Data Arrays)

Type III patterns occur when we detect data in our environmental monitoring and scanning that are not already known to us. They may be variations on existing Type I patterns, or they may be substantially new patterns. They may be Type II events. Because of the uncertainty, we have to continue tracking the data and arraying them in categories, clusters, arrays, lines, or whatever geometry we use on graphs to recognize any emerging patterns. The array becomes a Type III pattern which in time may conform to a familiar Type I or a significantly different Type I or an incidental Type II pattern.

Historians and trend analysts are typically most interested in Type I and Type II patterns, while futurists and intelligence analysts are most often interested in TypeII and Type III patterns. The futuring manager is interested in all three types of pattern: Type I to understand stable market conditions and the corporate culture; Type II to detect early significant changes that might create business opportunities or threats; and Type III to grasp new business conditions and to adjust as soon as possible to changing business models and paradigms.

Naturally, pure data arrays might appear as chaos with no apparent pattern. But the rewards come with recognizing and correctly interpreting patterns, not in just recording random data. Every profession has its own preferred geometry. Accountants, financial officers, and marketers look for lines; statisticians and psychologists use bell shape curves; and economists and historians seek cycles. There are numerous mathematical tools, like regression analysis, Box-Jenkins, econometric equations, and trend projections to give us the two-dimensional graphs that we crave. In truth, the world is full of all kinds of shapes with lots of different geometries. Alphabetical letters, words, abbreviations and acronyms, encrypted messages, numbers, music, colors, drawings and paintings, fingerprints, voices, motions, clothes, and faces are patterns, too.

In 1987, I asked Joe Martino, a pioneer in the field of technology forecasting, what was the most common forecasting method that he had observed in his military and corporate consulting careers. He immediately responded "trend projections." At that same time, I was managing a group program to review commonly used technology forecasting methods in business, and we came to a similar conclusion that trend analysis, often linearly projected, especially as derived from financial and econometric models, was the most frequently employed forecasting method. When you look at demographic, economic, and technological forecasts, you more often than not see linear forecasts entirely based on historical (time series) data.[60]

Professor Steven Pinker of Harvard has observed that people typically think of chains of cause-and-effect events that lead to linear projections into the future. Pinker points out that in our use of language we are constantly using geography as a metaphor for time: a point in time, an event that is behind us now, looking ahead, the time has arrived, etc. His observation on the mind processing time like space reminds us of Einstein's physical theory of space-time. No wonder that we reduce historical data, time series projections, and trend analysis to the graphs of plane geometric space. In addition, the perception of time as a consistent progression from the past to the future may be based on the same mental processes that lead us to think in the manner of inductive logic – that the accumulation of events and data leads to valid generalizations and expectations for the future. Sometimes this mode of thinking works well, and sometimes it does not. Over 200 years ago, Hume argued that inductive logic can be wrong in projecting the future from the past – but it can also be right. This applies to futuring, too.[61]

In the religious beliefs of predestination and in the secular philosophies of determinism, new data are continuously being interpreted according to preconceived expectations for Type I patterns. In this sense, a Type I pattern might be the background of history and experience, but it might also be the background of mental models. In general, all belief systems and mental models are Type I patterns. The person who believes in *The Book of Revelation*, for example, sees every natural disaster, catastrophe, or world crisis as the "writing on the wall"

---

60 Joe Martino was a retired Air Force officer and a professor at the University of Dayton. He wrote one of the earliest textbooks on technology forecasting. See Joseph P. Martino, *Technology Forecasting for Decision Making*. Second Edition. New York: North-Holland, Elsevier Science Publishing, 1983. Also see Stephen M. Millett and Edward J. Honton, *A Manager's Guide to Technology Forecasting and Strategy Analysis Methods*. Columbus, OH: Battelle Press, 1991.

61 Steven Pinker, *The Stuff of Thought. Language as a Window Into Human Nature*. New York: Viking, 2007; pp. 188-233.

indications of the forthcoming Day of Judgment. Likewise, the Marxist interprets every economic crisis as one more sign of the failure of capitalism.

Putting philosophical matters aside for the moment, a major practical question for trend analysis concerns how many data points constitute a trend line. I was visiting the R&D center of a global corporation to discuss technology forecasting methods, and an engineer asked me how many points I needed to plot a trend line. I suspected that he was toying with me, so I responded "at least two." He looked at me with a straight face and replied, "That's funny, we use only one." The joke that we shared was over the very common propensity for people, even very sophisticated scientists and technologists, to jump to a preferred conclusion from very little evidence. Maybe such behavior served our species well in the past to avoid or get quickly out of trouble, but today the mental processes of well concerned expectations for the future require a great deal more conscious effort.

The most common quantitative form of linear forecasting is the two-dimensional graph, which comes from basic analytical geometry. The x axis is typically time (t) and the y axis is usually some quantitative parameter (p), which might be dollars, percentages, miles per hour, degrees of heat, etc. The function lines might be straight, but they can curve, too, like cycles, sine waves, bell curves, and S curves (see Figure 5.1 below.)

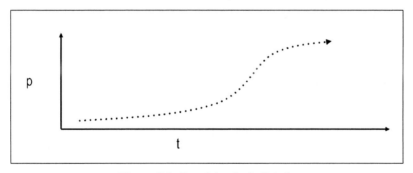

Figure 5.1: Trend Analysis Graph

Graphical trend analysis can be very simple displays of data, or they can become quite complicated using the advanced statistical methods for regression analysis. It is also possible to use words in place of data points and employ tables and charts as replacements of graphs.

To seriously answer the question about how many data points are required for a trend line, the rule of thumb is to use at least as many years in the past as you forecast into the future, and twice as many years is even better. So, for a 10-year forecast, you should do trend analysis for at least the previous ten if not 20 years. For long-term generational trends you should go back at least 80 years (two to three generations) and cultural trends should go back at least 100 if not 1,000 years. I recently heard of examples of forecasting public school budgets five years into the future using only the last three years of data. There may even be organizations using only one year of data to forecast the next five years. The shorter the period of trend data that you use for forecasts, the more you exaggerate the recency effect. In addition to graphs, trends may also be displayed qualitatively as chronologies, tables, time lines, and narratives. Both quantitative and qualitative approaches are generally better than one alone.

Of course, rarely does a single trend exist alone in such complex systems as economics, politics, social relationships, and business. An example of multiple trends plotted on a single graph appears as Figure 5.2 below. In the past, managers typically looked at a relatively small number of trends and isolated them as though they were totally independent of each other. What becomes tricky with multiple trend analysis is integrating the trends into net results, because some trends reinforce other trends positively and some negatively. You not only have to consider the trends but their interactions with each other, too.

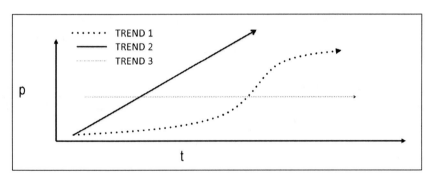

Figure 5.2: Prototype Graph of Three Trends

Second in common usage only to linear projections in Type III pattern recognition of trends is cycles. These cycles are not circles, but curved lines stretched out over time with periodic ups and downs. A symmetrical cycle on a graph would be a sine wave (sinusoid). It is easy for us to think in terms of cycles, because we experience the natural cycles of daily light and dark, the days of the week, phases of the moon, tides, and the seasons as well as many biological functions. Projected upon the life of societies and cultures, the 14th century Muslim philosopher and historian Ibn Khaldun talked about natural cycles of civilization, a theme picked up by numerous Western historians in our own times. If historical cycles existed and if we could track them, then we could make predictions about the future of politics, societies, and economics based on our location in any given cycle. Cycles can be just as deterministic as straight lines.

One particularly famous proponent of cycles to explain American political trends, for example, was the historian Henry Adams, the grandson of President John Quincy Adams, who identified alternating periods of vigorous and passive power assertion and leadership by the Federal government relative to states' rights or private interests. He thought the cycle was as regular as the swinging of a pendulum with each cycle lasting 12 years. Adams' cyclical pattern analysis was continued by the esteemed Harvard history professor Arthur M. Schlesinger (Senior), but with modifications. Schlesinger concluded that the historical data roughly but not precisely fit Adams' model, so he rejected the regularity of the clock's pendulum. He also changed Adams' characterizations of the political swings as the action-reaction phenomena of liberalism and conservatism. His analysis resulted in identifying periods of American liberalism and conservatism that roughly corresponded to Adams' analysis of the early years of the republic, but became longer as time passed. He concluded that the average life of a cycle was about 16.5 years. As enamored as he was with cycles, however, Schlesinger had to admit that some periods of American history did not neatly fall into his pattern. Toward the end of his career, Schlesinger gravitated toward a more complicated theory of spirals rather than regular oscillating cycles.[62]

The potential periodicity of American politics may be a reflection of a particular design element in the American national government: regular elections and fixed terms of office. A member of the House of Representatives is elected for only two years and the entire House is up for re-election every two years. A Senator is elected for a term of six years and one-third of the Senate is up for re-election every two years. The convention was that a President served at most two four-year terms until President Roosevelt won an unprecedented third term of office in 1940 and a fourth term in 1944. Since 1951, a President may not serve more than two terms of office according to the XXII Amendment.

Professor Schlesinger's more famous son, Arthur M. Schlesinger, Jr., who was the Kennedy court historian, further refined his father's cyclical theory. But as the younger Schlesinger grew older, he had more doubts, as had his father. He redefined the concept of alternating periods of political conservatism and liberalism to changing periods of national emphasis on private interests and values versus public interests and values. He extended the periodicity to 30 years, corresponding to a pattern of generations (which traditionally has been measured as 40 years). There would be a roughly 15 year upsweep of one cycle, then another approximately 15 years of decline before the next cycle emerged. Even with these adjustments, however, Schlesinger could not fit all data points on a cycle. In later

---

62 Arthur M. Schlesinger, Jr., *The Cycles of American History*. Boston: Mariner Books, 1999, pp. 23-48. The entire discussion of the Schlesinger theories of American historical cycles in my above text are taken from this source.

life, he thought that technology, especially the information technologies of the 1990s, changed the timing of the cycles.

One major conceptual problem with the theory of American political cycles is the presumption of regularity in the cycles. All data are expected to fit the curves, but they don't without having to "tweak" the data to make them fit. There are always "outliers," as statisticians dismissively call errant data that have to be explained away. There may be a pattern within the data, but it is far more complicated than sine waves. A more abstract way of interpreting cycles would be the consideration of repetitive variations of behavior within the boundaries of a closed system or a fixed set.

Another conceptual problem concerns the definition of terms. In the examples of American political cycles, what constitutes "conservative" and "liberal" or "public" versus "private" interests and concerns? The meaning of these terms shifts over time. In the present, these terms are often abstractions and highly biased and subjective. The classification of political periods always appears more obvious to an historian in retrospect than they do to a politician in the present, and can be very misleading when projected into the future.

A third conceptual concern is that no period of history is exactly the same as previous periods due to the arrow of time. Fashions, technologies, and issues will vary over time, to say nothing of the tremendous variations in the personalities of players in national political life. Certain fundamental ideas and behaviors may transcend any particular time period, but the time period provides context for the particulars.

The most serious objection to the literal interpretation of historical cycles, as the Schlesingers – father and son – discovered, is that they are not particularly predictive of the future except in very general ways. To use Bayesian logic again, the pattern of cycles in American politics helps us assign an *a priori* probability to future elections and administrations based on preceding trends and events, but the *a priori* probability would be much less than 100%. In addition to the challenges of defining the same political terms in different historical periods, American elections are rarely clean mandates for any particular issues. American politics and government policies are strange mixtures of ideas and interests spiced by personalities and fueled by cash. Governmental policies and laws end up as odd compromises of many voices.

To illustrate the point, the Schlesinger-Schlesinger cyclical pattern of American politics claims that the administrations of Franklin D. Roosevelt could be called a period of "liberalism," or a period of emphasis on public interests and values during the Great Depression, although they contained elements of both progressive and cautious aspects of social and economic policy. According to the 16.5 year cycle, the "public values" of the Roosevelt period that began in 1933 ended in 1949 or 1950. Then there should have been a conservative, or "private values" period from 1950 to about 1966, followed by another cycle of "public values" from 1966 to 1982. The historical facts, unfortunately, do not fit the pattern. In 1952 Gen. Dwight D. Eisenhower won the Republican nomination against the staunch conservative Sen. Robert A. Taft. The Eisenhower years from 1953-1961 are generally considered to be a time of political moderation with a liberal upswing occurring in the 1958 congressional elections. In retrospect, John F. Kennedy, who was elected in 1960, is viewed as a liberal, although at the time a lot of Democrats saw him as moderate to conservative (although still well to the left of Taft and Taft's conservative heir, Sen. Barry Goldwater). The turbulent politics of the 1960s were driven primarily by the Civil Rights Movement, the war in Vietnam, and Lyndon Johnson's Great Society. They are considered more liberal than conservative, and the landmark election of 1968 was hardly a turn to the left, as expected in the cyclical model.

The next landmark national election came in 1980. According to the model, the turn to the political right should have occurred in about 1983. Most historians and politicians would agree that the election of Ronald Reagan and the resurgence of the conservative wing of the Republican Party would constitute a shift to private concerns. It came three years early according to what the cycle led us to expect. You could say that being off by just three years is remarkably accurate, but the cycle also said that the conservative period would last about 16-1/2 years, so adjusted for the 1980 election the conservative era personified by Reagan should have lasted from 1981 to 1998 and then we should have entered a liberal phase from 1999 or 2000 to 2016 or so. Not exactly! Of course, you could argue that President George H. W. Bush (the first President Bush) should have been re-elected in 1992 and a "liberal" should have won the White House by the year 2000. You could argue that President Bill Clinton was "counter-cyclical" and that Al Gore should have become President in 2001, but you could not argue such without also generating a lot of partisan heat. The facts just do not fit the model; the model broke down and lost any predictive value it might have had.

As a former scientific colleague once remarked to me, more than once data have ruined perfectly good models.

Another example of cyclical trend analysis was offered by William Strauss and Neil Howe. Their book *Generations* in 1991 became a best seller and had an enormous impact on business marketing, advertising, and new product development. They discovered a pattern of American political and social behavior in generations. Going back in history as far as 1584, they identified four generational types:

Idealist, Reactive, Civic, and Adaptive. Each generation has had a particular style contrasting it with other generations. Furthermore, Strauss and Howe claimed that they had found a particular sequencing of generational types that they called a "four stroke cycle:" Reactive, Civic, Adaptive, and Idealist. They argued that the generations were based on sets of historical circumstances that shaped personalities during formative years. For example, the 20th century began with the G.I. Generation, which was born between 1901-1924. It was a Civic generation molded by the experiences of the First World War and the Roaring Twenties. It was the generation that entered adulthood coping with the Great Depression and then fought the battles of the Second World War. The next generation was called the Silent Generation, born between 1925 and 1942, and categorized as Adaptive. They were molded by the tragedies of the Great Depression, to which they had to make many uncomfortable adaptations both materially and emotionally. The next generation was the Boom Generation, born between 1943 and 1960. They are Idealist. This is roughly the same generation that is more commonly called the Baby Boomers, born between 1946 and 1964. They were raised with high expectations for the future and with high ideals that took them into both community-oriented and selfish directions during the infamous 1960s and 1970s. The Thirteenth Generation, born between 1961 and 1981, is Reactive, particularly to the exuberant idealism of the Boomers. This generation corresponds roughly to the very cautious, self-reliant, and often detached Generation X. The last generation analyzed by Strauss and Howe is the Millennial Generation, born from 1982 into the 1990s. It is a Civic generation with many uncertainties but with the expectation of repeating themes from the last Civic generation, the G.I. Generation. Based on this pattern, Strauss and Howe expect a general repeating pattern of American generational behavior out to the year 2069.[63]

Strauss and Howe acknowledged their intellectual debt to Arthur M. Schlesinger, Jr., who mentioned the analysis of generations as an approach to understanding and anticipating American historical cycles. Their characterization of the behavior of generations living today has been remarkably predictive to the extent that market research has validated many of the consumer trends inferred from general generational trends identified by Strauss and Howe. A particularly influential book on generational marketing based on the behavior patterns of generations was published by Yankelovich Partners in 1997.[64] The earning, spending, and (not much) savings behavior of the Boomers is now well documented for the 1990s and the early 21st century. We will see to what extent these same behaviors continue when the Boomers reach the life stage of retirement and old age during

---

63   William Strauss and Neil Howe, *Generations. The History of America's Future, 1584 to 2069.* New York: Quill/William Morrow, 1991.

64   J. Walker Smith and Ann Cluman, *Rocking the Ages. The Yankelovich Report on Generational Marketing.* HarperBusiness, 1997.

the period of 2008 to 2026. An additional influence, unexpected by virtually everybody, will be the long-term effects of the Great Recession.

I use these rather famous examples of forecasts to make the point that rigidly interpreting trends as cycles with regular periodicity and predictable outcomes, much like linear trend projections discussed above, may lead the futuring manager to the common mistake of assuming that the future will be a continuation of an historical (Type I) pattern and missing the emergence of a new (Type III) pattern where "outlier" data may be indicative of important changes that should not be lightly dismissed. As I said previously, I think cycles have some empirical validity, but they should be thought of as abstractions with many possible exceptions rather than as hard-and-fast laws of nature.

Turning to personal experience, in the futuring project on American consumer value in personal transportation to the year 2050 presented as a case history in Chapter 2, the futuring team that I led experimented with a combination of linear and cyclical American consumer trend projections to the year 2050. We decided that generational analysis would provide us a valid long-term trend whose momentum would be at least partially predictive. The consumer value trends for the World War II generation had been consistent over decades, and those of Boomers have been, too. But generational analysis alone is not enough; you have to understand the needs of different life stages, which each generation goes through but may react to very differently. For example, it is very doubtful that Boomers will respond to the life stage of retirement the same way that the World War II generation did. Many of them will not enjoy the pensions of their parents' generation and many did not save much over the years (and for others, much of what they did save in their 401(k) plans at work got highly discounted by the stock market in 2008-2009). Boomers with a life-time of spending may well continue their habits into their 70s, with one implication being that they will have to work longer than their parents did. You also have to consider long-term economic trends, which can be viewed both linearly (the long period of consistent US economic growth) and cyclically (periods of high growth followed by declining growth rates and recessions). Finally, we also looked at very long-term American cultural trends that provided a Type I pattern for understanding why Americans act like Americans. From the perspective of other customs and social norms, Americans act as strangely as aliens from another planet; yet Americans often act in patterns that are very well established in the historical experiences of people in the New Land.

Asian companies typically use technology roadmaps for long-term planning. It is a more or less linear approach to futuring (the self-fulfilling prophecy) and visioning (strategic planning) in the sense that they visualize R&D targets and work very hard to make them. They plan for a succession of technologies, one building upon others. They also foresee a progression of products. One common approach that I have seen involves the visualization of an ultimate, "perfect" product that cannot be made today but could be made in the future, even decades in the future. They know what the technologies and products are today, so they extrapolate a succession of technologies and products over the period from the present to the future product target date. Each product is spaced about two or three years from each other. The companies have an R&D plan with specific milestones; they also expect to periodically have new products to continue to generate sales and build consumer interest and brand loyalty.[65]

We took the method of technology and product roadmaps and created a new variation of them, the consumer value roadmap. We were able to identify the principal American consumer values in personal vehicles decade by decade from 1950 to 2050 and we were able to forecast how the values would likely shift in the future. For example, vehicle style and power were highly valued by consumers in the 1950s and 1960s, but they gave way to fuel efficiency and environmental quality in the 1970s and 1980s. Comfort and safety were major values in the 1990s and they have continued to be so in the 21st century, although fuel efficiency came back as a major benefit in 2008. In the meanwhile, rapid communication (microchip controls and diagnostic, computing, GPS, and Internet and mobile phone connectivity) emerged as a principal value and will likely remain so for the next 50 years. Since our clients relied heavily on visual representations rather than text on slides, we displayed our consumer value map with pictures and lines with arrows to illustrate the trends and our expectations for the future. In some cases, the consumer values were linear across decades, but in other cases we showed lines crisscrossing with some old values dropping out, new ones emerging, and old values taking on new meanings over time. We had trend lines, semi-cycles, and other geometrical patterns. The approach went over very well with the clients.

A variation on trend lines and cycles is the S Curve analysis for technology development and commercialization introduced by Fisher and Pry in 1971.[66] They presented a particular type of trend analysis that looks like an "S" rather than a

---

65 The Japanese origins and uses of technology roadmaps have been related to me numerous times from Japanese companies and American companies that worked with them. Also see Aklo Kameoka, "Road-mapping for corporate strategy," *Tech Monitor,* July-August 2003, pp. 35-40. The technique became very popular with the US government, especially the US Department of Energy. See Marie L. Garcia and Olin H. Bray, "Fundamentals of Technology Roadmapping," Strategic Business Development Department, Sandia National Laboratories, Albuquerque, NM, 1998 at www.sandia.gov/Roadmap/home.htm (accessed October 2003).

66 J. C. Fisher and R. H. Pry, "A Simple Substitution Model of Technology Change," *Technology Forecasting and Social Change,* Vol. 3 (1971), pp. 75-88.

straight line or a bell-shaped curve. Fisher and Pry asserted that technological innovation was fundamentally a matter of substituting a new approach, product, or service for older ones to better satisfy consumer needs. They came up with a formula for technology substitution that, when plotted on a two-dimensional graph, looks very much like an S (like Figure 5.1, which might be seen as a "lazy S"). Fisher and Pry were very bold in asserting that a relatively small amount of data provided enough information to make a prediction about the slope of the curve. S curves were very popular in the 1970s, but they declined as a business forecasting tool during the 1980s. The problem was that in practice rather than in theory no general formula worked to fit all topical data points – each curve and each plot, according to the subject matter, was different. The theory had much qualitative appeal, but mathematically it often forced the data to fit the curve. Yet the S curve concept matches with much experience in technology and product innovation: difficulties proving the efficacy and value of the innovation in the beginning mean that new technologies and products typically get off to very slow starts, then they experience gradual penetration of the market until a critical point is reached (a point that is very difficult to forecast), may (but not always) enjoy a period of exponential growth, and finally flatten out at some saturation level before declining.

An extraordinary example of S curve analysis emerged in 1993 in a surprisingly popular book called *The Great Boom Ahead* by Harry S. Dent, Jr. He combined trend analysis, S curves, and cycles into an interesting hybrid method for anticipating stock prices. Dent emphasized the importance of demographics, especially Boomers, and their impacts on spending. He also placed importance on technological S curves. Using his unique approach, Dent predicted that the Dow Jones Industrial Average would hit a high of 8,500 by 2007 (it hit a high at about 14,000 in October 2007), but then decline with a recession beginning no later than 2008! While wrong on many details, he got the story basically correct: the extraordinary American economic boom came to a screeching halt with the stock market crash beginning in late September 2008. He also correctly identified, but somewhat understated, the spectacular economic growth of China and the giddy real estate market in the US in the first decade of the 21st century. On the other hand, he missed the energy story by predicting that oil prices would stabilize in the range of $15-$22 a barrel (they actually rose to about $147/barrel in July 2008). He correctly anticipated the run up of the stock market in the second half of the 1990s; he also anticipated that the great boom of the 1990s would lead eventually, by the year 2007 or 2008, to a global depression that might last until as late as 2023![67]

---

67 Harry S. Dent, Jr. *The Great Boom Ahead. Your Comprehensive Guide to Personal and Business Profit in the New Era of Prosperity*. New York: Hyperion, 1993, especially pp. 15-19 and 187-188.

In 1998 Dent followed up the success of his first book with another book, called *The Roaring 2000s*. Reflecting the optimism of the times, his second book was even more exuberant than his first. "The simple but powerful truth," Dent shared with us, "is that we can easily project long-term economic trends. Our economy is fundamentally driven by the predictable family spending cycles of each new generation and the predictable movement of new technologies and industries into the mainstream of our society." He also told us that the biggest mistake in forecasting is to draw linear trend projections when in reality trends move in curvilinear ways. Dent provided many graphs of generational spending cycles and S curves for new technologies and industries. Combining these methods, he predicted that the Boomer cohort spending spree and its corresponding strong national economic growth would last until maybe mid-2009, during which time period the Dow Jones average would hit at least 21,500 and possibly surge to 35,000! Although he was off on many details, as he was in his first book, he warned that the US was headed for the first of a series of market "corrections" from about 2009 to 2023. The first correction, he wrote in 1998, would occur in 2009-2010. He implied an upturn in 2011-2015 with a second and perhaps deeper recession in the period of 2015-2023. Yet, the focus of the book remained on his characterization of the economic boom times, which he saw as having a defined periodicity. His book was remarkably bland in its expectation for a big bust following the big boom. Unfortunately, having told us how high the Dow Jones was going to go, he did not inform us how low it would go and when the strong economic growth would return after the Great Recession.[68]

From one perspective, the S curve looks like a partial bell-shaped curve, which is one of the most popular ways to display data for the past, present, and future by traditional statisticians, demographers, actuaries, and psychologists. Bell curves may work well for large numbers and for "normal" distributions, but they rarely figure prominently in the graphs of product sales, market penetration, and profitability. If they did, the bell curve plotted over time would predict that all organizations, institutions, and businesses will decline and eventually fail – not a message that typically goes over well with executive managers and owners. But from another perspective, one partial bell curve may be extended to another partial bell curve, as though we added another graph to the right, and then we see a succession of partial bell curves that looks somewhat like continuously upward semi-cycles or a spiral.

---

68   Harry S. Dent, Jr. *The Roaring 2000s. Building the Wealth and Lifestyle You Desire in the Greatest Boom in History.* New York: Simon & Schuster, 1998; quote on p. 30. See pp. 31-32, 41, 45, 293, and 297-298. For his analysis of the economy in 2009 and beyond, see Harry S. Dent, Jr. *The Great Depression Ahead.* New York: Free Press, 2009.

In the context of business futuring, I must return to the ever-popular concept of business cycles and recap my discussion of Joseph Schumpeter from Chapter 1. Many times the array of apparently random economic data in Type III trend recognition will get reduced to a cycle according to the theory of inevitable business ups and downs (the theory constituting a form of Type I pattern recognition). In 1939 Schumpeter (an eminent economist) published his two-volume work entitled *Business Cycles*. His goal was to document the ebb and flow of capitalism as opposed to a linear path of progressive economic growth. He based his theory upon a succession of cycles named for Joseph Kitchin (a 40-month cycle), Clement Juglar (8-10 years), and Nikolai Kondratieff (50-60 years). In regard to the Juglar Cycle, Schumpeter identified four basic stages: 1) expansion, 2) crisis, 3) recession, and 4) recovery. He added to the work of others his own notion of creative destruction, or the phenomenon of innovation that is always changing the nature of business competition and economic growth. The concept of the business cycle is now commonly used to explain business fluctuations, although, as with historical cycles, it is difficult to fit particular facts and data with precise cycles. Juglar and Schumpeter both expressed reservations about taking cycles too literally and assigning a precision to them that the data did not support. Again, the concept of the business cycle is more a metaphor for generally repeated variations within a closed system or a fixed set of data than a deterministic phenomenon that can be predicted.[69]

Like Schlesinger Senior, I see a lot of merit in the metaphor of a spiral. This is because the perception of good times leads people to spend money and enjoy life, thereby stimulating further economic growth, which in turn reinforces the psychology of optimism. We saw this in the American economy in the 1990s during the digital 'gold rush' of the Internet. The information bubble then burst in 2000, when the Y2K catastrophe did not materialize, although the recession in information technology companies was rather short and not too deep. The real estate boom of the first decade of the 21st century is another example of spiraling optimism. Then came the real estate bust of 2008 followed by a severe bear market on Wall Street from late September 2008 to March 2009. The Great Recession is an example of a negative spiral, in which pessimism reinforces more pessimism leading to higher unemployment rates and lower consumer spending.

Less popular but arguably more insightful than linear and cyclical projections are data arrays shown as scatter diagrams. (see Figure 5.3) They plot data as received according to two axes, the x axis usually being time and the y axis usually measuring frequency or intensity (or even location) of the data. The axes might be determined by experience or parameters of particular interest. Many

---

69 Thomas K. McCraw, *Prophet of Innovation. Joseph Schumpeter and Creative Destruction.* Cambridge, MA: The Belknap Press of Harvard University Press, 2007, pp. 251-278.

statisticians see arrays as chaos and they want to reduce variation into a line through regression analysis. Futurists might make the same mental errors by reducing Type III data arrays into Type I patterns, or known trends. I prefer the arrays, because I find stories in the spread that get lost in a line – the significance of a scatter is that the data do not fall into a line or cycle or any known pattern; the array is far more meaningful for anticipating the future than extracting the average of variations.

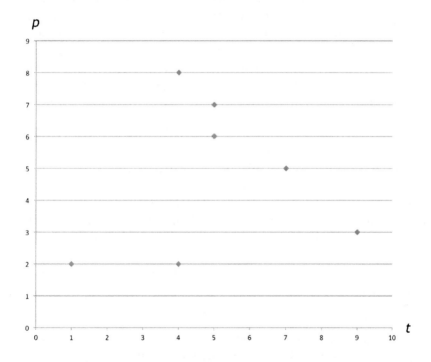

Figure 5.3: A typical scatter diagram, or array, of data in Type III Pattern Recognition

Of course, there may be many kinds of patterns that emerge from the array of data beyond lines and cycles. Historical patterns can be every bit as complicated, if not more so, as the flight of bees, the work of ants, the scores of music, and lines of computer code. The danger of Type III pattern recognition is to jump on a small sampling of data and immediately project unknown data to conform with a pre-existing Type I pattern. In a rush, it is very tempting to take an emerging Type III pattern and claim that it is a repetition of a known Type I or Type II pattern. This is an application of a metaphor that limits rather than expands our thinking. It is the danger of the false historical analogy. I love scatter diagrams, because I see a story in the spread of the data. I hate regression analysis because it flattens all the variations in the data into a synthetic line that gives me only an average. The story lies in the spread, not the flattening, of the data.

The trends that we observe in the past and project into the future may be similar to evolution on a grander scale. For example, as I discuss in Chapter 2, Professor Stephen J. Gould of Harvard argued in favor of the principle of punctuated equilibrium, in which a species may live for a long time with little or no change until a huge disruption, like a natural disaster, occurs to force it to adapt to new circumstances in order to survive (or perish). The life of a species was compared with the life of a soldier: long periods of monotony punctuated by moments of stark terror. Gould also argued that evolutionary trends exist without presumed destinations. He rejected the idea that the evolution of any species, including our own, progressed in any linear fashion and certainly was not moving toward a glorious conclusion. "A trend," Gould wrote, "is not a march along a path, but a complex series of transfers, or side steps, from one event of speciation to another." He objected strongly to treating evolution as only averaged, linear stages, because he felt that the variations, not the lines, supplied the most meaningful stories of evolution.[70]

Another approach to Type III pattern recognition as applied to trend monitoring and scanning is modeling and simulation. Models provide a powerful tool for organizing data and gaining foresights into the future if future data are consistent with present data. Yet, once we have a model of the past and the present, we can play with it in any number of ways that it might move in the future. Models are fundamentally examples of Type I patterns, but they can be used as templates for Type III patterns to provisionally organize and simulate random data pending conclusive categorization as a variation on an old Type I or the emergence of a new Type I pattern.

You can easily fool yourself by jumping too soon with too little data into declaring an emerging Type III pattern as a more or less Type I pattern when in fact it is its own pattern, a new Type I pattern for the future, but not a Type I pattern of the past. Unfortunately, this premature classification of patterns has been a major problem for the intelligence community for years. For example, armed with too little information, some people concluded that the terrorist attacks of September 11, 2001, were essentially a Type I pattern of the Pearl Harbor sort. I made this mistake, too, but learned that 9/11 was a new Type I pattern with its own unique implications for future American defense and homeland security policies. Some people predicted that the American military incursion into Iraq in March 2003 was akin to the American liberation of Paris from the Nazis in August 1944 – with images of adoring crowds greeting American GIs with American flags and flowers, admiring local women, and smiling children being asked to be held or given chocolate bars. Not exactly. The subsequent insurgency in Iraq looked

---

70 Stephen Jay Gould, *Full House. The Spread of Excellence from Plato to Darwin.* New York: Harmony Books, 1996; quotation on p. 63. Also see "Stephen Jay Gould" at www.wikipedia.org

more like Vietnam of the 1960s rather than France in 1944 but with its own complexities, making it very much a Type III pattern on its way to becoming a new Type I pattern. Such is the fallacy of mistaken historical analogies.

In poetry, the analogy is captured by the metaphor, and the great American 20th century poet Robert Frost warned us that the living metaphor has its mental limitations as well as its literary strengths. Frost warned that all metaphors eventually break down when carried too far. Likewise, historians and political scientists have shown the potential strengths and dangers of using historical analogies as inputs to policy decision-making, which also break down when stretched too far.[71] The abuse of metaphors and historical analogies can be viewed as a potential danger of too quickly jumping to the conclusion that an emerging Type III pattern is the repeat of a known Type I pattern when actually, given more data and time for analysis, it may be a new pattern with peculiarities of its own.

In conclusion, the comparison of trends with patterns and the classification of three different types of pattern can be very useful to the futuring manager in both the preparation and monitoring of forecasts, especially trend analysis and trend tracking. There are times and circumstances when lines and cycles are justified, but generally be skeptical of mechanical approaches to futuring. They are more justified as concepts than predictive tools for interpreting data. In terms of well considered expectations for the future, they make for better metaphors than mathematics.

A Case Study: The Updating and Pattern Recognition of Economic Growth in India

In the previous chapter, I shared with you the case history of a futuring project on the prospects for continued economic growth in India. The forecast was prepared in 2002 and it generated well considered expectations to 2012. The client continued investing in the Indian market and made several significant changes in its production and marketing processes to better reach prospective Indian consumers. The economy of India showed strong growth, as we expected, throughout the first decade of the 21st century. Even when the global recession hit in 2008-2009, India did not suffer as much as other countries did. Over the years

---

71   Robert Frost, "Education in Poetry. A Meditative Monologue." Amherst Alumni Council Address, November 15, 1930. In Robert Frost, *Collected Poems, Prose, & Plays*. New York: The Library of America, 1995, pp. 719, 723. For treatments of metaphors, similes, and analogies in history, see Ernest R. May, *"Lessons" of the Past. The Use and Misuse of History in American Foreign Policy*. New York: Oxford University Press, 1973; and Richard E. Neustadt and Ernest R. May, *Thinking in Time. The Uses of History for Decision Makers*. New York: The Free Press, 1986.

I had numerous occasions to monitor trends and to update the baseline forecast (Type I patterns) with new information, as described below.

In 1991, the world's attention was largely focused on the monumental changes occurring in Europe. Before the unbelieving eyes of Western observers, the Soviet Union and its Communist Party disintegrated along with other Communist regimes in Eastern Europe. Considering the background (Type I pattern) of the Soviet role in world affairs as a super power after World War II and the Cold War with the US, the change in governments, political states, and leaders from Berlin to Moscow shocked most people in the West. The events in Moscow during the summer of 1991 were viewed as unimaginable black swans. For people monitoring the political shifts from state-dominated to free-market economic systems, the changes in Russia constituted a Type II signal and the emergence of new patterns.

Another, less publicized, Type II change also occurred in 1991 in India, where the national government teetered on the verge of financial collapse. A political crisis occurred with the assassination of Prime Minister Rajiv Gandhi, who was the son of a previous prime minister, Indira Gandhi (who had been assassinated in 1984) and the grandson of the first prime minister and founder of the republic, Jawaharlal Nehru. The new prime minister was P. V. Narasimha Rao, a Nehru-Gandhi family loyalist and long-time political leader of the Congress Party. Along with his finance minister, Manmohan Singh, Rao decided to push harder the economic reforms begun by his predecessor. Major changes in the socialistic, central-planning economic system were begun, including gradual privatization of state corporations, liberalized licensing and deregulation of private enterprises, and tax reforms. Foreign trade and investments in India were encouraged. The market-driven private economy took off and India started to experience an economic growth spurt somewhat like China's.

By the year 2000, India was emerging as a potentially attractive market for foreign investment and business. The big question centered on how strong the economic growth might be in the future. Would new governments in the future continue the economic reforms of Rao and Singh? Would the Indian people tolerate aggressive entrepreneurs and evolve into assertive consumers? Would a strong middle-class of consumers emerge in India and would their consumption patterns and tastes parallel those of China, Europe, and the US? In our forecast of 2002 we concluded that the most likely future would provide the answer "yes" to all of these questions.

Looking back over about 3,000 years of Indian history, we were impressed with the resilience of Indian society and culture to foreign invasions and influences. India had been occupied by Alexander the Great, Arabs, great hordes from Central

Asia, Muslim potentates, and the British. Indian society accommodated many foreign incursions, but remained uniquely Indian. There had always been a strong commercial tradition in India; Indian merchants were almost as famous as Chinese merchants around the world. While there were Hindu elements of self-denial, there were also the traditions of the householder with worldly responsibilities and desires. In general, the Indians have loved the comforts of the material life as much as most other people in the world. We found no underlying historical or cultural trends that would sabotage a free market economy and sustained economic growth at the beginning of the 21st century. To the contrary, there was a long history that suggested that India could adapt to foreign investments, global trade, consumer economics, and information technologies and still remain uniquely Indian.

A. B. Vajpayee led the BJP Party to victory over the Congress Party and served as the prime minister continuously from 1999 to 2004. As the leader of many economic, political, and religious conservatives, Vajpayee vigorously continued the economic reforms begun in 1991. Vajpayee's party, however, was defeated by the Congress Party and a new Congress prime minister came to power in 2004: Manmohan Singh, a professional economist and a former architect with Rao of the paradigm-shifting reforms of 1991. Singh showed a concern for social issues of equity and equal opportunity for all, but his fundamental political philosophy was to continue strong economic growth, driven primarily by the private sector, in order to improve people's standards of living. The more or less free enterprise economy would drive economic growth and wealth accumulation, not the state. The personalities and parties of power changed, but the fundamental direction of the Indian economy continued on the course set in the 1990s.

The political, economic, and social trends from 1991 to 2011 indicate that India has indeed developed a new Type I pattern that is likely to endure for decades in the future. India has remained the largest democracy in the world, with the ability to make major political shifts without military coups, revolutions, and civil wars. The people generally support the economic reforms of the national government. The Indian economy continues to grow, achieving a 9.2% GDP growth rate in 2007, second only to the frantic economic growth rate of China. In the midst of this economic boom, a new middle class, called the "consuming class," has emerged. Their size has been estimated as 300 million, which is still only about 25% of all Indians but about as many people as the whole population of the US. They are proving to be just as entrepreneurial and just as consuming, relative to their socio-economic conditions, as middle classes in other parts of the world. They are seeking new homes and apartments with Western-style furniture, accessories, and electronics. They are vigorous users of laptop computers and the Internet; highly educated and English-speaking, the young middle class has driven a boom in Indian computer and Internet services, providing many with outsourced work for American corporations. They are also vigorous users of mobile phones. There is a strong market for all sorts of entertainment, including pop music, movies ("Bollywood"), and video games. They seek to own their own automobiles and enjoy the freedoms of personal mobility much like Americans. They are upgrading their diets to include more Western style packaged foods and beverages. And they are enthusiastic consumers of American fashions and fads.

Entering the second decade of the 21st century, India has a GDP of roughly $1.25 trillion (compared to the GDP of about $15 trillion in the US). In terms of nominal GDP growth, India is now the 11th biggest economy in the world. In terms of purchasing power parity (PPP), the Indian economy ranks fourth in the world. Yet, India is still a very poor country. Over one-third of India's huge population (over 1.1 billion people, second in the world only to China) remains below the official poverty level. Unemployment has risen above 10%. The conclusion is that the Indian economic reforms of 1991 and the subsequent strong economic growth rates are "real" and sustainable for many years to come. Having said this, India is still a developing country; it offers many exciting business opportunities and it is an emerging consumer market for American goods and services, but it is still modest compared with the higher standards of living enjoyed generally in Europe, North America, and South America.

Most importantly, the Indian people remain generally optimistic about their future and invigorated to achieve new level of economic development, despite the effects of the Great Recession on other countries. In particular, the positive attitudes in India stand in stark contrast to the feelings of frustration and fear in the US.

Having stated above the case for continued growth in the Indian economy, the annual growth rate, as measured by real GDP growth rates, has not been linear. In 2002, it declined relative to what it had been in 2001, and did not change in 2004. At that point in time, one might have said that the Indian GDP growth rate had flattened. The data for 2005-2008, however, showed an annual GDP growth rate that varied between 6.2% and 9.2%. The rate declined to about 7% in 2009 and 2010, but is expected to exceed 10% in 2011. This is a Type I pattern of sustainable economic growth, but it illustrates the point that growth can be inconsistent from year to year and that annual projects based only on data from previous years can be misleading. This illustrates the importance of continuing the futuring process beyond forecasting. In this particular case, the continuous monitoring of trends further validated the general expectations of the 2002 forecast, although a Type III pattern might have emerged but did not with the global financial crisis of 2008.

As for our clients, they continued their commitments in the Indian market. With increasing confidence about the prospects of future economic growth derived from the monitoring process, they increased their investments in India to maintain a long-term presence in the Indian market. They enlarged one major manufacturing plant to produce a product for the upper levels of the consumer class. They also invested in a new product that was less expensive than previous products, thereby reaching across a broad spectrum of potential buyers. They changed their making to make more effort to appeal to women as well as men. Consistent with our forecast, they have encountered no deeply rooted cultural problems with Indians as either employees or as consumers. They also have suffered no particular political or social discrimination by Indians. They continue to monitor trends closely, but new information so far fits with their well considered expectations for the future.

Chapter 6. Managing Futuring

Up to this point, I have shared with you the five basic principles of futuring. You can be your own best futurist, as anticipating the future is a skill that will help you achieve success in your career. You are already expected to be your own best planner, so you need to learn the theories, skills, and knowledge base of futuring, too. You may wish to employ these principles yourself and generate your own forecasts and plans; alternatively, you may wish to delegate some of these responsibilities to selected staff or consultants. Either way, you have the responsibility to see that well considered expectations for the future are crafted to reach your business goals.

The focus of this chapter is how to manage the futuring process, including projects that generate forecasts and trend tracking. The assumption is that you will have periodic futuring projects, maybe one major project every two or three years, and that you will have continuous trend (and black swan) monitoring and scanning at one level of effort or another. In addition, you will likely have the job of generating annual budgets and plans within the context of your forecasts and corporate goals. Managing visioning, including planning, will be the topic of Chapter 7.

I do not expect "perfect" forecasts or plans. No ideal futuring project has ever occurred with ideal results and I expect that none will ever happen in the future. Knowing all the things that can go wrong, both within and outside of my control, I am delighted when my forecasts or plans work out reasonably well in "the real world." I believe, however, that certain best practices, in particular those drawn from my own experiences and those related to me by other managers and futurists, are likely to improve the content and use of both forecasts and plans.

Step 1: Identification of the Project Goals, Resources, and Assignments

Every futuring endeavor begins with a customer to satisfy and a need to fulfill. In some cases, the "customer" may be senior executives or division heads. They may need your expectations for the future of your business to input into larger corporate planning. As a manager, you may be your own customer – you may need a forecast to enable you to make a decision, plan your strategy, or calculate your budgets. In other circumstances, the customer may be your business customer who asks you to engage with him or her in concurrent planning.

At the very beginning of a futuring project, you must identify: 1) who needs the forecast, and 2) what useful purpose the forecast will likely serve. These are the goals of the project. Having done this, you need to budget and allocate resources to conduct the project so that it meets its goals. As part of this process you will need to think about a time schedule, milestones, the forms of the deliverables, money, materials, and what staff you will need. If you are using others, be sure to give explicit assignments, just as you would for any other task that you would manage. If you are not managing the project yourself, then a critically important element is to assign a project manager, who will report directly to you.

How long and expensive a futuring project may be depends entirely upon the circumstances for it. A "quick and dirty" forecast could take as little as a month or two to prepare, while a major forecast can require six months to a year to craft. It all depends upon how much detail you need and whether the research materials and methods are readily available or take time to track down. It also depends upon your time availability and that of your staff. You may need one or two people dedicated to the effort to keep it on schedule. Obviously, the budget depends upon the amount of time required, the number of people committed to it and their personnel costs, and the costs of materials and tools that will be employed to get the job done. In any event, you should be careful to represent forecasts for what they are: quick and dirty (gross approximations) or thoroughly researched and thought out.

How specific the forecast will be should be determined at the very beginning of the project. You may need only a general background forecast, or you may need a rather specific forecast to use as an input to an important decision. I have asserted that it is not unreasonable to spend at least 3%-5% of the value of the decision at stake on a due diligence fund, including futuring and visioning. That would mean investing about $300,000 to $500,000 for due diligence on a decision worth potentially $10 million. Nobody has yet argued otherwise with me.

Step 2: Topic Question

It has been said that a question well stated is half answered. Every futuring and visioning project should have a focus or topic question, which should become the North Star for guiding all steps toward satisfying the customer and objectives of a futuring project. A well structured topic question should have at least four primary elements and a follow up element:

1. A focus descriptor (trend, issue, factor, variable, etc.)

2. A definition or metric for the key descriptor

3. A geographical scope

4. A time frame in the future.

The follow up question should be "and what are the specific implications for the company or organization?" "Implications" might be emerging opportunities or potential threats. I often ask my client managers "If you had the answer to this question, what would you do with it? Does it meet your needs as an input to a decision, an investment, or a strategy?" The implications of a forecast provide the bridge from futuring to visioning, as they become contextual inputs to your planning process.

The topic question must be responsive to the purpose of the forecast, as defined in Step 1. In a sense, it is a mission statement, the answer to which will provide a benefit to you as a manager for a practical application.

Oddly, many managers do not know at the beginning of a futuring project what the topic question should be. It is very easy to pose the wrong question. I am continually amazed that many managers who cannot frame a topic question simply ignore this critically important step. How could you justify a forecast that had no focus and no use to you? Many times I have struggled along with managers to hit upon the right focus descriptor. Some managers want to know everything about everything, which is not only very challenging but also very expensive. Impossible, too. You need to understand that the futuring or visioning project will involve many descriptors, but you need one of particular importance to guide the project. In my experience, some managers need only a broad perspective, so they frame a rather broad topic question. They want to know "the lay of the land," so to speak, of a future market or service area without needing any particular input for a specific decision. This is OK. In other cases, however, the manager may need a futuring input to a specific decision or course of action. He or she needs a well focused topic question in order to get what they need.

When you frame your topic question, you need to define the meaning of the topic question and/or provide a metric for it. The metric does not need to be a specific number; rather it may be expressed in a range to reflect uncertainty about the future. In addition, you need to specify the geography. Is the forecast to cover the whole world, the US, or a specific market? The amount of research and the nature of expert judgments will vary greatly depending upon whether your topic is in the US, the EU, the Middle East, India, China, Japan, Latin America, or the whole world.

The timeframe also makes a huge difference in futuring projects. Are your expectations calibrated by 10, 20, 50, or 100 years into the future? The time frame will drive the expectations of both trend analysis and expert intuition about potential changes – the longer the timeframe the more uncertainty there will be and more opportunities for radical changes to occur. When asked about the future of a topic just five or fewer years into the future, you may narrow your thinking and emphasize current trend projections (the recency effect) with little or no consideration of potential changes, unless there is a milestone event expected within a shorter timeframe. This is why so many annual budgets and operational plans get stuck in the "business as usual" mode. They are too often merely projections of last year's performance to next year's expectations. On the other hand, the longer the timeframe the more flexibility there will be for creative thinking and potential innovations. I typically recommend that a futuring project for an American corporation should be at least 10 years in the future to get away from the recency effect and to encourage the creative thinking that comes with both uncertainty and the opportunities for innovation. Asian companies like to think 20 to 50 years in the future. Looking too far into the future, however, should be avoided – really long-term forecasts suffer from too much uncertainty, doubts of prescience, lack of relevance to today's challenges, and the exaggerations of science fiction.

I express topic questions with an end date in the future and generate the forecasts for a range of years, such as "from now through to the year 2020". I do not try to forecast year-by-year. This looks too much like a linear projection of trends. I also do not try to forecast exact cause-and-effect sequences of trends and events. This is valid for planning the things that you will do (the self-fulfilling prophecy), but it is way too speculative for forecasting. Rather, I forecast for a target year without knowing exactly what outcomes will most likely occur in what given years So, for example, a forecast of GDP growth or the annual sales of a product will be given as an amount, or better yet a numerical range to properly reflect uncertainty, by 2020 and not for each year up to 2020. I have done highly speculative forecasts whereby I have interpolated hypothetical events between now and a forecasted target date, but in the context of visioning rather than futuring.

I have enjoyed many discussions (sometimes arguments) with my futuring colleagues on the most important determinants of a successful forecast. I am absolutely convinced from experience that the topic question determines everything that follows. If you ask different questions, you may reach radically different results. After the topic question, the most important determinants of a successful forecast include the amount of time and resources given to it, the people involved in preparing it, the experts used for expert judgments, and the methods employed.

Some typical topic questions are as follows:

- What new patterns in consumer behavior (spending preferences and shopping habits) might occur in the US from now to the year 2020? The follow-up question might be: What new business opportunities might emerge from them? The timeframe is expressed as a range of years rather than a particular date. You will be describing future conditions, but may or may not attempt to identify specific sequences of events (which would be extremely difficult to do and highly speculative).

- What will likely be the GDP of the US, as measured in constant 2011 US dollars, by the year 2015?

- To what extent will the EU likely reach its unification goals by the year 2020 and will reaching those goals result in a "Fortress Europe" mentality in foreign, defense, financial, and trade policies?

- What will likely be the sales of commercial fuel cells to commercial customers in the US between 2011 and 2020? This question addresses how rapidly and under what conditions fuel cells will be commercialized with a particular type of customer – "commercial customers" in the parlance of electric utilities include shopping malls, department stores, warehouses, small shops, dry cleaners, etc.

- How many combat troops will the US likely have in Afghanistan, and under what circumstances, by the year 2015?"

- What limitations, controls, and penalties will the US government likely impose on carbon emissions and under what circumstances by the year 2030?

Of course, it is possible to have more than one answer to a question since multiple possible future outcomes exist. Scenarios provide alternative views and alternative answers to a topic question.

The topic question for a futuring project should have a focus on the external environments of the enterprise to qualify as "futuring." The samples of topic questions above are futuring topic questions. Entirely different questions might be asked for visioning, including planning, such as:

- What are the current strategic assets and technologies of the company and how can they be leveraged for sales growth in the US by the year 2020?

- In what ways does the corporate culture need to change in order to be better aligned with changes in customers and markets and how can we best affect those corporate culture changes around the world within the next three years?

- Given a forecast for a product that we see as having great opportunities in the American market over the next decade, how do we optimize our resources and what do we need to do to position ourselves by 2015 to fully exploit that business opportunity by 2020?

As I have argued before, it is potentially dangerous to address the investment and strategy issues of visioning with little or no prior work in futuring. Without the boundary conditions or sample space of futuring, the plans that emerge from visioning in a vacuum can be full of wishful thinking and other biases.

Step 3: Selection of Descriptors

Having established the topic question, the next step is to identify the descriptors that are most relevant to it. "Descriptors" are trends, issues, factors, variables, elements, etc. They are the things that go into the analysis that will lead to an answer or answers to the topic question. In systems analysis and model building, this step is generically called "the specification of the model." It might also be considered as setting up a closed system or fixed set to improve predictability. Theoretically, a specific question that leads to a perfect set of descriptors (meaning highly relevant to the topic question with no serious omissions or redundancies) would be a closed system and might be highly prescient. Such is the ideal. Even when we fail to achieve perfection, we are still learning along the way to form better considered expectations for the future.

You should include the focus descriptor among your total set of descriptors, especially if you intend to do cross-impact analysis. At this stage of work, you cannot presume to know yet which are independent or dependent variables, or, in the language of cross-impact analysis, which descriptors will be drivers with strong impacts on other descriptors and which will be driven, meaning those descriptors that will be highly impacted. A manageable number of descriptors for a relatively simple problem might be in the range of 8-12. For mid-level complexity, you may want up to 18 descriptors. I have worked with as many as 24 descriptors, but that is about the limit of useful complexity. Beyond two dozen descriptors, models can get so complex as to become virtual black boxes. Also, models with too many variables tend to include repetition, with multiple descriptors appearing as really only variations on a theme. Repetition leads to redundancy, which in turn leads to skewed (tightly clustered or even monolithic) results.

Descriptors can touch on all kinds of matters as long as they are judged to be relevant to the topic question: economics, government policy, regulation, law, politics, demographics, social dynamics, consumer behavior and values, competition, trade, terrorism, national security, public health, and technologies of all sorts. They may be qualitative as well as quantitative since we do not have to reduce them to a formula if we do not want to.

Descriptors may be objects as well as "free agents." I realize that some systems analysts draw a distinction between a "variable" and an "agent," whereby a "variable" is an inanimate "thing" and an "agent" is a proactive, evolving, living agent that itself has some element of free will. As I argue at length in Chapter 2, there are fundamental theoretical, methodological, and practical differences among the systems approaches of the MIT school of cybernetics and systems dynamics based on the work of Jay Forrester, Donella Meadows, and Peter Senge; the University of Pennsylvania school of operations research and systems analysis as constructed by C. West Churchman and the "ideal-seeking system" concept of Russell Ackoff; and the school of complex adaptive systems (CAS), especially formulated by John von Neumann in his concept of "cellular automata" and as presently championed by the Santa Fe Institute. These approaches result in significant differences in orientation of forecasting vs. planning and in degrees of predictability. Some system models are more valuable as learning rather than forecasting approaches, and some are better for the design of a new system than analysis of an old system. It has been further argued that it may be possible to anticipate with high probabilities a future state of a system containing "variables," but it is extremely difficult if not impossible to anticipate the future state of a living system wherein the agents are continuously changing and may not be known, or even knowable.[72]

Unless you are performing very sophisticated modeling, the theoretical distinction between inanimate variables and animate agents may not make too big a difference for your purposes. They are all "descriptors." These distinctions in systems theory have not figured prominently in my experiences of futuring. I have followed a more qualitative approach to systems analysis with an emphasis on conceptual modeling in order to understand the past and the present and to anticipate likely future outcomes. I have never been enamored with mathematical and statistical methods of quantitative forecasting. I use a very generic concept of a model: as a representation of a state of nature in which there exist things that have relationships with each other in the form of inputs, processes, outputs, and feedback. I have always had my theoretical reservations about the MIT school of systems dynamics. I like it conceptually, but I don't care for its mechanics, which I see as being both too simplistic in its fundamental assumptions and

---

72 I thank Dr. Peter Bishop for bringing these distinctions in systems analysis to my attention in a face-to-face conversation that we had in Columbus, Ohio, on November 2, 2009. See Peter Bishop, "Teaching Systems Thinking," *Futures Research Quarterly*, Summer 2008, Volume 24, Number 2, pp. 7-38.

hidden biases and too complicated in its calculations. (As an aside, I also like the concepts of supply and demand, historical and economic cycles, and S curves, but I seriously question the results of quantitative forecasts of them in the future – for me, they are metaphors, each with illustrative strengths and weaknesses.) After all, we must always keep in mind that in any form (including systems analysis) models, both formal and intuitive, are representations of reality rather than reality itself. When we use them for futuring, we are modeling our thinking and our expectations for the future, not the future itself (which does not exist yet).

The selection of descriptors in *all* systems, fixed sets, models, and formulas is a matter of expert judgment. The problem is that, in much model building, the method and rationale for selecting the variables are not made explicit. A lot of assumptions and biases can be buried in models. Somebody has to decide what to include within the scope of the topic question (boundary conditions that lead to a closed or quasi-closed system and a fixed set of descriptors) and what not to include. I have never seen any "objective" way to do this. Some statisticians and econometricians may claim objectivity in their data, models and formulas, but they had to select the variables, so they were exercising their expert judgment without necessarily justifying their selections to anybody else. It is therefore terribly important that you put in place a process to sample expert judgment that is explicit, more or less comprehensive, bias-balancing, and participatory.

In some cases, you will be your own expert. Especially in "quick and dirty" futuring exercises – the ones that are meant to be gross approximations for your own eyes – you will select the descriptors based on your current (*a priori*) knowledge and maybe a little extra research on the Internet. For major futuring projects, however, you need to reach out to other experts, through a variety of means, to solicit expert judgments from a variety of sources.

You can access expert judgment through secondary research using books, articles, reports, and papers on the topics of interest to you. A literature search is always recommended for any research project. You, or one of your subordinates, will be overwhelmed by the amount of potentially useful material that you may find on the Internet.

I highly recommend that you perform primary research to gather judgments from experts through interviews (face-to-face, by telephone, and by e-mail), questionnaires and surveys (hardcopy, e-mail, or website), and expert (as opposed to consumer) focus groups. The experts may be other managers and staff throughout your organization; they may also be outside consultants, journalists, scientists and engineers or professors. You are asking them to identify the most important descriptors relative to a topic question, not a forecast in and of itself.

You are asking them to make their expert inputs into a larger futuring process that will result in a forecast.

Expert focus groups provide a surrogate for consumers when thinking years ahead. That is because the experts think more about emerging consumer behavior than consumers do. I define "experts" very broadly to include people who have studied consumer behavior from any number of perspectives, such as academic research, R&D, market and consumer research, demographics, and economics.

Remember that when you are sampling expert judgment, no expert, contrary to what he or she may assert, knows everything, and that all experts have biases, whether they admit them or not. To guard against these potential problems, you need to sample the views of many experts, both outside and inside your organization.

My experiences with experts are largely consistent with the findings of James Surowiecki: that sourcing an opinion from large numbers of diverse and independent experts will give a significantly more prescient view than approaching a few specialists. In addition, the most famous experts, especially those great authorities who tend to dominate conversations, are usually not the best experts for participating in expert judgment groups. As Surowiecki observed, "...we don't always know where the good information is... it's smarter to cast as wide a net as possible, rather than wasting time figuring out who should be in the group and who should not."[73]

For years I preferred to conduct real-time and in-person expert focus groups when identifying the most important descriptors going into a "top 10" technology forecast or scenarios analysis. One of the advantages of real-life expert focus groups includes the experts hearing and interacting with each other – they stimulate everyone's creativity in thinking about the future. Using the Nominal Group Technique, I could get a lot of expert opinion and a rank-ordered list within about two-and-a-half hours. There are, however, disadvantages to expert focus groups, including the difficulties in scheduling the participants for the same time at the same place, expenses associated with having any meeting, and the limitation of participation to a manageable number of experts. The optimal number of participants is roughly 12. To manage this limitation, we often held more than one expert focus group on any given topic and this way we could see whether other experts came up with different items on their list. This is good research, but also time consuming and expensive.

If I have the time and resources for only one focus group, I like a mixed group including some participants from inside the company or organization and some

---

73   James Surowiecki, *The Wisdom of Crowds.* New York: Anchor Books, 2005, p. 276.

outside experts (from a university, an R&D center, a supplier, or another company or organization similar to the client). I like to use a broad representation of the entire company, including experts from R&D, manufacturing, accounting and finance, and marketing. If I have the time and resources, I like to do two expert focus groups on the same question. One expert focus group does not literally "validate" another, but it does supplement. A second focus group may confirm the importance of descriptors from the other and it may generate potential descriptors that were missed previously. On a single topic, I have done as many as six expert focus groups in six different places in the US and Europe with six different groups of experts who brought us a particularly wide range of points of view.

In recent years, I have used more frequently virtual expert focus groups and online surveys. The Internet provides an excellent vehicle for surveys. I can reach dozens if not hundreds of experts. I can e-mail my question to whomever and they can respond when it is most convenient for them. I can set up a chat room or a blog whereby they can see each other's responses and we can make the process iterative by allowing experts to express their views repeatedly in reply to what other experts write.

The question for the expert focus group is a derivative of the primary topic question. It typically begins "What are the most important descriptors (trends, issues, and factors) that will directly affect x [the topic question itself]." For example, the topic question for a futuring project might read "What long-term changes are most likely to occur in American consumer behavior from 2011 to 2021?" To identify the most important descriptors through expert judgment, the question for the experts would be "What are the most important descriptors (trends, issues, and factors) that will drive American consumer behavior from 2011 to 2021?" We would also follow up with a definition of what we mean by "American consumer behavior": i.e. the predominant ways in which Americans will shop and purchase goods and services and the aspects of products and services they will most value (with value equaling benefits less price). The experts might come up with the following list of descriptors:

- GDP annual growth rate.
- Household income.
- National unemployment rate.
- Number of new jobs created.
- Dow Jones Industrial Average of stocks on the New York Stock Exchange.
- Availability and cost of consumer credit.
- Predominance of "big box" retailers.

- Predominance of shopping malls, department stores, and other major retailers.

- Volume of Internet sales.

- Housing values.

- Fuel prices (including gasoline, natural gas, and electricity).

- Inflation rates.

- Interest rates.

- Willingness of consumers to spend.

- Benefits of product quality, performance, and utility.

- Benefits of product durability and longevity.

- Retail prices.

- Importance of shopping convenience to consumers.

- Ratio of sales of luxury goods to day-to-day commodities.

- Immigration.

- Average age of American population/consumers.

- Importance of novelty and entertainment in products and services.

- Technology breakthroughs in materials design (such as nanotechnologies), genetics, and energy storage.

- R&D spending levels and priorities as indicators of future technological advances.

- Patents as indicators of emerging products and services coming onto global markets.

Such a list could include 60 or more potential descriptors, depending upon the topic question, the experts, the number of expert focus groups, and the time available for the exercise. In the language of idea-generation techniques, the initial brainstorming of potential descriptors is the divergence phase. You want to encourage as many responses to the question as seem reasonable given the time and circumstances. But you have to have a means of paring them down, too. This is the convergence phase. It can be done by any of a number of voting procedures to enable the experts themselves to do a screening. They can vote according to a prepared set of criteria or by their own judgment (a cerebral black box). The team can also sort the descriptors according to frequency of words or concepts mentioned by the experts. There may also be a reduction in descriptors through consolidation and elimination of redundancies. Another approach concerns the fact that some potential descriptors may not actually be separate descriptors, but rather potential alternative states of a descriptor.

You would hate to go through this process of generating a master list of descriptors and consolidating them into a manageable set only to find out later that you had left some important descriptor out and included others that were indeed redundant. Unfortunately, this happens. Futuring projects are always a learning process; therefore, they often are iterative and cyclical rather than linear.

In my experience, executive managers love to see the results of expert judgment exercises. They have never complained that we conducted too many interviews, surveys, or expert focus groups. You can take the results of each exercise and rank in order of importance the resulting descriptors to give you a "top 10" list. This packaging is always popular and generates much interest and discussion. Even though they may or may not be used as inputs to larger futuring projects, a top 10 list stands on its own merits as a valued deliverable of information on various perceptions of what is important.

Because expert judgment plays such an important role in futuring, I would like to take a short diversion to explore it more thoroughly. We see expert judgment used in crafting the topic sentence (principally, your own as the responsible manager), selecting the descriptors, making projections and imagining alternative outcomes for descriptors, evaluating forecasts (and scenarios), and drawing business implications from the forecast to use in decision-making, strategy development, and planning.

The social psychologist and political scientist Philip Tetlock, as well as Stephen Jay Gould, characterized experts as "foxes" and "hedgehogs." The former are those experts who may have an area of expertise but also an unusual amount of familiarity with a broad spectrum of topics (known as "generalists"), while the latter possess well defined and circumscribed areas of expertise (the "specialists"). Tetlock concluded that in most situations of political forecasting, the "foxes" outperformed the "hedgehogs."[74] One explanation might be that the "hedgehogs" knew too much and over wrought their predictions for the future.[75]

---

74 Philip E. Tetlock, *Expert Political Judgment. How Good Is It? How Can We Know?* Princeton, NJ: Princeton University Press, 2005, especially pp. 67-120. Also see John T. Jost, "The Perils of Prognostication," *Science*, Vol. 312, June 30, 2006, pp. 1876-1877.

75 Gerd Gigerenzer, *Gut Feelings. The Intelligence of the Unconscious.* New York: Penguin Books, 2007, pp. 16-19, 147-151; Michael Shermer, "Patternicity," *Scientific American*, December 2008, p. 48. Also see William Ascher, *Forecasting. An Appraisal for Policy-Makers and Planners.* Baltimore: The Johns Hopkins University Press, 1978. Ascher concluded that experts with deep knowledge in selected fields had a poor track record of making predictions in their own areas of exceptional expertise.

My experiences with experts and their judgments, however, suggest other reasons for preferring "fox experts" over "hedgehog experts." The "foxes" typically show an ability to identify and interrelate multiple trends coming together from many directions, while the "hedgehogs" emphasize just one or a few trends about which they have exceptional knowledge, comfort, and interest. I, too, have found that the generalists tend to outperform the specialists in futuring. In addition, the "foxes" can be professionally humble and respectful of the uncertainties of the future, while "hedgehogs" can display great confidence in their ability to predict the future due to their own expertise, not seeing their own biases and knowledge limitations.

What makes expert judgment prescient if not predictive? What is the theory that stands behind the methods and techniques of expert judgment? Experts have exceptional knowledge and mental processes that we simply call "intuition." Experts are aware of the momentum of many trends and their interactions with each other. They unconsciously see complex patterns. Experts know how to rely appropriately on proven cause-and-effect relationships, and they draw logical inferences from closed systems and fixed sets. They know enough from years of study and experience: to realize what is possible and what is more likely than not; to deduce from science and technology what could be according to the laws of nature; and to appreciate from works of fiction what has been imagined as possibly happening in the future. They may also have insights into the intentions and plans of key players. Experts are not always correct, but they have been able to anticipate the future, if not in precise details then in many general ways (and with Bayesian probabilities), as opposed to those who have little or no knowledge of trends and conditions.

One theory asserts that intuition is subconscious pattern recognition. It consists of heuristics, or "rules of thumb," that may be based on evolution. These heuristics have become part of the "hard wiring" of human brains. According to this theory, intuition likely developed in our distant ancestors as a survival mechanism in reaction to sudden crises. Intuition may be an aspect of our instinct to think quickly just to stay alive. Pattern recognition, or the ability to relate a perception of sight or noise to the behavior of predators, became a heuristic for survival. Such pattern recognition often rewarded speed rather than thoroughness, so it became something we do automatically, without requiring conscious thinking. Therefore, reaction stemmed from stimulus without the agent logically knowing exactly why they did, or concluded, what they did.[76]

---

76 Gigerenzer, *Gut Feelings*, pp. 47, 82-86, 146-151, 182-85, and 192; Shermer, "Patternicity." [See Footnote 75.]

It is possible that the intuitive powers of subconscious pattern recognition, logical inferences, and the recognition of early stages of cause-and-effect sequences may account for the phenomena that we commonly call premonitions, hunches, extrasensory perception (ESP), the sixth sense, and second sight. When these powers are exercised by serious academics, analysts, and experts, we call it "expert judgment."

Tetlock's study of political predictions concentrates largely on futuring in the field of world affairs. Tetlock places grave doubts on the prescient powers of experts, especially "genius forecasters," to generate accurate political forecasts. One methodological problem of his study, however, is that he was asking experts to make predictions about future events, like black swans, more than future conditions. As I mentioned above, it is more practical to anticipate general conditions as the context for possible events than it is to predict precise events. Tetlock concluded that most experts, regardless of their credentials and confidence in themselves, and including those with big reputations as authorities in their field, typically had no better record of success than trend extrapolations in anticipating the future. While I agree with Tetlock on many points, especially concerning the poor track record of highly respected "hedgehog" experts in giving political predictions to government decision-makers (like the President), I want to go beyond his study to assert from my less lofty experience that using many experts is much better practice than using a single expert and that using groups of experts interacting with each other is better than using multiple experts one-by-one in isolation. I have also found that it helps me most to use experts to make inputs into formal futuring processes (like trend analysis, modeling and simulation, and scenario analysis) rather than to ask the experts to make their own predictions from the black boxes of their intuition.

Experts may rely on the talent of imagination, but a type of imagination tempered by information and the laws of physics. My good friend and colleague David Staley has argued that highly educated and informed individuals (experts, specialists, and authorities) bring a disciplined imagination to futuring. Experts have the capacity to generate mental maps of how the future might look based on extensive knowledge of trends, cause-and-effect relationships, and historical precedents. They have an acute feel for what is possible and what is more likely than not in the times ahead. Staley calls this capability "restrained imagination," because it is disciplined by scientific methods of inquiry and evidence.[77] I would add from my experience of using scientific and technical experts that they have a talent for anticipating the outcome of trends and separating the "science" from the "science fiction."

---

77   David J. Staley, *History and Future. Using Historical Thinking to Imagine the Future.* Lanham, MD: Lexington Books, 2007, pp. 101-127.

I disagree with those who have asserted that less knowledge is better than more knowledge when it comes to anticipating the future. There is a school of thought that asserts that an expert might know "too much" and that less knowledge might lead to better forecasts. I do not accept that point of view as it is often stated. My experience has taught me that experts are most often specialists who have deep knowledge of their own specialty but not a lot of breadth of understanding across many other specialties. They may "know too much" about "too little." My experience is that generalists, or diverse groups of specialists, generate better forecasts because they consider many variables and how each interacts with the others. In this context of forecasting based on broad information, I disagree with Gigerenzer's *take the best and leave the rest* approach, summarized by his statement: "Intuitions based on only one good reason tend to be accurate when one has to predict the future (or some unknown present state of affairs), when the future is difficult to foresee, and when one has only limited information."[78]

Of course the heuristic "Take the best" assumes that in any number of cases you actually know "the best" in order to leave the rest. In some contexts of individual behavior, especially survival moments, Gigerenzer may be correct. But in the circumstances of the futurist whose task is understanding trends and anticipating future outcomes, I take strong exception. According to his argument, knowing only one trend gives you sufficient information upon which to frame an expectation for something happening in the future. I have argued consistently that the integration of many trends is much more likely to be prescient than a focused concentration on just one. I agree that some trends are always more important to a topic of inquiry than others (and maybe that is the interpretation of "take the best," referring to a cluster rather than a single trend), but there are very few instances where one trend, issue or factor is a sufficient basis for futuring.

In addition, many of the most important futuring failures have been due to a lack of information. Virtually everybody – experts and dilettantes, professionals and amateurs, futurists and policy-makers, intelligence analysts and freelancers – missed foreseeing the fall of the Berlin Wall and the reunification of Germany in 1989-1990, the collapse of the Soviet Union in 1990-1991, the terrorist attacks of 9/11 in 2001, and the stock market panic of 2008-2009. From one point of view, these were exceptional events, indeed black swans, and by their very nature could not have been predicted. But from another point of view, these great surprises were serious gaps in our information and understanding of others' capabilities and intentions, much like our ignorance of the pending Japanese attack on Pearl Harbor in 1941. Some experts might have anticipated these extraordinary events

---

78 Gigerenzer, *Gut Feelings*, pp. 144-157; quotation from p. 151. The original quotation appeared in italics.

if they had had intelligence of the intentions of some of the key players and imagined accurately the cause-and-effect sequences of events.

It is the confluence of the conscious analysis of trends with subconscious pattern recognition and imagination that provides *a priori* Bayesian probabilities for trend outcomes and events in the future. With more information, we change our judgments – based on both rational thought and intuition – about how likely a trend is to unfold or an event to occur.

I am not willing to go so far as to claim that intuition involves innate knowledge or mental representations of universal forms. As a product of 20th century materialism, I have a hard time taking seriously the mystic metaphysics of ancient Greek philosophers like Pythagoras and Plato. I even have trouble with the archetypes of the psychoanalyst Karl Jung. While I accept the evolutionary origins of human behavior, especially to the extent that a certain type of behavior can be closely associated with a particular gene or with a "hard wired" region of the brain, I still hesitate to accept the conclusion that people are born with knowledge as opposed to the fundamental capabilities of perceiving, storing, processing, and using information that we characterize as "knowledge." I am willing to accept the concept that we process knowledge both consciously and unconsciously and that the unconscious processing of information is what we call "intuition."

While I can't explain intuition exactly, I know it when I see it. I also know from both theory and experience that only with expert judgment, which employs intuition, can one imagine potential changes in the future. As I have said before, you can capture the continuities with trend analysis and tracking, but you cannot use them to anticipate discontinuities. Even Type II pattern recognition is a form of expert judgment: somebody had to decide what signals and signatures had to be watched. In so many aspects, managers have to rely on their own expert judgment to make important decisions, but in the process of doing so they often seek expert judgment from others as inputs to decision-making.

Turning back to a consideration of expert judgment methods and techniques for futuring, one very common method of seeking expert judgment is interviewing in person, by telephone, or by e-mail. The technique is well known. The interviewer poses questions, which the interviewee attempts to address. "Closed end" interviews keep rather rigidly to a prepared script. "Open ended" interviews begin with prepared questions and then progress to a conversation. The interviewer can be either active (provocative) or passive. A passive interviewer will ask the prepared questions and pose follow-up questions for more details and depth, but rarely if ever expresses an opinion of his or her own. The active interviewer, on the other hand, may ask questions and may also make statements inviting, even provoking, the interviewee to respond. The risk of the active interview is that the interviewee may be put off, even offended, by the aggressive style of the interviewer. The advantage is that the interviewer may prod the interviewee into expressing a view that the interviewee may not have intended to have revealed.

The "gold standard" in interviewing would be to have access to key players in a future situation and have them tell you what they plan to do in the future. Imagine the potential implications if a reporter had had an interview with Osama Bin Laden before 9/11 in which the Al Qaeda leader had announced his intention of hitting targets inside of the US! The next best situation would be an interview with people who have interactions with key players. And you can still gather important information by interviewing people who are very knowledgeable about the trends and circumstances that influence the key players.

Another approach to soliciting expert judgment would be to conduct a survey of many experts. You ask a group of experts, more or less at the same time, a set of questions and then you tabulate their responses, much like any other method of doing surveys. Surveys typically use questionnaires prepared by the researchers. You can also do live surveys, which I call expert focus groups.

One the of the best known modern methods of sampling multiple expert judgment is the Delphi Method, which originated at the RAND Corporation in the 1950s. One of its originators was Olaf Helmer, who later pursued cross-impact analysis and probabilistic scenarios at USC. The Delphi Method is a variation on a survey limited to recognized experts, specialists, and authorities on the subject matter. The designers of the survey frame the questions and submit them to a pool of participants, who are usually not told who the other participants are. They complete the survey and return it. The survey team tabulates the responses with no attribution to any of the participants and sends them back to the participants for a second round. Typically, a Delphi survey is repeated at least twice, maybe even as often as five times. With each iteration, as the experts see the responses of the others, a convergence takes place. The consensus results of the survey constitute a forecast.[79]

I still see examples of the Delphi Method used in Europe, but I rarely see it anymore in the US Delphi surveys proved to be too expensive, too time consuming, and not very predictive. There has been a theoretical argument that a consensus of expert judgment in and of itself has no predictive value to it – there has been demonstrated no positive correlation between consensus and accuracy of a forecast. Of course, expert consensus enjoys an aura of authority and may influence decision-makers to act upon it, making it a form of the self-fulfilling

---

79   Harold A. Linstone and Murray Turoff, eds., *The Delphi Method. Techniques and Applications.* Reading, MA: Addison-Wesley Publishing Co., 1975; Harold A. Linstone, "The Delphi Technique," in Fowles, *Handbook of Futures Research,* pp. 273-300.

prophecy. My experience is that expert consensus has proven very successful in the identification of descriptors to be included in a forecast, if not in generating the forecast itself.

I used the focus group method to generate expert judgment forecasts for the 14 "top 10" technology forecasts that I managed for Battelle from 1995 to 2008. Some years we ran only one expert focus group to generate our top 10 list; in other years, we used only virtual focus groups so that we could sample dozens of expert judgments from across the country; and in some cases we used a hybrid of both actual and virtual focus groups. These top 10 lists became very popular with the media and with millions of viewers on the Internet. The lists were rarely backed up with detailed trend analysis, but the experts participating represented literally hundreds of years of accumulated experiences in research, teaching, and technology management. See Chapter 8, pp. 245-246, for a summary of the Strategic Technologies 2005 top 10 list.[80]

Many techniques and methods of idea generation can be used in expert focus groups. Some are loose and some are structured; I prefer the structured type in order to get the information that I need and to give a sense of closure to the exercise for the expert participants. As in all such situations, you need a divergence phase, when the participants are generating many responses to the topic question with little or no filtering, and a convergence phase, when the group selects the responses that they judge to be the best ones. This is typically done through some kind of voting exercise. Of all the methods that I have seen and used, I much prefer the Nominal Group Technique.[81] It consists of the following steps:

1. Introductions, including self-introductions of the participants.

2. The topic question.

3. Silent generation of responses to the topic question, with each participant making his or her own list.

4. Round-robin sharing of responses, involving one idea per participant per round. This allows each person to participate in order. Questions for clarification of meaning are welcomed, but verbalized evaluations of the responses should be avoided. The facilitator or scribe will write each idea/response down with a sequential number for identification on large sheets of paper as a master list posted to a wall

---

80   The Battelle top 10 technology forecasts from 1995 to 2008 are posted on the Battelle website: www.battelle.org under "Technology Forecast Archive" under "News."

81   Andre L. Delbecq, Andrew H. Van de Ven, and David H. Gustafson. *Group Techniques for Program Planning. A Guide to Nominal Group and Delphi Processes.* Glenview, IL: Scott, Foresman and Company, 1975.

for continuous viewing. A typical session will last four or five rounds, after which the process may be opened up to random additions to the master list.

5. Consolidation of ideas to reduce redundancy but not to categorize or cluster. I prefer to do the clustering into major themes after the voting, so that I can see more nuances of judgment with the benefit of knowing how each participant voted before clustering.

6. Voting. This may be done in many different ways. I prefer to have enough time to give eight index cards to each participant. I ask them to make eight selections from the master list hanging on the wall. They should write the number of the idea from the master list and at least a few key words if not the whole idea as it appears on the master list. This should be done at the top of the card. Then, having made eight selections, the participants are asked to give each of his or her eight a score in sequential order from 8 points, high, to 1 point, low. These votes can be tabulated immediately upon completion. There will be scores based on the frequency of votes and scores based on the sum of the point values.

7. Review of the results and follow-up discussion following the tabulation of votes and points.

An expert focus group employing the Nominal Group Technique with an ideal number of 12 or so participants usually requires 2½ hours to complete. If more time is available, I recommended that the group take longer to evaluate the results of the first voting and as small sub-groups evaluate in more detail each of the top choices. I find that expert judgment works best for me when it is layered – in the sense that we start with a coarse cut of judgment and work sequentially down to finer judgments. The experts seem to work better this way and the process of intuition and imagination is more open and subject to questions and explanations.

I strongly recommend that you thoroughly document expert focus groups. All the ideas in response to the topic question should be written down as well as the voting and the resulting rank order of the top 10 or so. This documentation should be shared with all the participants to allow them to double-check what they offered and to make any further inputs to your process. Sharing the results is also a courtesy to the external participants, and so the documentation should be open and not restricted as "business sensitive."

You may never know whether the selection of descriptors by expert judgment will be correct or not. You always worry about the sins of omission and redundancy. You do the best you can with what you have at the moment, and then you continuously review the judgments with new information as time passes. You should be flexible enough to be willing to add new descriptors and drop (or combine) initial descriptors as changing circumstances dictate. If more judgments have value, then hold more Nominal Group Technique sessions with more experts. I have done as many as five different expert focus groups using the Nominal Group Technique on the same topic question with five different groups of experts from Los Angeles to London.

I conclude this section by repeating the very important point that all futuring exercises and all resulting forecasts include expert judgment to one extent or another. The intuition of experts is a powerful component of any futuring endeavor, but like so many other aspects of intellectual life, it has to be disciplined and channeled toward useful purposes. The challenge is to manage the process of soliciting expert judgment in such a way that the expert opinions are as complete and balanced as possible given the circumstances, allowing for such limitations as access, time, and expense.

Step 4: Descriptor Research and Analysis

Having identified the most important descriptors, you need to become better informed about them before trying to forecast them. Descriptors in most cases are known trends with uncertain outcomes in the future. The theory is that information supplies a sustainable understanding of precedents and possibilities that lead to foresights of more prescient merit than hunches, lucky guesses, and appeals to the occult. All futurists and futuring managers use trend analysis to understand what has happened in the past, how things are today, and how likely continuity may be in the future.

Research and analysis into the descriptors can range from scant to thorough. An essay, or white paper, should be prepared for each descriptor. Typically, a descriptor white paper of two or three pages is sufficient for most futuring projects. I like to see essays of up to five or six pages, but that may not be possible given limited resources. This is the step that typically requires the most time and expense for a project. Regardless of length, a descriptor essay should contain the following elements:

- Definition of the descriptor – what it is and how it is being described or measured.

- Why it is relevant and important to the topic question – justification for why it is being included in the forecast.

- Past trends – the trend analysis should capture the main milestones in graphs, charts, and other visuals in addition to narration. You will recall from previous chapters in this book that trends teach us what happened in the past and what is reasonable to expect for the future based on trend momentum. The analysis should also describe contemporary conditions.

- Alternative states in the future – rather than project just one outcome for a descriptor by the target year, you should project two, three, or four alternative descriptor states in the future. The alternative states reflect the inherent uncertainty of the future by offering alternative outcomes by the target year established in the topic question. States should be mutually exclusive and exhaustive of all possible outcomes; therefore, they are typically expressed as ranges rather than points.

For example, a descriptor might be Average Annual GDP Growth Rate in the US and its alternative states might be a) high (more than an average annual rate of 5% to the target year), b) middle (an average annual growth rate of 2.5%-5% to the target year), and c) low (an average annual growth rate of less than 2.5% to the target year). Admittedly, the ranges are very broad, so the resolution of the forecast will be rather grainy. To provide more resolution, however, would be to risk over-constraining the descriptor states and promising more precision than warranted. On the other hand, more specificity is generally appreciated even at the risk of error.

Using the same example, you could have four rather than three alternative states, such as "very high" (an average annual growth rate of 5%-7%, which might be considered low for Chinese GDP growth but very high for the US, especially sustained over 10 years), "high" (an average annual growth rate of 3%-5%), "middle" (1%-2%) and "low" (-2% to +1%). It appears very unlikely that the US GDP, as large as it is, would have an average annual growth rate above 7%, so the "very high" state may be virtually exhaustive at that end of the range. But at the other extreme, the "low" might be too constrained and mis-specified. In addition to specifying the states, an *a priori* probability can be assigned to each state. These Bayesian probabilities are based on existing information (the trend analysis) but may also include, if made explicit in the white paper, adjustments made by the expert judgment of the person writing the descriptor white paper.

Using the first, three-state example above, "high" might have an *a priori* probability of 0.25, "middle" 0.40, and "low" 0.35. The probabilities of the states must have a total sum of 1.0. The probabilities help quantify, at least in a general, estimative way, the expert judgment as to what states are more likely than others, based upon trend analysis as adjusted, with reason, by the expert. The probabilities say that the "middle" state is the most likely and that the low state is more likely than the high state. Of course, all white papers, alternative states, and *a priori* probabilities must be peer reviewed and challenged; they may also be revised according to new sources of information. In summary, one descriptor among a set of descriptors would appear accordingly:

"GDP Growth Rate for the US (average annual growth rate from 2012 to 2020 expressed in constant 2011 dollars)"

High (>5%)	0.25
Middle (2.5-5%)	0.40
Low (<2.5%)	0.35

Like any research paper, the expert should include a list of references for the facts and figures given in the descriptor white paper. All quotes and graphs should have attribution.

The proper place to introduce Bayesian probabilities is in the *a priori* probabilities of the descriptor outcomes. It makes little sense to me to place the *a priori* probabilities on the descriptors themselves. In Step 3, the experts have given a virtual 100% probability to the expectation that the descriptors are trends, issues, and factors that will be important to the topic question in the future. I think the same descriptors should be addressed for the same topic question; the outcomes may vary, but the issues are elements of continuity. I especially do not care for intuitive scenarios in which different descriptors are addressed in different scenarios. I think the same descriptors, but different outcomes, need to be included in each of several scenarios.

Step 5: Interactions Among Descriptors

Too often managers think about trends in isolation and have no way of integrating them together except through highly qualitative and implicit intuition. Yet, how many times in our casual conversations do we say, "If all other things remain equal, then..." But so many times "all other things" do not remain equal. In technical terms, this every day expression reflects an attempt to predict the future based on a closed system or a fixed set. I have asserted that all forecasts are conditional: outcomes depend upon certain sets of circumstances happening and these circumstances can vary. You have to consider the interactions of many trends with each other, and it is more scientifically sound to do this explicitly rather than just implicitly.

I have seen many examples of technology forecasts that were too optimistic in the sense that the forecast anticipated technology successes sooner than they actually occurred. Or, the forecast anticipated the successful commercialization of a technology sooner than what was realized in the market. These mistaken expectations may have been due to biases, self-interest, or wishful thinking. I do not believe that they were caused by the participating experts knowing "too much" about the topic. The major cause of error in so many technology forecasts is that the futurists involved in generating them did not adequately take into account other trends and factors upon which technology development and successful commercialization depend. Technology development, for example, depends upon R&D funding and the talent of the developers. It also depends upon the company or organizational mission. It may even depend upon luck, such as an unexpected but very interesting result of an experiment or an unanticipated observation. The commercialization of technologies depends upon many factors that are beyond science and technology: benefits and prices (value) offered to consumers, consumer expectations and preferences, distribution chains and retail outlets, market positioning, competition, regulation, etc. These multiple conditions involved in technology commercialization must be blended together into a comprehensive view of the future.

Models, both qualitative and quantitative, provide a way to integrate descriptors and show their impacts on each other. These models can be qualitative in the form of systems flow charts that show the elements of the model (whether variables or agents), inputs, processes, outputs, and feedback. When descriptor A, for example, has a direct impact on descriptor B, then it may be an input to B; and if B has a consequent impact on A, then it is a feedback loop. A model is a representation of a state of nature, a problem, or anticipated conditions in the future. It is very useful to visualize and to comprehend a topic of inquiry. It is also very useful as a platform for simulation of expected future outcomes.

Games are simulations upon a model. For hundreds of years, war gaming has been a standard military method of planning and rehearsing potential future battles. A game is a model with a fixed number of elements and rules; these features constitute a closed system or fixed set for purposes of predictability. The players make their moves in a sequential scenario in order to achieve a defined result: a win or a loss. Then the players may do it all over again with variations in actions to see what variations in results may occur. The model and its roles stay the same, but the scenarios change to see whether and under what conditions the results may change. With computers, these games are typically called "simulations." They can be very complex and highly quantitative. Board games are analogy models for simulations. Both types have become popular as a business strategy and planning method.

In the context of futuring, a systems model, whether quantitative or qualitative, with a fixed set of descriptors provides the foundation for what are commonly called "baseline" forecasts. You can use a model to perform any number of simulations of potential changes to the descriptors (changes within the context of trends as Type I patterns) and potential disruptive events, or black swans. If you can imagine a black swan, you can simulate its potential impact upon a baseline forecast.

In most traditional forecasting methods, the descriptors are quantified and formulas and models are used to integrate them into a single coherent forecast. There are qualitative ways to integrate descriptors, too. A common method is to take the descriptors and their alternative outcomes and intuitively arrange them according to your (or others') expert judgment as to which are most likely to occur. The most likely to occur might be called "the certainties," because you do not expect much variation from a trend projection. Then you could also rank the descriptors by those that are most important. The most important and the most certain are called "drivers" or "pre-determinants." Qualitatively you can then make a forecast based on the drivers. A more rigorous approach, however, is to use cross-impact analysis to systematically array descriptors and interrelate them, with the use of a matrix. This approach still relies on making many expert judgments about how descriptors impact upon and are in turn impacted by other descriptors, but it forces you to make all of those judgments explicit for others to review and critique. I prefer to use cross-impact analysis as a method of systematically integrating descriptors. Although it may appear as a table or matrix, it is a model of a kind and can parallel in many respects a visual systems diagram.[82]

Step 6: Forecasts

Forecasts, which provide well considered expectations for the future, are the products of the futuring process. They may provide either a single expectation (consistent with common usage of the word "forecast" as one expectation for one future) or multiple expectations (scenarios) as possible alternative outcomes for the future. Forecasts can be either qualitative or quantitative, although in most cases they will be some hybrid of both: some qualitative forecasts may contain

---

82 John G. Stover and Theodore J. Gordon, "Cross-Impact Analysis," in Jib Fowles, ed, *Handbook of Futures Research*. Westport, CT: Greenwood Press, 1978, pp. 301-328; Wendell Bell, *Foundations of Futures Studies. Human Science for a New Era*. Volume 1: *History, Purpose, and Knowledge*. New Brunswick, NJ: Transaction Publishers, 1997, pp. 265-269; Stephen M. Millett, "Interactive Futures Simulation (IFS)™ Theory and Computational Method," December 16, 2008, on the website of Futuring Associates LLC: www.futuringassociates.com/thoughts.html

trend data and some calculations while all quantitative forecasts include qualitative definitions and assumptions. While they can take many forms, forecasts must convey views of the future that have meaning to the clients who asked for them. They must answer the topic question and fulfill the purposes that launched it.

All you can say for a forecast based on a specific set of descriptors is that there is a future that is more likely than other possibilities: a statement based on the assumption that all known descriptors play out as expected at the time that the forecast was generated. Such is a baseline future, or a surprise-free future. However, you must go a step further to simulate, in one way or another, imagined disruptive events (outliers, black swans, wild cards, or exogenous variables). In some cases, the disruptive events may not change the baseline forecast much, if at all; but in other cases, they may shift the forecast considerably, possibly creating significantly different scenarios. No baseline forecast, in whatever form or generated by whatever futuring method, is complete without the due consideration of potential disruptive events.

My experience has been that baseline forecasts may get close but rarely play out exactly as expected over time. You have to continuously watch for biases, omissions, and disruptive events. You should use the baseline forecast as a platform upon which to run many simulations of what could happen in the future and how that might change expectations. You should also update the baseline with new information as it becomes available. In my experience the biggest cause of errors in forecasts come from the sins of omission. Let me give you two examples to illustrate my point.

In 1986, not long after the breakup of the old AT&T that created the regional "baby Bells," my futuring team worked with a regional telephone company to forecast business opportunities based on the transmission of non-voice information across telephone networks. We used probabilistic scenarios for forecasting future business environments in order to test the assertion by Alvin Toffler that the US was entering the digital Information Age that would take it beyond the 19th century industrial age.[83] We crafted a topic question with the client managers and we held expert focus groups to identify the descriptors, which included Federal telecommunications regulations, economic growth, competition, technical standards, demographics, and market demand for information services. I remember vividly several discussions about whether regulation or market demands would be more important drivers of the future (I argued for market demands, but the telecommunications veterans argued for regulations). We also performed a cross-impact analysis with Bayesian probabilities of the alternative descriptor states and a computer software program to generate scenarios.

---

83   Alvin Toffler, *The Third Wave*. New York: Bantam Books, 1981.

We were well aware of trends in personal computers (PCs) and we knew about the possibility of sending digital information from one PC to another using telephone wires. We also worked with a technology concept of a "public switched network." We correctly identified this thing as being extremely important in the future to enable Toffler's image of the "electronic cottage." But we missed the Internet, which burst upon the cyber scene in 1995 with the introduction of the World Wide Web. We got the basic idea right, but there were a lot of details we just did not know about. Having said that, when the Web hit, the client could say "That's It! That's our big opportunity in information services!" Although we missed the Internet *per se*, we did anticipate the kind of service that would fit the convergence of many trends toward virtual work, shopping, and communicating. The story served the company's business strategies and investments well. What we missed entirely was the emergence of extensive wireless communications and cell phones. This is exactly why a forecast is never complete – as long as the future continues to expand, so do forecasts, too, through continuous monitoring, updates, and revisions.

Another example of omission occurred in the forecast of future American consumer value in personal transportation, a project that I have now mentioned several times in this book. In retrospect, I can see that we made a major omission by the very way we defined "consumer value." We took a narrow definition that I call "transactional value," meaning the benefits and value seen by the consumer when he or she buys a personal vehicle. We did an excellent job of specifying style, power, comfort, safety and security, reliability, environmental quality, information access, etc. But we missed what I now call "intrinsic value," or the inherent value of the thing itself. This is so often assumed in the minds of consumers without necessarily ever being articulated. The consumer might express value in the convenience of the purchase experience and the pride of ownership of something very stylish. But we learned in the futuring process that there are intrinsic benefits in transportation, including freedom of movement; access to distant locales; site seeing; and the physical sensations of motion and speed. Americans love their cars because they provide the personal flexibility to go to work, shop, date, visit other people, and just to go wherever, whenever one wants to do so. The car provides an enormous degree of personal freedom. It also provides the pleasure, even the thrill, of power. Yet, even though we missed this important aspect of personal transportation, the intrinsic value remained constant across time and our explicit omission of it did not materially change our conclusions or potential business opportunities.

To our credit, we did include in our forecast the uniquely American aspects of personal transportation, so we tangentially hit upon the freedom of movement issue in the broader cultural context. We identified several American cultural characteristics based on some 400 years of historical experience. This perspective may seem excessive to American companies, but Asian companies are very sensitive to what they perceive as the social and cultural peculiarities of Americans. One such characteristic is the restlessness of Americans dating back to the earliest colonies of Jamestown, Plymouth, and Massachusetts Bay. No sooner had some immigrants set foot in the New World, they wanted to move on to new, unexplored territory. Land is so vast in the US that people think nothing about crossing long distances. Furthermore, the personal freedom of moving, both daily commuting and semi-permanent relocation, is ingrained in the American sense of self. In many other places in the world, people feel very fixed to a sense of place: to the land upon which they were born and upon which their ancestors lived. When the sense of self is detached from the land, then individual mobility grows in value. We see this in India and China now with the restructuring of societies according to the dynamics of 21st century global economics.

A successful forecast or plan is a learning experience, so one metric of achievement is how much you learn from the experience and how you use that learning to make better decisions in the future.

In previous days, forecasts were largely narrative. They were packaged as reports, even as books. The narrative tradition, however, is waning in the current era of the quick-questions and quick-answers of television sound bites, text messaging, e-mails, and Internet searches. Executives in particular simply do not have the time or patience to wade through tomes. Forecasts must convey stories in easily accessible and compelling ways. They must also provide a framework that can easily transition from concepts and strategies to actions.

Yet cognitive styles vary throughout any corporate culture, so for forecasts to reach the greatest number of people they must be packaged and delivered in a variety of ways. There must be a presentation with a limit of about 20 slides for the prevailing cognitive styles of most executives. The presentation should present relevant information in a few words supplemented by illustrations, graphs, charts, and other pictorial representations. I have found that in most cases a well-received presentation begins with the conclusions and then works backward to justify them. Executives may enjoy reading mysteries, but they like to see "the solution" up front in their business communications.

In addition to a presentation, there should be a written report that looks more like an executive summary than an academic dissertation. It should be no longer than three to five pages. Supporting information and data can be attached. Increasingly, futurists and researchers build electronic libraries where information supporting forecasts can be stored and accessed as required.

Forecasts as well considered expectations for the future should guard against all the common fallacies of futuring. As final results of a lot of work, your forecasts should ideally include the following best practices:

- Identify underlying assumptions and points of view that reflect deeply held biases, self-interest, mental models, and values. Identifying the perspective taken in the futuring process goes a long way toward establishing its credibility.

- Be as precise as possible in defining terms and their metrics.

- Explain the theory and mechanics of the futuring methods employed – in most cases, make this explanation relatively short and put the details in an appendix or post them on a website.

- Consider multiple trends, issues, and factors (descriptors) and their relationships with each other.

- Thoroughly research and document descriptors as the elements of continuity and sources of potential changes. While only a few salient facts and figures may be included in a presentation or a report, the body of research should be readily available, in hard copy or electronically, or both, upon demand.

- Explain the reasoning behind trend projections and their *a priori* probabilities of occurrence.

- Use your disciplined intuition – your imagination bounded by science, the precedents of history, and the rigors of sound logic – to identify plausible changes in known trends and potential disruptive events.

- Be careful not to jump to the conclusion that an emerging Type III pattern is a repetition of a known Type I pattern.

- Present the results first as the most likely, or baseline, forecast – based on known descriptors and their interactions – and also provide alternative future outcomes (scenarios) rather than a single view of the future to reflect various degrees of uncertainty about the future.

- Identify potential disruptive events (wild cards, outliers, or black swans) and perform simulations on how they might change the baseline forecast.

- Subject all trend projections, analysis, and forecasts to periodic peer review and constructive criticism.

- Provide numerous opportunities for other managers, staff, and consultants to participate in the futuring process. For other managers and staff, participation should lead to feelings of ownership of the process and the resulting forecasts. Consultants may bring new sources of information, different perspectives, and other biases to balance yours.

- Since no forecast is ever "finished" until the forecasting target date is reached, monitor and scan trends and make necessary updates and revisions to the forecast over time.

- Answer the topic question (with one or more answers) with sufficiently warranted precision and suggest practical implications for strategy. Forecasts have little practical utility unless you draw implications from them for strategy-making, decision-making, and planning.

- Package and present forecasts as attractively and as compellingly as you can.

Scenarios

Before concluding this chapter, I want to say something more about scenarios, which present forecasts with alternative outcomes rather than a single expectation for the future. I have mentioned them several times, but now I wish to define them and show their advantages as an approach to futuring as well as visioning.

The underlying benefit of scenarios is that they offer multiple views of the future rather than a single forecasted outcome. They reflect the uncertainty that existed at the time they were generated and the uncertainty that lies in the future. They also encourage you to think of alternative actions associated with alternative outcomes. Scenarios lead to contingency planning and flexibility.

Perhaps no other method of futuring has caused as much confusion as scenarios because of variations in definitions of them and the methods of generating them. Virtually every manager may say that he or she understands and uses scenarios, but few really do.[84]

"Scenario" is an Italian word that originated in the theatre. It means an outline or synopsis of a play, movie, TV show, or game. It typically provides an overview of the script that shows the progression of the plot through a sequence of scenes. Choreography of dance is a variation on a scenario. Today, if you were to use the

---

84 Stephen M. Millett, "The future of scenarios: challenges and opportunities," *Strategy & Leadership*, Vol. 31, No. 2, 2003, pp. 16-24; Ron Bradfield, George Wright, George Burt, George Cairns, and Kees Van Der Heijden, "The origins and evolution of scenario techniques in long range business planning," *Futures, 37* (2005), pp. 795-812; Peter Bishop, Andy Hines, and Terry Collins, "The current state of scenario development: an overview of techniques," *Foresight*, Vol. 9, No. 1 (2007), pp. 5-25.

word "scenario" on Broadway or in Hollywood, people would understand you to mean a concept or overview of a dramatic work.

More than any other individual, Herman Kahn transposed scenarios from the theatre to government and corporate planning. While at the RAND Corporation in Santa Monica, CA, during the 1950s, Kahn used scenarios as a method for thinking through alternative military strategies. He formulated scenarios as hypothetical sequences of cause-and-effect steps from a starting point to a conclusion of a military situation, such as a global nuclear war. In some respects, Kahn's scenarios were conceptual war games. He demonstrated to the US Air Force that there were many different ways to achieve a mission and that some planned missions were not well thought out and might not have the desired outcomes. In the hands of Kahn, scenarios became a way to think about and plan military operations based on well considered expectations. This meaning of the word in the Department of Defense continues today – scenarios are used as hypothetical sequences of military actions to achieve a defined mission in education and training, war gaming and rehearsals, and planning. Others in Washington have picked up on the same word and meaning, so that we hear about energy, economic, and political scenarios as well as military scenarios.[85]

So, one meaning of "scenario" used in the entertainment industry and in government refers to a hypothetical chain of events from a starting to an ending point. It is primarily a planning (visioning) rather than a futuring method, unless the scenario planners and implementers can make their own desired scenarios come true as examples of self-fulfilling prophecies. In the theatrical sense, "scenarios" are highly imaginative and creative in the best traditions of the performing arts; they can be equally imaginative and creative in the performing arts of government.

Kahn provided the link between the military and business worlds. In 1961 he led a team that founded the Hudson Institute at Croton-on-Hudson, up river from New York City. The Hudson Institute used hypothetical scenarios as well as game theory and systems analysis to perform all kinds of projects for both government and corporate clients. Ian Wilson, a corporate planner from nearby General Electric corporate offices in Connecticut, befriended Kahn and talked with him about how scenarios might be applied to the business world. Kahn and Wilson were joined in their conversations by Pierre Wack from the international oil giant Royal Dutch/Shell in London. Both Wilson and Wack decided to initiate scenario projects as an innovative approach to traditional corporate and financial forecasting, which was dominated at the time by quantitative time-series trend projections and wishful thinking. Wilson and Wack, however, changed the

---

85 Arguable the most famous example of military planning scenarios appeared in Herman Kahn, *Thinking About the Unthinkable*. New York: Avon Books, 1971 (1962).

meaning of scenarios so that they became alternative sets of future market and business conditions. "Scenarios" thereby became static in the sense that they were alternative outcomes by a designated future date, regardless of any specific and hypothetical sequences of events to reach them. Although conceived as a planning tool, depending upon how they were generated, scenarios could also be used for futuring. In some scenarios, companies might be able to influence future states, but in other scenarios there might be circumstances beyond their control; in corporate scenarios, one might be both proactive and reactive. This new approach to scenarios appealed particularly to Wack, who wanted to change the corporate culture at Shell to introduce more flexibility in planning and operations to deal with any number of possible futures. For Wilson and Wack, the central question for corporate planning shifted from "what do we want to do and what will our future profits be?" to "what are the potential future business environments and what do we need to do to be successful in each one of them?" Wilson's first scenarios were rolled out at GE in 1971 and Wack with his team produced their first scenarios at Shell a year later.[86]

Wilson assigned expert judgment probabilities to the first GE scenarios, but Wack did not. Wack did not want scenarios to be seen as traditional forecasts; rather, he presented scenarios as an alternative planning method to what he saw as an over-reliance on numerical forecasts. He defined a "forecast" narrowly, as a series of quantitative expectations, and he urged that planning at Shell be more qualitative and flexible than using time series trend projections. The first Shell scenarios provided only two rather extreme views of the future environment for the oil industry projected out to the year 2000. These two scenarios provided the structure for a conversation of possible scenarios between the two extremes. Wack emphasized the importance of the stories in order to make impressions upon the mental models of Shell executives. He also wanted to discuss the potential discontinuities that he felt intuitively were lying in wait to ambush Shell in the future. Like military planning, Wack wanted to prepare Shell's management to deal with potential disruptive events before rather than after they occurred.

---

86 Much of the anecdotal history of the origins of corporate scenarios was told to me in telephone conversations and e-mail exchanges with Ian Wilson. I did not have the pleasure of meeting Pierre Wack, but I met his principal associate Ted Newland, who told me that the Shell scenario method was so grounded in the particulars of the international oil business that he had a hard time seeing the application of scenarios for other industries. For Wilson's pioneering scenario report, see Environmental Task Force of the Corporate Executive Staff, General Electric, "Four Alternative World/U.S. Scenarios 1971-1980," January 21, 1971; Ian Wilson, "Scenarios," in Jib Fowles, ed, *Handbook of Futures Research,* pp. 225-247; Pierre Wack, "Scenarios: Uncharted Waters Ahead," *Harvard Business Review,* September-October 1985, pp. 73-89, and "Scenarios: Shooting the Rapids," *Harvard Business Review,* November-December 1985, pp. 130-150.

In 1973, just a year or so after Wack's team presented their first scenarios at Shell, came the so-called Energy Crisis. The OPEC countries placed an embargo on their oil exports, resulting in the global price of a barrel of crude jumping about four-fold. The oil industry was turned upside down and many companies had no idea what to do in times when old business models failed. Wack proved to be extraordinarily prescient and Shell demonstrated that it was better prepared to deal with the new situation than most other global oil players. As it was told to me by Shell scenario planners in the 1980s, the traditional business model at Shell had been to sell oil products principally at the retail (downstream) level, but the scenarios prepared Shell managers to sell oil at several different points of the upstream and downstream spectrum, making money at the points where profit could be maximized due to volatile market prices.

Shell has continued to generate scenarios since the early 1970s. Their approach to scenario writing evolved over time and spread to other corporations around the world. Because their scenarios were closely linked with energy, some Shell scenario practitioners questioned whether or not the method might be valid for other topics in other realms, both corporate and public. It turned out that the method proved useful regardless of the topic. The success of scenarios as a futuring or visioning method depended more upon corporate culture and leadership than the topic or the industry.

Arguably the most famous alumnus of the Shell scenario shop has been Peter Schwartz, who came to Shell from the Stanford Research Institute (SRI) International. Shell used experts from SRI to supplement their own relatively small staff of scenario planners. One of them was Ian Wilson, who left GE on the East Coast to join SRI in the San Francisco Bay area. I have been told at various times that the scenario method originated at Shell and transferred to SRI and that it began at SRI and transferred to Shell. Either way, the scenario method became entrenched at Shell and became a consulting business at SRI. Schwartz was a veteran of both companies, and he and his closest associates created their own scenario consulting firm called Global Business Network (GBN). Their scenario method evolved and procreated many scenario offspring over the years. There are now dozens of scenario methods. Today we call the Shell/SRI/GBN family of scenario methods the "intuitive" scenario approach or "scenario writing."

There were several similarities but also marked differences between the GE and the Shell scenarios of the 1970s. Both contained alternative portraits of the future rather than hypothetical sequences of events. Both contained extensive amounts of trend analysis – of many different trends beyond familiar products, markets, and customers. Both contained heavy doses of expert judgment, largely that of the scenario team. Both the GE and Shell scenarios were heavily qualitative in their descriptions of the future, which was given as 10 years (to 1980) by the GE scenario team and 30 years (to 2000) by the Shell scenario writers. A significant difference, however, was that GE considered four comprehensive alternative futures, while Shell generated only two, which were the two extreme ends of a spectrum of possible (not likely) scenarios. In later years, the Shell/SRI/GBN scenario method called for four prmary, more nuanced, scenarios, and with spinoff scenarios as variations of the principal four. More significant than other differences in style, the GE scenarios included probabilities of occurrence and the Shell scenarios did not.

The use of probabilities with scenarios has been controversial for decades. It is the principal difference between scenarios as qualitative forecasts and scenarios as conjectural planning. Wack was strongly opposed to using probabilities with scenarios in the context of the Shell corporate culture. He felt that as soon as his team expressed the weighting of one scenario over another, management would gravitate to the single, most likely scenario and ignore other possibilities. His goal was to open up, not channel, corporate strategic thinking. He further wanted to differentiate clearly the difference of scenarios as descriptions of alternative futures versus single point quantitative forecasting. Wack and his successors have consistently argued that scenarios are a way to do planning and not forecasting. He even allegedly denounced modeling as "an enemy to thinking." The GBN associates have persistently said that "you cannot predict the future" and that all scenarios that are plausible are equal in consideration, with none designated as more likely to occur than others. Wilson, having used probabilities in the first GE scenario project, stopped using them when he went to SRI International.[87]

For many practitioners, the intuitive scenario method developed by Shell, SRI International, and GBN is the only scenario method for corporate planning that has ever existed. They continue to ignore the earlier contributions of Wilson and GE or any of the alternative methods developed at the Futures Group, the University of Southern California (USC), and Battelle. The intuitive scenario approach has many attractive features: it is non-proprietary and open to anyone to do; it can be taught to students and professionals in futuring, strategic planning, and group facilitation; it requires no particular equipment, props, or computers; it is highly adaptable to particular circumstances; it can be applied to virtually any topic and any participants; and it does not claim to be predictive, only provocative in stimulating people's thinking about future possible environments. Not to be underrated, scenario exercises are supposed to be entertaining with the participants getting very enthusiastic about their work.

---

87 Stephen M. Millett, "Should Probabilities Be Used With Scenarios?," *Journal of Futures Studies*, Vol. 13, No. 4 (May 2009), pp. 61-68.

The intuitive scenario method as practiced today has countless variations ranging from very casual to rather complex. Typically, there will be a facilitator, a few experts, and a selected group of people from the company or organization that is hosting the scenarios exercise. Participants today are not nearly as well prepared in the trends as the original Shell scenario writers were. In many cases, the social experience of generating scenarios is of more importance than the scenario content because the participants are learning to work together in exchanging ideas and realizing possibilities. They may be the same people who have to work together to make things happen in the future.

The scenarios are typically generated in a workshop setting. The workshop might be just a half-day, one full day, the better part of two days, or spread out at selected intervals over several weeks. The method usually consists of the following steps:

1. Compose a topic or focus question for the scenarios that has meaning for the hosting company or organization. This may be achieved by the team leader and the corresponding executive or it may be done collectively with the participating group.

2. Generate a list of the most important trends, issues, and factors relative to the topic question (usually with a voting procedure to converge on a selected few). This is typically achieved with one of several techniques for managing group dynamics, such as Idea Generation, Brainstorming, the Nominal Group Technique, etc.

3. Reach group consensus on just two trends, issues, or factors from the list generated above that are viewed as being *both* the most important *and* the most uncertain in the future. For example, the two might be US GDP growth rates and Achievement in US Education. Of course, terms should be defined as carefully as possible.

4. Structure the scenarios based upon the two most important and uncertain trends, issues, or factors, which are arrayed orthogonally to each other as axes of a symmetrical matrix with four sectors, or quadrants. Each axis is viewed as a continuum from one extreme (such as "low" or "negative") to the other (such as "high" or "positive"). This becomes the structure for writing four scenarios relative to each of the quadrants created by the axes. Each template corresponds to the four quadrants: "low, low," and "low, high" and "high, high" and "high, low."

5. Generate stories, or scenarios, for each quadrant. This can be done collectively or by sub-groups with one scenario for each sub-group. The stories are generated in an intuitive way with a heavy

emphasis on imagination. These scenarios are descriptions of a future environment that incorporates as many story elements (including other trends, issues, and factors) as possible.

6. Discuss business implications and potential strategies and plans for each of the scenarios, whether probabilities are used or not.[88]

When I facilitate this type of intuitive scenario generating exercise, I begin with the orientation of futuring, with the topic question focused on some major aspect of the market or operational environment of the participants. Steps 1-5 should stay centered on that environment and not introduce, yet, the desires of the participants. Then Step 6 becomes an exercise in visioning within the context of having done the preceding futuring. This approach tries to maximize "objectivity" and minimize the dangers of context-free, wishful thinking.

The intuitive scenario method places a heavy emphasis on the intuitive qualities of the participants. One might argue that the intuitive scenario method places a heavy emphasis on the expert judgments of the scenario-generating team. Some participants may be very knowledgeable about trends and well prepared to create scenarios, but others may not. It has even been argued that the emotions of the participants and their commitments to the scenarios and their business implications are far more important than the cerebral quality of the scenarios. Maybe, but I prefer high quality scenarios from which we can derive well considered expectations for the future.

Whether a scenario is "good" or "bad," or "best case" or "worse case," is purely a matter of perspective. They are "good" or "bad" relative to biases and wishes. The reality is that in every economic or market situation, somebody makes money while others get hurt. The proactive challenge is to recognize emerging conditions and position yourself to maximize what opportunities there are to make money and to minimize the threat of losing money.

Scenarios can be predictive within the boundary conditions of trend momentum, cause-and-effect relationships, closed system or fixed set, and self-fulfilling prophecy. They can also provide foresights from the visioning perspective, which is why people often call them a "scenario planning tool."

There is a more rigorous and analytical approach to generating scenarios than the Shell method that relatively few practitioners know. Analytical scenarios can be

---

88 The Shell/SRI International/GBN scenario method has been described in dozens of articles and books. One of the earlier accounts is Peter Schwartz, *The Art of the Long View*. New York: Currency/Doubleday, 1996 (1991), pp. 227-248. I recommend Bill Ralston and Ian Wilson, *The Scenario Planning Handbook. Developing Scenarios in Uncertain Times*. Mason, OH: Thomson South-Western, 2006.

generated by using cross-impact analysis, modeling, and simulation, usually but not necessarily with the help of computer software tools.

The creation of cross-impact analysis as an alternative to the intuitive method of generating scenarios is credited to a group of highly innovative analysts at the RAND Corporation in the late 1950s and early 1960s. Two of them in particular, Olaf Helmer and Theodore Gordon, developed cross-impact analysis to generate multiple forecasts (alternative futures or scenarios) as an alternative to Kahn's hypothetical, sequential planning scenarios. Helmer left RAND to go to USC, where he and his academic team created a scenario method called INTERAX. Gordon left RAND to organize his own company, the Futures Group, in Connecticut. His team developed a variation of cross-impact analysis and scenario generation, also with the use of a computer, that they called Trend Impact Analysis. Their approach migrated to the consulting practice of Deloitte. Gordon himself moved on in later years to the Millennium Project of the World Federation of UN Associations.[89]

Selwyn Enzer, a colleague of Helmer at USC, was the principal agent of the INTERAX technology transfer to the Battelle Memorial Institute in the 1970s. He worked with Battelle mathematicians and computer technologists at Geneva, Switzerland, to develop the algorithms of calculating Bayesian probabilities and cross-impact values. The Battelle approach differed from other cross-impact and scenario methods in that it identified alternative outcomes, each with its own *a priori* probability, for each alternative state of each descriptor (as opposed to just one outcome for each descriptor) and its algorithm was deterministic, not Monte Carlo, in the sense that it did not use random number generators and adjusted the *a priori* probabilities up and down according to the cross-impact values in always the same way. This approach allowed simulations where the analysts knew that changes in outputs were due to changes in inputs and not to variations in Monte Carlo number sequences. In addition, the Battelle Frankfort laboratory provided the method for employing group dynamics, or expert focus groups, to determine the most important trends, issues, and factors (called "descriptors") to be used in the scenario analysis. The Columbus laboratory provided the systems integration, packaging, and marketing. The Battelle method was called BASICS (Battelle Scenario Inputs to Corporate Strategy) and was rolled out publicly in 1980. In the mid-1980s the Columbus laboratory developed the first personal computer version of the software program, called BASICS-PC. About a decade later, it reprogrammed the software for Windows and changed the name to Interactive Future Simulations (IFS)™ It used the analytical modeling approach with its

---

89 William R. Huss and Edward J. Honton, "Scenario Planning – What Style Should You Use?," *Long Range Planning*, Vol. 20, No. 4 (1987), pp. 21-29; Millett, "The Future of Scenarios;" conversation and subsequent e-mails with Jerome C. Glenn, Director, The Millennium Project, September 2008.

various computer software programs as both a forecasting and a planning method for over 100 corporate and government clients around the world. [90]

While there are some important similarities, particularly at the beginning and the ending of the processes, between analytical and intuitive scenarios, there are some very important differences, especially in the procedure used to generate the scenarios. A typical analytical scenario project consists of the following steps:

1. Formulate a topic question that has practical value for the hosting company or organization in much the same way that it is done in the intuitive scenario method.

2. Generate a list of the potentially most important descriptors (trends, issues, and factors) relevant to the topic question. Vote, consolidate, and select as many as 20 descriptors (with 12-16 descriptors usually optimal).

3. Research and prepare a white paper on each descriptor that includes definitions, importance, trends, current conditions, alternative outcomes, and *a priori* probabilities of occurrence for each of the alternative outcomes for each descriptor (summing to 1.0). These descriptor white papers support the judgments that will be made in the cross-impact analysis of the descriptors. They also provide a library that can be shared widely and periodically updated with new information that comes from trend monitoring.

4. Create the cross-impact matrix and perform the cross-impact analysis with or without a laptop software tool.

5. Generate scenarios (alternative sets of concurrently occurring descriptor states) and consolidate and select about five for further analysis.

---

90 I practiced the BASICS method as a manager and consultant with Battelle from 1983 to 2006. I knew and worked closely with several of the developers of BASICS, the BASICS-PC, and IFS. I continue to consult through my own company, Futuring Associates LLC. For documentation of the Battelle approach to scenarios, see A. Duval, E. Fontela and A. Gabus, "Cross-Impact Analysis: A Handbook on Concepts and Applications," in Maynard M. Baldwin, ed., *Portraits of Complexity. Applications of Systems Methodologies to Societal Problems* (Columbus, OH: Battelle Memorial Institute, 1975), pp. 202-222; Huss and Honton, "Scenario Planning – What Style Should You Use?; E. J. Honton, G. S. Stacey, and S. M. Millett, "FUTURE SCENARIOS: The BASICS Computational Method" (Columbus, OH: Battelle Columbus Division, October 1984, Revised July 1985); Stephen M. Millett and Edward J. Honton, *A Manager's Guide to Technology Forecasting and Strategy Analysis Methods*. Columbus, OH: Battelle, 1991, pp. 63-75; Stephen M. Millett, "Interactive Futures Simulation (IFS)™ Theory and Computational Method, December 16, 2008, on the website of Futuring Associates LLC: www.futuringassociates.com/thoughts.html

6. Perform simulations with variations in *a priori* probabilities and cross-impact values and the introduction of hypothetical disruptive events (or black swans).

7. Discussion of the business implications and potentially effective strategies for each of the five principal scenarios.

The analysis of business implications is extremely important for scenarios. If you had only the scenarios, what would you do with them? You might see alternative future outcomes, but so what? You have to also derive specific opportunities and threats from each scenario. You have to build the bridge of scenario implications analysis to connect futuring with visioning in order to get to planning.[91]

The Shell/SRI International/GBN school of intuitive scenario writing stresses that a company or organization must develop strategies and plans based on each of the scenarios. Using that method, there would be four sets of strategies and plans based on four different scenarios. Wack's original intent was to force managers to draw up multiple business plans, not just contingencies from one primary plan. In this regard, Wack was trying to do with business people what Kahn had shown to Air Force generals. But I rarely got my corporate managers and clients to go that far. It involves too much effort, time, and expense. The best that I could realize was the analysis of implications for each scenario and then the clustering of implications into one or two particularly robust strategies that would be a response to several scenarios.

Of course, no forecast is ever complete and requires continual monitoring and revision, as discussed in previous chapters. At this point, we should transition from futuring to visioning to pick up the elements of planning, which is the conjunction of futuring and visioning.

---

91 Stephen M. Millett, "How Scenarios Trigger Strategic Thinking," *Long Range Planning*, Vol. 21, No. 5 (1988), pp. 61-68; Michael E. Raynor, *The Strategy Paradox*. New York: Currency/ Doubleday, 2007, especially pp. 177-230. Raynor argues for probabilistic scenarios as an input to the calculations of real options analysis.

Chapter 7. Managing Visioning

Having provided you with advice on how to manage futuring projects or tasks, based on proven best practices, I now want to switch to the topic of best practices in managing visioning. You recall the differences between futuring and visioning covered in Chapter 3. To be successful in the future, you will have to do both futuring and visioning and blend them effectively (Futuring Principle #3). But always keep in mind the differences between, on the one hand, the trends that impact you which you may have little or no direct control upon (futuring) and, on the other, the issues that you manage in the context of forming your corporate culture and goals (visioning). Just because you want something to occur in the future does not mean that it will occur.

Preferred Futures

I have taken the perspective that a futurist is like a scientist in that he or she gathers and interprets information along with reasoned hypotheses to generate well considered expectations for the future. Like any other scientist, for the futurist to be most effective – even prescient – he or she must be open-minded, thorough, and critical. As a futuring manager, you have to look at information as objectively as possible so that you can recognize the most important trends relative to your interests and concerns and see them for what they are, whether you like what you see or not. In some cases, you will become better informed about trends beyond your control; you will learn to optimize situations in order to take advantage of them. In other cases, you may have some control over circumstances; in this case you will need to figure out what moves will most likely result in the maximum benefits for your company, institution, organization, or agency.

Furthermore, the futurist is also like a scientist in regard to Heisenberg's uncertainty principle: the very act of investigation opens up opportunities to influence the subject being investigated. At some point in time, futuring has a practical purpose. Just as in science, when we have a better knowledge of what is happening or what is likely to happen, we are empowered to make a better future happen. Of course, "better future" is very normative and subjective relative to the beliefs and values of the observer. As soon as we say "better," we are crossing the line, sometimes obscured, between futuring and visioning. The argument of this book is that you should do the analytical futuring first in order to grasp trends, to understand how they affect each other, and how they may impact you in the process of visioning, in order to see how you might best survive, if not thrive, in future conditions.

There is another point of view, however, that must be considered. Some futurists and futuring managers do not want to be analysts, scientists, or detached observers. They would rather act like the prophets of ancient times. They have a cause, and they see the future largely within the value-laden context of how the future *should* be rather than how it might likely be. They may employ trend analysis, but only as evidence for what they argue, as a lawyer might argue a legal case or a politician might debate an issue in an election campaign. Futuring has no trappings of objectivity or uncertainty for them; their mission is to preach their cause and convince others to see and act upon the future in highly prescribed ways.

I have encountered many normative futurists who behave more like visionaries than scientists. They are often engaging, typically enthusiastic, but too often detached from the constraints of everyday reality. They are inspiring, but not entirely convincing. They typically are also highly idealistic. Many of them are descended intellectually from the futurism of the 1960s, when there was a strong sense of optimism, based on modern science, technology, and mathematics, that we could successfully re-engineer society with the same effect as landing a man on the moon. Many bold visions of distant futures came out of the 1960s, including the works of noted science fiction writers like Isaac Asimov, Arthur C. Clarke, Robert Heinlein, Ray Bradbury, and Gene Roddenberry. These works of science fiction were highly imaginative and entertaining, but they were not analytical – there was in their characters, plots, and props more fiction than science. It is from the experiences of the 1960s that the title "futurist" suggests a wide-eyed seer of glorious if not fantastic tomorrows.

The normative futurists typically over-emphasize future changes to the detriment of continuities. They tend to dismiss the apparent blemishes of the present and dream of perfection in the future. They latch on to the exceptional possibilities of new science and technologies without considering the barriers of finance, laws, and social conventions. They exaggerate trends and they focus on only the trends that interest them most. They embrace values of their own that they will generously share with others, whether some values are welcomed or not. Normative futurists may be agents of change, and they may contribute much to breaking down the mental models and attitudes that we so often display as defense mechanisms in reaction to the fears of uncontrolled change; but they can be just as annoying as the prophets of ancient times.

A normative futurist behaves like the champion of a cause, and as such may be willing to bend the facts and force data into a perceived pattern (Type I), or model, whether or not the data fit well. Maybe this behavior is to be expected from a visionary, but it typically does not transfer well into business. A business visionary may argue for a point of view, but he or she has to continuously back up the vision with facts and figures to get others to go along with the same point of view. As a visionary leader, you have to convince other people that your vision is desirable for them as well as for you and also that it can be done, given reasonable resources, hard work, determination, and even a little luck.

Entrepreneurs, of course, are champions of their new enterprises. They expect success because they so desperately desire it. They cannot be detached analysts or business futurists. Therefore, while you should listen to them, you should also keep in mind their biases.

In addition, I have found that, in general, middle managers in large corporations are the least receptive to futuring – they already know what future they want and what future they are working toward, contrary to what anybody else may think. Like entrepreneurs, middle and aspiring managers are champions of their interests and careers.

On this point I have my own convictions (or biases), as you may have detected by now. As a pragmatist, I know that I have my own values and mental models, but I must explicitly admit them as a warning to others. I myself may argue for a normative future, but only after I have been through the rigorous process of forming well considered expectations for the future based on the best practices of futuring. I want to see the opportunities and threats of the external environment with as much detachment as I can muster before I make recommendations for other people's investments, strategies, and plans. I think it is unethical to accept pay for my work just to advocate my own personal values and objectives. My conviction is that this attitude applies to you, too.

There is a proper time and place to project your biases. When you are thinking about the future as trends and events external to your own business or organization, you need to recognize and control your own biases and self-interests. When you are thinking about the future in terms of what you yourself can do, the resources that you have at your command, and the degree of influence you can exert over other people to do what you think they should do, then you are channeling biases into potentially productive visionary leadership.

Visionary Leadership

Normative futurists are one thing, but visionary leaders and managers are very much a different story. They have the means and the courage to invest and pursue their own visions of the future. They are examples of self-fulfilling prophets: they not only see a future that others cannot, but they go forth to make their own future, potentially impacting millions of other people. They are not just telling others how wonderful the future could be, they are leading others to that future, by a combination of their energy, encouragement, and resources.

To recap from Chapter 3, successful visionaries certainly have active imaginations, but unlike so many people they have the ability to go far beyond just wishful thinking. They have exceptional intuition to see many trends, recognize patterns, understand cause-and-effect relationships, and anticipate critically important changes. They have bold goals and they know how to achieve them. They are very well informed about economic, market, industrial, demographic, social, consumer, and technological trends. But they also see opportunities that others miss. They not only have a vision of a desired and possible state in the future, they have specific ideas about how to achieve it.

A dramatic example of a visionary leader's thinking was provided by Sen. Edward Kennedy when he attributed a saying to his slain brother Robert borrowed from George Bernard Shaw that: *some people see things as they are and ask "why," but I see things as they could be and ask "why not?"*[92]

The key to visionary leadership through the processes of visioning is the combination of extraordinary intuition and supreme practicality. Intuition along with imagination provides the mental images, or mental models, of what could be; practicality based on education and experience provides the guidance as to how to gather and use resources for achieving aspirational goals for the future.

Visioning begins with the founders and the owners of most enterprises. Entrepreneurs are visionary leaders by definition: they start up new businesses based on their mental visions of emerging opportunities to make a lot of money. Most of them are wishful thinkers; they convince themselves that they will be successful. Unfortunately, most wishes do not come true. It has been estimated that in the US at the end of the 20th century, four out of five new enterprises failed after five years. People forget that business failure is the norm and business success is the exception. The few successful companies endure because they correctly (or fortuitously) estimated their customer base and customer value, recognized unmet opportunities with little or no effective competition, and contained their costs to align with available resources for longer than expected. In many cases, successful companies are those that are asked to provide a certain product or service by customers looking for something that they can't find elsewhere.

The vision is typically wrapped inside a mission statement, which says in one or two sentences why the enterprise exists, what it does, for whom, and why. The

---

92 Sen. Edward Kennedy attributed the saying to his assassinated brother in his eulogy for Sen. Robert F. Kennedy on June 8, 1968. Whether Robert Kennedy ever said this is now a matter of debate. The original saying came from George Bernard Shaw in his collection of plays titled *Back To Methuselah* (1918-1920). See http://en.wikiquote.org/wiki/Robert_F._Kennedy.

mission statement may appear in the original articles of organization, incorporation, or partnership. In some cases, the mission statement of the founders may be very specific, and in other cases rather vague. In any case, it may well change over time due to changing business circumstances.

The visionary leadership of the enterprise founder and owners determines corporate culture, which is the sharing of the sense of mission, vision, values, and behavior norms among all the individuals of the organization. The mission, including the vision, is the frame of reference for judging what is good and bad. The cultural foundation of an enterprise can be learned by others (by example and by both positive and negative reinforcement of desired behavior) and transferred from one generation to the next. In the beginning, the enterprise founder typically brings along others who share his or her own aspirations; they may be experienced business partners, trusted associates, and family members. If they incorporate, they write articles of incorporation, articles of organization (like a corporate constitution), by-laws, policies, and plans. The inner circle may expand to a board of directors based on the distribution of stock. The personality and values of the founder prevail; others around him or her imitate the behavior and embrace the values and practices of the corporate culture. The behavioral norms and values spread in turn to new employees, who learn to adjust by training and by imitating. If the vision of the founder proves to be aligned with the market, there will be business success, which in turn provides powerful reinforcement of the vision, the values, and the behavioral (operational) norms. Thus a corporate culture is born.

Let us look at three famous case histories of how visionary leadership created huge corporations and corporate cultures.

In 1837 two brothers-in-law in Cincinnati joined together in a business partnership built on pig fat. At that time Cincinnati, located on the Ohio River in the middle of the developing American heartland, was called "porkopolis," because it was the leading center of pig slaughtering and fat rendering in the country. William Procter was an English-born candle maker who had settled in Cincinnati and married Olivia Norris. He needed fats to make his well-respected high quality candles. James Gamble was an Irish-born soap maker who settled in Cincinnati after graduating from Kenyon College. He married Elizabeth Norris, the sister of Olivia Norris Procter. He needed fats to make his high quality soaps. As the story goes, Procter and Gamble, encouraged by their father-in-law, joined forces with each other in order to purchase larger quantities of pig fat at lower prices. Then they decided to combine their products into one consumer product company, which they called Procter & Gamble (P&G). They successfully transitioned their personal trade skills to technology-based manufacturing.

The vision of Procter and Gamble was to make high quality products in large quantities and to market them as widely as possible. They wanted to make a lot of money for themselves and their investors while meeting the commercial needs of society through a free market system. They learned how to make products with controlled costs to be sold at reasonable retail prices with attractive profits. They served the needs of a rapidly expanding American population fueled by heavy immigration after 1848. They may have anticipated the growing market of immigrants, but they did not anticipate the Civil War. However, they were quick to seize the opportunity of supplying soap and candles to the Union Army. The soldiers liked their products and continued using them as consumers after the war.

Procter and Gamble's vision of sustained business success was predicated on their dedication to quality, strong branding and marketing, and product differentiation through continual innovation. Again, according to corporate lore, the demand for Procter's high-quality candles meant that he had to mark them so that the consumers who asked for them would know what they were buying. Procter marked boxes of his candles with a half crescent moon, which evolved into the world-famous P&G brand label. The brand became a promise of quality and product differentiation to consumers among competing, but ultimately less desirable products. Procter & Gamble's soaps were no less renowned than their candles. In the 1880s they introduced a light bar soap that could float in water. They called it "Ivory" soap, probably because it was so white, and they marketed it as "pure." Its branding made it innovative, and it was a huge success all over the world.

The succeeding generations of P&G perpetuated the values and corporate culture of P&G's two founders. The company aggressively pursued global marketing and product innovation. In 1911, the company began to migrate from its base in pig fats to alternative vegetable oils. This innovation broadened its natural resource base while offering more variety to consumers at competitive prices. Their culinary product Crisco proved to be as successful for cooking as Ivory soap was for washing.

During the 20th century, P&G perpetuated a corporate culture that valued strong R&D for product and process innovations, consistently high quality with cost controlled manufacturing, expanding distribution channels and extensive marketing, including advertising through a succession of public media: from newspapers and magazines to radio and TV.

After World War II, P&G took advantage of two decades of chemical research to develop synthetic alternatives to animal and vegetable fats. It also diversified into other types of consumer products for cleaning and personal hygiene. In 1946, the company introduced Tide, a chemically derived detergent for washing machines.

In 1957, P&G launched Crest, the first commercial toothpaste to contain fluoride to strengthen the enamel of teeth to resist tooth decay. In 1961, it introduced the first successful disposable baby diaper, Pampers. In the meantime, the company experimented with mass advertising through radio and television. It sponsored daytime dramas with commercials for soaps and detergents and these dramas came to be known as "soap operas."

The culture of product innovation, product category leadership, exceptional value to consumers (often at value-added prices), branding, and aggressive marketing characterized P&G from the time of its founders to the present. Yet, not every product was successful. Innovation runs the risks of failure, and P&G has had more than its share of disappointments over 17 decades. One such disappointment was the commitment to a synthetic fat substitute generically called olestra (brand name Olean). It was expected to sweep the market for cooking fats by offering health benefits with good taste. However, the fact that, by design, the substance would not be absorbed by the body, coupled with undesirable side effects, alarmed some consumers and affected sales. Nonetheless, P&G moved on to other successful products in household cleaning and personal hygiene. Today the legacy of William Procter and James Gamble is a global corporation, still headquartered in Cincinnati but with manufacturing and marketing around the world, with an annual turnover of over $80 billion.

The second historical case study concerns another 19th century immigrant and aspiring entrepreneur. Andrew Carnegie, the man who created the largest American steel enterprise by the turn of the 20th century, was an impoverished 13 year old immigrant from Scotland in 1848. That year, his weaver father and mother brought him to the New World, where he began his industrial career as a bobbin boy (or what we might call a "go-fer") earning $1.20 a week in a textile mill. Then he worked as a messenger boy for the Pittsburgh telegraph office, where he became exceptionally adept with the emerging telegraph technology. He allegedly could identify the letters corresponding to the clicks of Morse Code and verbally translate them "in real time" into English text. In 1853, at the age of 18, because of his exceptional skills, hard work, and charm, Carnegie became the personal secretary and telegrapher of the general superintendent of the Pennsylvania Railroad in Pittsburgh. His talents and connections took him into the ranks of senior management in the railroad business. During the Civil War, he also managed the eastern telegraph operations of the Union Army.

But Carnegie saw other opportunities beyond managing railroads. He knew that railroads were hungry for quality rails. He foresaw a period of American territorial expansion and unprecedented economic growth following the Civil War. When he learned about emerging innovations in steel production, especially the Bessemer process, he was convinced that new technologies could produce high quality steel rails (and other steel products) in large quantities at profitable rates. He left the railroad and communications industries and entered the steel business in 1868. He also realized that he could finance a network of large, vertically integrated steel mills that would provide a large asset base as a barrier to market entry by potential competitors. Like other capitalists of his period, he was a ruthless competitor. His vision drove him to create the first billion dollar corporation in the US: the foundation of what became US Steel. Having achieved his business goals, he retired in 1901 at the age of 66 and dedicated the rest of his life to building a vast knowledge network with some 3,000 Carnegie libraries and generous endowments to universities around the world.

Using the language of futuring and visioning, Carnegie recognized macroscopic economic and technological trends and he knew the railroad industry from the perspective of its senior business management. He acquired a strategic competency in the evolving technologies of transportation and communication, which led him to explore new technologies in the emerging steel industry. He identified a specific opportunity, and he mustered the resources to pursue it. He had, at least in his own mind, a business mission statement, a customer value proposition, and long-term goals. He developed his corporate culture along with massive investments in steel-producing assets. For decades, he maintained strategic competencies and technologies in steel production. He had both short-term and long-term plans. With an estimated fortune in the hundreds of millions of dollars, the poor immigrant from Scotland had become one of the richest men in America by the turn of the 20th century, if not the richest. In sum, Carnegie was an extraordinary visionary.

Yet, one could argue that the initial vision of Carnegie was perpetuated by succeeding American steel executives for too long. Innovation is not static; today's innovation can be made obsolete by another innovation in the future. Such innovations can arise from emerging technologies, process reengineering that reduces costs, new value propositions for consumers, and new business models. Carnegie knew this principle in his times, but future generations of steel executives apparently forgot it. Following World War II, the American steel industry was so large, with such huge amounts of sunk capital (a Carnegie legacy), fixed distribution systems, and global market domination that it appeared unassailable for another century. Its global hegemony, however, lasted just another three decades or so. Japanese competitors took global steel market share away from the Americans through their own process innovations, lower labor costs, and redesigned mini-mills. The Japanese were joined in reducing the American global market share of steel by additional competitors in South Korea, Brazil, Russia and China.

The third business case history concerns the digital visionary Bill Gates, the co-founder of Microsoft and reputedly the richest man in the world at the end of the 20th century. Gates became fascinated with computers as a teenager in the Seattle area. He learned virtually all the languages for mainframe computers. As early as 1975, at the age of 20 and while attending Harvard University, Gates recognized the potential importance of the emerging micro-computer. He and his closest friends learned how to adapt languages for mainframes into a language for personal computers (PCs). The first application was in PC gaming, but Gates saw many other potential applications, both for business and individual consumers. More interested in computers and software programs than in his Harvard studies, Gates dropped out of college after about a year to join his friends in developing what they called "micro-soft" programs. They subsequently formed their own company, Microsoft. Their first big engagement was to write software for the operating system of the first generation of IBM PCs. IBM, thinking of itself as a hardware manufacturer and distributor, paid Gates' company for developing the operating system for IBM, but allowed Gates to keep the intellectual property rights to it. IBM apparently had no vision of going into the software as well as the computer business. This allowed Microsoft to reinvest in the software and sell it over and over again. Their product was called MS-DOS, from which later emerged Windows and various software applications.

Gates was exceptionally adept at articulating his view of the future, as evidenced in his bestselling book, *The Road Ahead*, in 1995. He identified early technology and market trends in the PC industry. Gates had exceptional foresight to recognize the potential spread of personal computers across the US and the rest of the world that most other people, including IBM, did not grasp. He knew the IBM computer technologies and markets intimately. Unlike Carnegie, Gates required very little capital, so assets became no barrier for his company. Physicals assets, likewise, would pose no future barrier to competitors. With proprietary knowledge, exceptional digital skills, legally defensible copyrights, and aggressive marketing, Gates built a business empire with strategic competencies and technologies. Like many other great business leaders, he thrived on competition and was not adverse to crushing competitors whenever he could. Like John D. Rockefeller in the years of building the Standard Oil Company, Gates has been accused of being ruthless. He enjoyed the powers of futuring and visioning like those at Procter+Gamble, and Carnegie. Even so, Gates failed to anticipate a very important parallel technology development and new business opportunity: the Internet and the World Wide Web. Microsoft caught up, but it never dominated the Internet as it had computer operating system software and various applications.

Visionaries exist today just as in the past. We see various qualities of visionaries in start-up companies and new ventures. As visionaries, they tend to do their own futuring and visioning in their own heads; they vary greatly in how well they can anticipate the future and articulate their vision to others. The visionaries like Carnegie and Gates are very rare; today, some will be successful in realizing their visions, but most will fail for any number of reasons, some of which are beyond their control.

While big successes are rare today, you can see visionary leadership operating every day at more modest levels. It may be argued that one of the most important responsibilities of senior managers and executives is to think about, and prepare for, the future. It is a responsibility that they acquire as heirs to enterprise founders and owners. Thinking about the future goes beyond annual budgeting, which (unfortunately) is where most operational planning begins and most strategic thinking ends. Visionary leaders as business managers should think at least 10 years, if not longer, into the future. Visionary leaders should address the following early stage challenges and opportunities. They should:

- Continuously align the enterprise with ever-changing market and customer conditions. The visionary leader must anticipate significant changes in the market environments and customer behavior and value. Operational managers should focus on business as usual; the senior managers must worry about how the business would be if it were not usual. Visionary leadership involves, to use the Wayne Gretzky analogy, skating toward where the puck is most likely to go, not where it has been. Visionary leaders have strong intuition about the future. Such executive intuition comes from years of experience and learning from both past successes and failures. It relies heavily on the astute recognition of the leading indicators for trend momentum and cause-and-effect patterns. Experienced and successful managers know that corporate goals may remain relatively constant, but business models have to continuously adapt to new circumstances.

- Prepare the enterprise for growth beyond familiar products, customers, and markets. The budget process should align resources with operational norms and annual goals. Successful managers, however, must think about the kinds of investments required today to provide the necessary resources for operations to achieve goals in the future. The imperative of any enterprise is to survive and to grow; to not grow risks decline and death. But growth may be increasingly difficult with the passing of time, unless the visionary manager is ready to lead the enterprise in new directions. To grow, every enterprise sooner or later has to expand into new technologies, processes, products, and services, even new customers and markets. Fundamentally, growth occurs when the enterprise can offer new products and services to an established market or base of customers or when it can offer the same or similar products and services to new markets and different bases of customers; the big stretch and risk, obviously, is offering new products and services to new markets and customers. Visionary leaders are the ones who see opportunities, assess risks, and prepare for future growth.

- Articulate and communicate the vision to others. The vision must be inspirational, but also based on compelling rational evidence and judgment. There must be a story for success. Visionary leaders and managers advance their vision repeatedly in conversations, memos and e-mails, reports, budgets, and presentations. They use relatively simple words to express complex thoughts and they use words that inspire. They employ the organization's values that everybody has already embraced to achieve new and exciting aspirational goals. Visionary leaders also explain how they are going to lead the organization to the visionary destination – they have to convince others that the objectives can be realized and show them how to participate in the adventure. They are able to convince senior managers and investors to take the path to success with them.

- Identify the resources and the personnel needed to fulfill the vision. Visionary leaders go beyond just wishing – they plan, they gather resources, and they recruit talent. They can construct mental models of how everything will come together to achieve the goal.

Visioning managers are much like successful athletes, performers, and soldiers, who can visualize a sequence of events in their minds long before they enact them. They see in their mind's eye the playing field or the stage; they see how they will line up and move; they anticipate the motions of others and how best to respond to them. They have a plan and they know what has to be done to win. And then they do it, making tactical and maybe even strategic adjustments along the way but staying focused on the mission.

Participatory Visioning

Visionary leadership may begin with the enterprise founder and his closest associates, but in order to endure it must spread to other stakeholders. No vision, no matter how brilliant or prescient, lasts forever. The founder and original owners will eventually age and die, or retire. Their successors may continue the original enterprise vision, mission, and values, but they may redefine them over time according to different personalities and changing circumstances. Over time, vision and values may still radiate from the top of the corporate hierarchy; or they may drift with no particular direction; or new values will emerge collectively from the bottom up. We see all three variations among corporations and non-profits today.

Since World War II, it has become increasingly popular among senior corporate executives and boards of directors to open up visioning, along with strategic thinking and planning, to middle managers and employees throughout the enterprise. Many corporations have over time transitioned from rigid, hierarchical organizations (like the Army model of World War II) to a more decentralized organizational structure that delegates responsibility (and the US Army, maybe to a lesser extent, is also changing itself in similar ways). The traditional command-and-control structure may be too slow in making decisions, responding to changing customer demands, and thwarting competitor threats. A chain of command, where each level has its own staff, adds overhead costs, too. The so-called flattening of corporate organizations, however, reduced redundancies and forced planning as well as execution to lower levels of management. In a way, using the Army analogy, corporate captains took on the traditional roles of colonels. Many of these new managers decided to share planning with their subordinates. At the same time, Japanese companies encouraged employee-led inputs in solving day-to-day production problems to a much greater extent than seen in typical American companies. Over time, employees were allowed to make inputs to strategic as well as operational issues. Corporate planning, and the vision, mission, and values behind it, became increasingly participatory within enterprises.

Typically, corporate boards and executive managers will define the nature of the business or organization and set long-term objectives. This function is the legacy of the founders and the most influential owners. Increasingly, boards and executives set high level expectations for the future, both qualitatively and quantitatively, but delegate much of the strategy and execution to operational managers, from division presidents down to mid-level managers. As the delegation for strategy, planning, and goal achieving travels down the chain of command, the visioning function becomes more participatory with increasing numbers of managers and employees involved in planning. Divisions, product lines, and other operational units may have to develop their own specific mission statements, values, and strategies to support their plans.

Dr. Daniel Kim, a student of systems dynamics at MIT and a popular corporate consultant, asserts that management should share the process of generating vision and fundamental values with employees in order to fully engage them and to align everyone with common objectives. He observes that many employees may feel fundamental corporate values, but have a difficult time articulating them. He has a procedure that he uses to draw in a large number of people through an exercise of generating values in connection with a mission, which is the source of values. Kim further states that often disagreements among managers and employees over the most desirable strategies and operations may stem from a lack of clarity and consensus around fundamental values, vision, and model for success. Get the values and vision explicitly established by consensus, and the rest of planning flows, he finds. In the words of Peter Senge of MIT, value and vision are parts of the corporate mental model and the shared vision.[93] In my words, vision and values are integral to corporate culture, which consists of the prevailing attitudes, values, business model, mission, behavioral norms, and common work practices of any company or organization.

As discussed in Chapter 3, culture and assets provide the basis for visioning. I include the mission statement, vision, and values under "culture." Culture and assets contribute both positive and negative attributes to sustained success. Culture provides a motivating sense of direction for all stakeholders of a company or organization. It allows work to get done in an orderly and meaningful way. It provides stability and sustainability. It is difficult to see how annual goals and bonuses could be realized without the psychological, and maybe even physical, security of culture. In addition, assets provide the infrastructure, plant, offices, machines, tools, and equipment with which to do work. But both culture and assets are Type I patterns that drive toward continuity. They crave stability and resist deviation, including change. Culture supplies security and routine; acting like an organism, it sends out antibodies to eliminate threats to its sense of order and balance. Assets are more tangible, but they are just as resistant to change as culture is. Once a major investment has been made in an asset, financial managers wish to get the best return possible by assuring that the asset works for as long as possible. After an investment is paid for and generates positive cash flow, it is indeed an "asset" in all meanings of the term. To abandon an asset because of the apparent need for change is to walk away from the machine that has been minting profits.

Because culture and assets provide operational continuity and stability, they can get out of alignment with the external environment of customers, markets, competitors, etc., which change at a more rapid pace. The challenge for managers is to recognize external changes and periodically realign the enterprise with its evolving business environment. They must also provide opportunities for employees to see and understand changes, too, in order to get their full

---

93   Daniel Kim, *Foresight as the Central Ethic of Leadership.* Voices of Servant-Leadership Series Booklet 8. Indianapolis: The Greenleaf Center for Servant-Leadership, 2002; Daniel H. Kim, "What Is Your Organization's Core Theory of Success?," *The Systems Thinker*, Volume 8, Number 3, April 1997; Peter M. Senge, *The Fifth Discipline. The Art & Practice of the Learning Organization.* New York: Currency Doubleday, 2006 (1990), pp. 163-215. I had the great pleasure of watching Dr. Kim facilitate a large group in determining values and vision at the Governor's Institute for Creativity & Innovation in Education, Columbus, Ohio, June 19-21, 2008.

cooperation in making internal adjustments. The longer the enterprise is out of alignment with its business environment, the more difficult it will be to adjust. Major misalignments can be very expensive to correct. The ultimate disaster of misalignment is the termination of operations, the closing of facilities, and the mass layoff of employees.

One trend that we have seen repeated many times over the last 30 years in the US occurs when the corporate board of directors changes executive management and the new CEO goes about "cleaning house." The favored method for changing corporate culture is reorganization with personnel changes. This is popularly called "swapping out the monkeys," based upon an alleged but oft-cited psychological experiment that tested how many generations of monkeys in a cage had to be removed in order to make a complete transition from one mode of collective behavior to another (the answer is supposed to be three). The point of the story is valid, even if the story is distorted. Changing corporate culture may involve substantial changes in personnel, including middle managers. A new executive may bring in his or her own senior management team and frequently fires the previous one. It is assumed that it is better to have senior managers of a previous administration gone than to keep them around and risk them frustrating the transition to a new culture. The assumption apparently goes way back in history to when kings felt compelled to execute senior advisors whose policies had disappointing if not catastrophic outcomes. For example, in 1540 Henry VIII got rid of the overly Protestant and pro-German policies of his chief minister Thomas Cromwell, not merely by removing him, but by having him beheaded. Similarly, when Joseph Stalin conducted his periodic purges in Soviet Russia, he may have been responsible in one way or another for the deaths of as many as 20 million people. The purge of senior managers can easily extend to middle and lower managers and to the mass of employees.

A more humane, less disruptive and less expensive – albeit slower – way to change corporate leadership and culture is through continuous evaluations of the business environment and company performance. Dramatic changes in senior management and the firing of many lesser managers and staff feel like earthquakes on a par with that of San Francisco in 1906 and just as destructive and expensive. Such dramatic seismic events are not necessary in most circumstances. They can be avoided by making many little changes over time. These changes should be led by senior managers, by example and by instruction. Leaders must teach their subordinates to recognize changes in market conditions and customer behavior and adjust accordingly. The teaching process includes opportunities for employees to see the changes for themselves and to willingly change with them.

I agree with Dr. Kim's observation that purpose drives values. What is highly valued should be aligned and functional (as opposed to dysfunctional) with the mission and the vision – in business as well as in war, athletics, and other goal-oriented and competitive walks of life. If you accept this premise, then you should agree that the owners through the executive management team have the first, but maybe not exclusive, responsibility to determine the foundational mission statement, the vision for the future of the enterprise, and the core values of a company or organization. But they should seek inputs from employees and other stakeholders, too. Participation in the conversation about mission, vision and values may enrich everyone's understanding of them and their commitment to them. Correspondingly, strategy at the highest level comes from the top, but strategy is enriched by the contributions of others. Senior managers must have the final word, but the word does not have to come down cast in stone, especially in times of uncertainty, where changes come from various directions.

The way to generate mission statements, vision, and values through participation at various levels of the enterprise is to employ one of many techniques of group dynamics: small group discussions aggregated gradually toward a large group consensus; the Nominal Group Technique (see steps on pages 175-176); group writing and editing exercises, etc.

While the culture (including purpose as manifested in a mission statement, fundamental values, vision, and business theory, or model) provides the common level of visioning, the next level consists of strategic capabilities, competencies, and technologies. The determination and leveraging of strategic capabilities, etc., might be done by senior managers alone, but it is often better to let the most knowledgeable employees participate in this process, too, as they have day-to-day experience with them.

To summarize up to this point, the vision of a company or organization begins with its founders and is often perpetuated, with modifications over time, by successive generations of owners and managers. The vision typically becomes codified in a written definition of the business and its mission. A business definition contains a statement of what the company or organization does for whom and why. The mission might be stated broadly or narrowly. It is designed to reflect well on the company or organization for both external and internal consumption. The business definition and mission provide the North Star for guiding management principles, organizational structure, operating procedures, and corporate culture. The vision leads directly to both long-term and short-term goals, which are sometimes viewed as aspirations and sometimes as contracts. These are often written down and agreed upon by managers and employees at the same time as annual performance reviews. Goals and performance reviews are often associated with rewards and punishments. Performance that meets or exceeds the expectations of goals may lead to annual bonuses, pay raises, and promotions, while performance that does not meet goals may lead to the denial of these rewards. They may even lead, directly or indirectly, to severance.

Strategic Capabilities, Technologies, and Assets

I discuss strategic competencies and visioning in Chapter 3, and it feels appropriate to begin this section with a recap of that earlier discussion. Strategic capabilities and technologies fit into the middle rung of visioning. This middle rung merits more detailed explanation in the context of participatory visioning. It is the bridge from the abstractions of vision, values, and culture to specific business strategies and plans. The concept goes beyond just core competencies, which are too often interpreted to mean what one company or organization can do better than others. It is entirely possible that a company might provide a "best in show" product or service and yet nobody will buy it. A more complex definition of a core competency was offered in 1995 by management consulting gurus Gary Hamel and C.K. Prahalad: it is "a bundle of skills and technologies that enables a company to provide a particular benefit to customers." They went further to ascribe three attributes of a core competency:

- Customer value

- Competitor differentiation

- Extendibility, or the basis for new products and services.[94]

In the early 1990s, my colleagues and I developed a different approach, which we called "strategic technologies." We gave "technology" a broad definition so that it would include hardware, software, systems, and technical knowledge and skills. It could be applied to manufacturing and other processes as well as to products and services. Our definition allowed us to include what managers and employees know as well as what they do, with knowledge often being a highly under-leveraged resource. While applying our definition in projects with clients, we learned that most people related easier to the words "strategic competencies and technologies." To round out our method, we developed categories for "enabling technologies" and "commodities" in addition to "strategic technologies."[95]

---

94 Gary Hamel and C.K. Prahalad, *Competing for the Future*. Boston: Harvard School Press, 1994, pp. 199, 202-207; quotation on p. 199.

95 The visioning method developed by Battelle in 1992 was called STEP-UP. It was inspired by Andrew M. Messina, "Technology Management for the 1990s," *Manufacturing Engineering*, June 1989, pp. 49-51.

A strategic technology has to meet all of three criteria:

1. It directly provides benefits and value, through packaged products and services, to customers as seen by and paid for by customers.

2. It enjoys some kind of competitive protection through patents, copyrights, or proprietary information.

3. It fits squarely with the company's business definition, mission, and value propositions.

An enabling technology is one that fits any one of three criteria:

1. It is not seen by or necessarily valued by customers.

2. It enjoys no particular or sustainable competitive production.

3. It could be outsourced to other firms that could claim it as a strategic technology to them.

Finally, a commodity technology is one that meets any of two criteria:

1. It is rarely differentiated by quality, but usually by the lowest prices.

2. It is readily available on the open market.

A strategic technology, or a strategic competency for those who continue to think of technology as the tools but not the systems or know-how behind them, has to be more than just being able to do something better than anyone else can. It must, first and foremost, provide benefits and value to customers that customers can see, appreciate, and respond to.

A strategic technology can provide basically three types of value to customers.[96] The first is superior benefits through quality, utility, and design at "reasonable" prices, which can be wholly subjective to customers, although they must be affordable given customer resources and cannot be undercut by competitors. In this one case, a traditional core competency of superior capability, manifested in product and service quality, may indeed be the key to customer value. Or, secondly, a strategic technology, and its resulting products and services, might be virtually unique, such as an exciting new product to hit the market ("the best thing since sliced bread"), and highly desired by customers. Customers may be willing to pay premium prices. Or, thirdly, a strategic technology leads directly to lower production costs that can be passed on to customers in the form of lower prices.

---

96 The analysis here is leveraged from the concepts of competitive advantages and business strategies presented by Michael E. Porter, *Competitive Strategy. Techniques for Analyzing Industries and Competitors*. New York: Free Press, 1980.

In addition, strategic technologies must enjoy some kind of competitive advantage. We have previously mentioned that large capital investments provide one type of barrier to potential competitors. To recap, investments provided a huge barrier in the early days of the steel industry; they provide little or no barriers in the information and communication technologies today. Another form of competitive advantage is a monopoly, which was much favored in the past but illegal today. Traditional forms of legally protected competitive advantages include patents, copyrights, trademarks, and proprietary knowledge. In the US, we have seen many types of technologies and resulting products and services protected by patents. Many types of software programs are protected by copyrights. They are also protected by the fact that software companies typically sell the object code but not the source code to customers. Patents demand disclosure, so a company filing for patents has to tell the world what it is protecting. Consequently, we see many more product than process patents. If a technology or product is relatively easy to reverse engineer or replicate, then it will be typically protected by full-disclosure patents. On the other hand, if a technology or product were difficult to reverse engineer, then the company might be further ahead in a competitive advantage to keep the knowledge proprietary and secret.

Finally, a strategic technology has to be one that contributes directly to the corporate mission, goals, and business strategies. There must be a close fit among strategic technologies, corporate culture, and assets.

We should also amplify the meanings of "benefits" and "value" in the eyes of customers. Many times, companies confuse the terms "benefits" and "value." They are closely related, but not the same thing. Benefits include payoffs to the customer, both tangible and intangible. They include attributes such as utility, quality of performance, durability, longevity, etc. They also include pride of ownership, social status, and pleasure. Value, on the other hand, is the relationship between the benefits and the price paid. Did the customer feel like he or she got a "good deal" or got "ripped off?"

Value to the consumer is like profit to the producing company: it's the margin of advantage. Profits are easy to determine because they are measured in units of money. Customer value, however, can be very subjective to the customer. A simple formula is $V=B-P$, where customer value (V) is the relationship in the mind of the customer between benefits (B) received and the price (P) paid. The formula can also be expressed as $V=B/P$ when you are seeking a ratio or an index value. Benefits can be tangible, such as quality, performance, and utility. Sometimes they are highly psychological, such as pride of ownership, social status, convenience, and pleasure. Therefore, in some cases B can be directly measured, and sometimes it can only be measured indirectly through index numbers (or values in a different sense of the word). Price (P), on the other hand, is easy to measure in dollars and cents. You can also place price on an index ranging from very high to low with qualitative definitions and ranges.

Superior value is realized when the customer gets a lot of benefits at the lowest possible prices. To improve value, the company must increase the benefits, lower prices, or both. In retailing, for example, you see the expression "value priced," meaning that you are being offered a standard of quality, as represented in well-known brands, at lower than customary market prices. Japanese, South Korean, and Chinese companies with more modern facilities, the latest technologies, and lower labor costs can out-compete traditional American companies (such as we saw in the steel industry) through delivering acceptable if not even better quality at substantially lower prices.

When I was at Battelle, we developed a method, called STEP-UP, to apply the definitions of technologies to existing and potential company products and services. We facilitated expert focus groups of selected company managers and technical staff to identify a company's strategic technologies using the definitions given above. We used the Nominal Group Technique to generate a master list of potential strategic technologies and a voting procedure to identify the most important strategic technologies. A group might provisionally identify 10 or more strategic technologies, which would later prove to be too many. Most companies have barely three or four truly strategic technologies, and many successful companies have only one or two. We would array the provisional strategic technologies as the row heading of a matrix. We would, through prior research, present the company's leading products and services as column headings. (We often added information for each column heading for their primary customers, annual sales volumes, and typical margins.) Then we would go down each row of the matrix and ask the group to identify each strategic technology found in each product and service. The completed matrix displayed a map of how strategic technologies were deployed across products and services. The theory is that a strategic technology with many checks across the rows is a well-leveraged strategic technology; having few or no checks across a row indicates a poorly leveraged and possibly phantom strategic technology.

Likewise, a product or service with many checks down a column reflects one that is well supported by strategic technologies. We did have examples of products and services that had few, and maybe no, strategic technologies supporting it. The conclusion was that they either had other attributes supporting them (like brand and dedicated distribution channels) or that they were highly vulnerable to potential competition.

A hypothetical example of a STEP-UP matrix is shown in Figure 7.1, overleaf. In this matrix, the participants of a company in the STEP-UP method identified as many as 12 potential strategic technologies, but then they reduced the list to just three strategic technologies, represented by the row headings of the matrix. The column headings represent three existing products and one service. In addition to the identification of products and the service, the previous year's sales and profit margins were also provided. Working through the matrix with the participants, the matrix cells were filled in with either S (strategic), E (enabling), or 0 (not present). At the completion of the matrix, we stepped back to look at it as a general map of technologies and products and services and began to analyze the meaning of what we were seeing.

The history of the company provided much valuable background (Type I pattern recognition) for understanding the matrix, and through it the strengths and weaknesses of the company itself. The enterprise had been established in the 1920s to manufacture equipment sold to residential construction contracts for installing, for example, water and sewage systems. It made one principal product until the 1950s, when it began to diversify into other products for the same business customers. The culture of the company was very cautious; the second generation of owners wanted to largely preserve the company established by the founder (their father). In the 1970s, the third generation of owners was willing to take more risks and began an after-market maintenance and repair service for their manufactured products. The new leadership also launched a new product: direct sales of water purification and filtering products to residential customers. It was a "strategic" product with good profit margins, but it was experiencing a lot of competition and slow market penetration.

	Product A Sales: $500 m Profits: 1%	Product B Sales: $300 m Profits: 3%	Product C Sales: $50 m Profits: 9%	Service A Sales: $70 m Profits: 12%	
Tech 1	S	0	0	S	2 S
Tech 2	S	S	E	S	3 S
Tech 3	0	E	S	0	1 S
New					
Total	2 S	1 S	1 S	2 S	

Figure 7.1. A Hypothetical Example of a STEP-UP Matrix

Product A was the original product that the company produced from the days of its founding. Product A continues to enjoy the highest sales of any product or service, but also the lowest profit margin. The product had grown old and, from a marketing perspective, had deteriorated to a commodity with very small price markups. The innovation of the third generation of owners was to expand into the aftermarket service (Service A), where profits were much higher. I might have concluded that the company continued to manufacture Product A only out of respect to the company's legacy (and how much is that worth?) and to seize the opportunity of providing maintenance and repair services. (As the facilitator of the process and the outside consulting commentator, I actually said something to this effect and it was not well received by the client.)

Product B was a second-generation diversification closely aligned with Product A. It was doing better in its margins but had still not reached the sales level of flagship Product A. Product C was fairly new and went off in a different direction than Products A and B. It had good profit margins, but somewhat disappointing sales.

From the point of view of return on investment, one likes to have a strategic technology that is well leveraged across several products and services. In this illustrative example, Technology 2 was the most widely deployed strategic technology, while Technology 3 was the least well leveraged. From the marketing point of view, one likes to have products and services that are well supported by strategic technologies, on the premise that several strategic technologies in one product or service gives strength to competition and endurance over time in the marketplace. In this example, Product A and Service A were the strongest offerings of the company, with Products B and C potentially vulnerable to competition in the future.

The STEP-UP matrix may be used as a prognostic tool for the future as well as a diagnostic tool for the present. In this example, we could generate ideas about how existing strategic technologies could create new products and services. We do this by adding columns to a completed matrix. We also could brainstorm how existing products and services might be improved (e.g. providing more benefits to customers and/or reducing production costs) by adding new strategic technologies, or more rows to the matrix. The most exciting, and speculative, possibilities would be adding a new section to the matrix with both new columns and new rows.

The most effective STEP-UP projects that we managed included research beyond the expert judgment of the participants. In some cases, the research focused on market trends. The most fruitful projects, however, involved customers directly. The company would reach out to customers and ask their views on company products, benefits, and value. They would combine STEP-UP with traditional market research methods. This exercise would validate or modify the judgments of the participants on the first criterion of "strategic technology" (or "strategic competency"). In addition, the company in some cases would conduct detailed competitive analysis studies to validate the participants' judgments on the second aspect of the same definition.

Beyond learning that most companies overestimated the number and strength of their strategic technologies, we learned that many companies believe that their strategic technologies of today will remain strategic in the future. They fall into the trap of assuming that things as they are today will remain constant. This is almost never the case. Over time, all strategic technologies will erode into commodities unless they are continuously refreshed. Once a technology becomes well known it runs out of its freshness and can be widely imitated. Strategic technologies can degrade to enabling technologies and eventually to commodity technologies over time.

We also realized that products and services – the packages in which technologies and capabilities are offered to consumers – can be categorized as "strategic," "enabling," and "commodity," too. If a company does not innovate with its old products, let alone launch new ones with exciting benefits and new technologies, it will lose product differentiation and have to compete within a lower price bracket. Even successful products have to be periodically refreshed with new features and benefits. If not, consumers will take an old product for granted and expect more volume at lower prices.

Having done some two dozen STEP-UP projects with corporations and government agencies, we gained a very interesting insight: it is easier to add more technologies and benefits to existing products and services than it is to develop new products and services based on existing strategic technologies. This seems counter-intuitive, but it proves to be correct most of the time. The biggest barrier that we encountered in the consideration of new products and services was distribution. The participants in the STEP-UP process would throw their arms up and ask, "If we had such products, how would be sell them?" We also learned that companies that tended to be very strong in R&D, engineering, and new product development were often not equally strong in distribution and marketing. Conversely, we saw that companies that were very strong in distribution and marketing tended to be not as strong in new product development. This observation further explains why P&G, a company that historically has enjoyed parallel excellence in both new product development and marketing, is exceptional.

A further thought is that companies should have more realistic views of their own strengths and weaknesses and partner with other companies that have complementary strengths. We saw many times that companies often thought they could cooperate with other companies that claimed the same strategic technologies.

These prospective partnerships almost never work. By nature, same competes rather than cooperates with same. The match is between strategic and enabling. This is why some Japanese companies have been so successful in the last 50 years. They focused on just a few in-house strategic technologies and outsourced many of their enabling technologies to other companies that could claim them as strategic. Japanese companies were generally far more virtual and networked and less fully vertically integrated than American companies. Of course, the networked manufacturer had to worry about consistency of parts and sub-systems made by others. So the Japanese embraced Total Quality Management so that all players in the network performed at the same standards of excellence.

By way of example, a company that is truly excellent in product development but not so strong in distribution and marketing should team with a company that is very strong in distribution and marketing but not so strong in new product development. This generalization explains in part why many companies with strong distribution channels and marketing seek to outsource their R&D and new product development, or simply buy technical services and inventions in the global technical marketplace.

Can a company be successful without any strategic technologies? The answer depends upon how narrowly or broadly we define "strategic technologies." If we define the term narrowly, then the answer might be "yes," but then the same company would have to enjoy some strategic assets rather than strategic technologies. Such assets might include unique and very expensive capital investment, well-established brands, exclusive distribution channels and retail outlets, or particularly loyal customers. The definition of a strategic, enabling, or commodity asset would be the same as the definitions for the three categories of technologies. It is possible for a company to have two or three strategic assets and no strategic technologies, and vice versa.

To come back to the historical example of Carnegie's steel empire, the strategic technology was principally the Bessemer process. In addition to one very strategic technology, Carnegie also enjoyed several strategic assets: his huge physical steel mills, his financial genius for acquiring and merging many small steel companies into one large steel conglomerate (which evolved into US Steel), and his intimate knowledge of the railroad industry and other strategic customers for steel.

The vision, mission, values, and culture of a corporation or organization provide the ideas that drive thought and the inspiration that drives motivation behind work. Strategic technologies, competencies, and assets provide the processes and tools for work. Combined, they provide the basis for strategic planning, which provides the direction for work.

Planning

So much has been written on strategic planning that it seems unnecessary for me to cultivate further this well-plowed field.[97] American companies at one time had strategic planning departments and treated planning in general as an important staff function, particularly at the corporate level. This was the legacy of World War II. Then in the 1980s corporations sought to reduce corporate overhead and to diversify many management functions among operating divisions or subsidiary companies. This was largely in reaction to a wave of unfriendly corporate mergers and acquisitions and stiffening competition from abroad. So many companies dropped strategic planning at both the corporate and the division levels. "Strategic" planning shifted to operational planning. But managers at all levels still had to plan in order to reach their goals. Then when the dotcom boom hit in the 1990s, business planning came back into vogue, but as a tool for raising money from venture capitalists. No start-up enterprise could get external funding and no corporate unit could get re-investment budgets without a thorough and compelling business plan. Unfortunately, much of the staff expertise in strategic planning had been lost, leaving entrepreneurs and business managers with little more guidance for sound strategic planning than their personal familiarity with trends, their will for the self-fulfilling prophecy, or wishful thinking.

Strategic planning never died, it just changed. Like trends in manufacturing, the process had to be re-engineered to be lean and mean. It had to fit the more diversified and flexible organizational style of post-modern companies and get away from the vertically integrated, mass production style of the early 20th century. It also had to migrate away from the model of another important American institution, the military, which was organized and managed much like old-fashioned mass production factories.

Perhaps no American institution had more impact on business organization and management style in the 20th century than the US Army and Navy. The World War I experience affected millions of military personnel and civilians in the 1920s and 1930s, and corporations were organized, operated, and managed much like the military. It was a model that nearly every man had experienced, directly or indirectly, and understood. It had a mission, structure, discipline, rules, and a

---

97   Just a few examples of the extensive literature on strategic planning include Henry Mintzberg, *The Rise and Fall of Strategic Planning*. New York: Free Press, 1994; Ian Wilson, "Realizing the Power of Strategic Vision," *Long Range Planning*, Vol. 25, No. 5, 1992, pp. 18-28; Ian Wilson, "Strategic Planning Isn't Dead – It Changed," *Long Range Planning*, Vol. 27, No. 4, 1994, pp. 12-24; Daniel H. Gray, "Uses and misuses of strategic planning," *Harvard Business Review*, Vol. 64, Number 1, January-February 1986, pp. 89-96; and Kenichi Ohmae, *The Mind of the Strategist. Business Planning for Competitive Advantage*. New York: Penguin Books, 1987 (1982).

well-defined culture. World War II had an even bigger influence on American business. At least 15 million men and women served in the armed forces from 1941 to 1945, many of them young men who would eventually work for private companies. What they learned from the Army they carried with them into business. Such lessons included structures of strict command-and-control by a hierarchy of rank (CEO = CO, commanding officer, then executive officer = chief operating officer, etc.); obeying orders; following the rules; maintaining standards of dress; and organizational units focused on particular types of operations (infantry, artillery, engineers, etc. = manufacturing, marketing, accounting, etc.). The military culture passed into the corporate culture across America. No example had a more profound impact on the concept of strategic planning in business than the conventions of planning in the military.

During the world wars, the convention was that the commanding officer, his staff, and his immediate subordinates crafted strategy and gave orders to the planning staff to draw up the operating plans and official orders in great detail. In World War II, much of the military strategy was formulated at the very highest levels in Washington, primarily by President Roosevelt and his closest advisors: Secretary of War Henry Stimson and Secretary of the Navy Frank Knox, and Gen. George C. Marshall and his staff of general officers at the Pentagon. Gen. Marshall's career had advanced because of his superior capabilities in planning and staff work rather than his leadership daring in the field. Gen. Dwight D. Eisenhower likewise had an illustrious career as an organizer, planner, and staff officer who earned Gen. Marshall's trust prior to commanding American forces in Africa and Europe. They set the model for the Army and the Navy, which in turn set the model for strategy and planning in business for the next four decades.

After World War II, the prevailing practice in large corporations was that the senior executives made the decisions on business strategy and assigned planning to a dedicated corporate staff. Strategy, planning, and budgeting were largely hierarchical and top-down. Plans and budgets looked like command orders. Over time, however, the military model of planning deteriorated. Too often corporate planning staffs wrote the strategic plans which field managers increasingly ignored. Strategic planning acquired a bad reputation for being too esoteric, too idealistic, and too irrelevant to the quarterly challenges of corporate combat. Too little of strategic planning was really "strategic" and too much of it became operational planning and budgeting. Strategic plans were shelved and forgotten almost as quickly as they appeared. Strategic planners became politically marginalized, so that planning staffs were typically cut to reduce overhead in the business process re-engineering: something so many American companies had to endure in the 1980s to cope with Japanese and other foreign competitors.

Corporate planning continued to be done, just in different ways. Executive managers did their own strategic planning at the highest levels. As companies delegated more responsibility to divisional and major product managers, more strategic, operational, and budget planning got delegated, too. Each management level had its own plans, typically heavily operational, yearly, and budgetary. A slow yet dramatic change occurred during the 1980s with a shift from staff-generated strategic planning, as historically practiced, to manager-driven strategic thinking. All level managers were expected to have their strategies and to know how to best run their units in cooperation (hopefully) with other units for the greater good of the corporation. Strategic thinking became more visionary and inspirational. It actually had been such with Generals Marshall and Eisenhower in World War II; the rank and file had just not seen it as openly during the 1940s as corporate employees saw it in the 1980s and 1990s.

The general practice today is that senior managers, in cooperation with their boards of governors or advisors, are still responsible for corporate-level strategic planning. Strategic planning includes the broad elements of business definitions, mission, and goals. It is strategic in the sense of providing the "big picture" with basic business strategies. Operational planning, on the other hand, deals with day-to-day work procedures to implement the strategic plan. The corporate strategic plan sets the framework for operational plans at all levels. The plans are drawn up in conjunction with budgets, but the budgets are separate and meant to support the plans rather than the plans rationalizing the budgets. Or, that is the ideal. In reality, many companies focus on their budgets as their implicit plans and let the assumptions of strategic planning go unarticulated.

Planning can also work from the bottom upward as well as top downward, especially in large corporations with highly diverse operations and with non-profits and government agencies. The identification of strengths and weaknesses and opportunities and threats can percolate up from the lowest ranks of employees and managers. More commonly, there is a hybrid of both top-down and bottom-up planning.

I think the "strategic" in strategic planning gets over-emphasized and under-utilized. A lot of good planning is not necessarily "strategic." The legacy of the 1990s is to use the term "business plans." I will just refer to "plans" and to the process of "planning," with the understanding that planning can range in scope from large corporations to small enterprises, from organizations to individuals in their daily lives, and from big issues and large money to little issues and less money. The scope may vary, but the principles of good planning do not.

A common misunderstanding about plans is that once made they cannot be changed. That misconception apparently came from the World War II experience when military plans were official orders. It is easy to see how over time plans became ignored; if a unit or regional manager exceeded his goals, the plans looked too soft and if operations could not meet the goals of the plan then the plan was at fault for being out of touch with business realities. The blame for the shortcomings of planning got placed on the staff planners rather than the managers. At that point, CEOs and other executive level managers said that the lower level managers could be their own planners – and be held accountable for both the day-to-day operations and for achieving the goals.

Some managers have complained that business plans are constraints on flexibility. If the plans were viewed as orders, then the plans had to be executed regardless of whether or not they still made sense in the light of changing circumstances. But Gen. Eisenhower was well aware of that problem. He has been credited with saying that the plans are nothing but the planning is everything. He knew perfectly well from experience that the best laid plans could quickly be irrelevant because of changing battle conditions. He would have been the first to endorse the idea that strategic planning should lead to strategic thinking. An adaptive leader should learn from planning how to identify the goals of the mission, options to achieve those goals, and contingency plans to be flexible in reaction to changing circumstances without abandoning the goals of the mission.

A major pitfall of planning is wishful thinking. Plans have goals that are typically aspirational, but not necessarily realistic. Plans usually assume some degree of business growth over the years; using military terms, plans are more offensive than defensive. Corporate plans rarely if ever foresee stagnation and decline. They see growth! With bonuses! While incremental growth may be soundly based on trends, exponential growth can be wishful thinking bordering on delusional. This is exactly the point about futuring and why, in most cases, it should be done before visioning in order to provide an external frame of reference for internal goals and strategies.

On the other hand, a plan can be a rare example of predictability when it has the direction and resources for people to execute it successfully. Planning is an example of the self-fulfilling prophecy to the extent that one has control of sufficient elements to make a desired future happen. This is the goal of many futurists and planners: to be more proactive than reactive and to be winners rather than losers in the fortunes of fate. Well considered plans, including disciplined futuring, can deliver the dream of fulfilling one's own destiny (which can be our own rationalization, often *ex post facto*, of achieving more or less the desired effect in the future). This is exactly why athletes have game-plans and practices, actors have scripts and rehearsals, architects have blueprints and models, and generals have strategies to make their desired futures come true. Planning is ultimately preparing for the future, and the plans can be evaluated by judging how well they actually prepared you to make your own future.

The advice credited to General Eisenhower that the planning process is everything and the plan is nothing is frequently forgotten by corporations and government agencies that draw up elaborate plans and then slavishly pursue them. Eisenhower knew from experience that the planning process, rather than the plans themselves, showed people how to best achieve the mission in a variety of possible ways under all kinds of unforeseen circumstances using the resources at hand. Planning taught people to be more flexible and adaptive to things that could and usually do go wrong. Planning contributes to the organization's resilience in the face of uncertainties in the future.

Planning is fundamentally a thinking, learning, and preparing process. I would like to share at this point what elements I think characterize good planning and plans as well considered expectations for the future. We might call them the "dirty dozen" of planning.

1. *Mission Statement*
The mission statement includes the definition of the organization and its vision of the future based on a statement of the enterprise mission (its *raison d'être*, as the French say). It is ground zero for all planning. The mission originates with the desires, values, and future vision of the founders, owners, board of directors, and executive managers. While the business mission, definition, and goals must be articulated, the underlying vision, values, and corporate culture may not be. Sometimes the vision is stated very clearly, and sometimes it is merely implied. In addition, some companies have written their values down in their annual reports, on websites, and in various communications with employees and other stakeholders. I have seen signs in offices and on shop floors pronouncing corporate values as though they were political slogans. Such values, of course, must be internalized in order to become operational.

2. *Goals and Priorities*
According to the best military traditions, the goal determines the strategy. As with the identification of the mission statement and the business definition, the owners, the board of directors, and the executive managers determine the long-term and near-term (typically annual) performance goals. These may be corporate or divisional goals that will in turn lead to business unit and personal performance goals. Usually goals are expressed in the metrics of growth rates, sales, market share, and margins. They can also be expressed qualitatively, as in the language of corporate values, community service, and the national good. In most cases with American enterprises, the goals are included in budgets as revenue, costs,

to reward achieving goals. In both the setting of goals and the ̲ssociated with them, priorities are identified as a precursor to strategic ̲ormulation and plans.

3. *Current Business Lines and Their Performance*

An overview of the current business sets the frame of reference for strategies. It is a logical elaboration upon the statement of business definition and mission. It tells everybody where you are at this moment. The current business lines should be identified with performance metrics such as sales volumes, market share, and margins. This provides the starting point for the planned map of the future. The important point is whether the company appears to be on track to achieve its goals or not. If it appears to be on track, then the plan may be more or less a continuation of the past with some modifications. If it appears to not be on track, then get ready for some major changes.

4. *Strategic Capabilities, Technologies, and Assets*

The plan should explain what assets support the business definition, mission, and goals. This step provides further elaboration upon Steps 1 and 2 above. It lays out the foundation of how the company or organization achieves its purposes. This is the place to summarize the results from the STEP-UP method, as mentioned earlier in this chapter. I have seen some capabilities statements that are very dry, and I have seen others that bordered on chest-beating. Perceptive planners, influenced by marketers, realize that the plan is a public document and a marketing tool as well as an internal map.

Some planners omit this section in their written plans because it gives too much internal detail. I agree that in some business plans this section is more important than in others. In the plans of startup enterprises, it is very important to show investors how the goals can be achieved. Maybe not in all cases, but usually I think this section has value because it clarifies what the company or organization has to offer customers relative to competitors. I realize, however, that this material may be boring and distracting to potential external readers and might appear at the back of the plan as an appendix.

I must remind people that the plan is not the same thing as the annual report, which is definitely oriented to investors, regulators, and various stakeholders. Elements of the plan may be included in the annual report, but the annual report is not likely to contain the level of detail typically required by a plan. In addition, most companies do not want to broadcast their business strategies, which would be incorporated into a proprietary plan, to the world if they think competitors could benefit from such information.

5. *Customers and Markets*

Plans should provide qualitative information as well as quantitative data. In addition to the metrics of performance of existing products and services, you should also identify your current customers and describe the marketplace conditions in which you interface with them. What is the value proposition of the customers and what are their typical modes of buying behavior? What are the styles of shopping and buying in the marketplace? This is also a good place to discuss branding and market positioning, especially relative to the Michael Porter dimensions of competitiveness: differentiation, niche, or price.

This is one among several places to work futuring into planning. There should be a discussion of consumer behavior trends and how they are likely to evolve in the future. In other words, the assessment of customers should be dynamic over time and not just snapshots of the past and present. The same should be said for marketplaces, which also change over time. Just think about the last decade and how the Internet changed both consumer habits and marketplaces with more virtual shopping and in some cases less actual shopping.

A consideration of markets and marketplaces should include distribution chains and retail outlets for your products and services. The distribution network is extremely important, as it provides the conduit for you to get your goods and services before customers. In the "good old days," the provider of goods and services distributed them directly to customers at his or her home, shop, or place of business or fairs and open-air markets. Stores became popular in the 18th century. Companies making goods and providing services might reach out to customers directly or go through agents, wholesalers, and other middlemen and retailers for final sales to end-use customers. Then businesses such as Sears provided distribution through the mail, which became increasingly reliable and quicker through the use of railroads and later airplanes. Today, distribution might include all of the following options: a traditional distribution chain with wholesalers and retailers, direct sales to end-users through outlets and special opportunities, Internet sales, mail order sales, and the use of courier services, like FedEx, UPS, etc. Which options are most attractive must be considered thoroughly and included in any comprehensive business or strategic plan.

Some planners prefer to place this section earlier in the plan, especially if the plan becomes a public document. I agree that every company and organization should have a central focus on customers, but sometimes the elaboration upon the business definition and mission makes more sense earlier rather than later in the plan.

6. *Competitors, Competitive Advantages, and Market Positioning*

There should be a discussion of the competition – who they are, what they do, why they have success, etc. What alternatives to your products and services are offered to customers by others? What is a comparison of their quality and prices relative to yours? In conventional SWOT (strengths, weaknesses, opportunities, and threats) analysis, this is the place to identify strengths and weaknesses of your business lines relative to those of the competitors – in the eyes of customers (not just in your eyes). This is also the place to discuss the three basic types of competitive advantage: differentiation, niche, and price. Like the element above, this discussion should be dynamic and contain expectations for the future.

This material would typically be deleted in any strategic plan that might be seen externally, especially in an annual report or statement of future intentions, but it is vitally important for internal managers and employees to understand the competition in order to strive for superior benefits and value for customers.

7. *Significant Trends and Their Potential Impacts*

This is the primary place to work futuring into planning. This step requires a consideration of trends in the economy, demographics, technologies, specific markets, and consumer behavior – the environments beyond the enterprise not just as they have been or are presently but as they appear to be moving in the future. This part of the plan should present a view of the future that sets a forward-looking frame of reference for company plans and future operations. How likely is it that consumer behavior and value will change in the future, and what might those changes be? Are trends presenting new opportunities and threats? Are old competitors changing and are new competitors emerging? And a big question for the futuring manager: is the enterprise still well aligned with the external market environment? Will changes in the market require changes in the enterprise's basic business model and value proposition for customers?

8. *Strategies*

While it may have seemed like a long time getting to this point, the identification and explanation of strategies have to appear within a broad context of external and internal corporate factors. Michael Porter characterized strategy as the rejection of some possible actions in favor of those moves that are best suited to deliver superior value to customers and to counter the likely moves of competitors.[98] Strategies must be identified along with expectations given the conditions covered in the previous sections of the plan.

---

98   Michael E. Porter, "What Is Strategy?," *Harvard Business Review*, November-December 1996, pp. 61-78.

I have seen some strategic plans that provided an overview of most if not all theoretical strategy options, just to show what choices are available. In such plans, there will be a discussion of the pluses and minuses of each option, thereby reducing the various possibilities down to just one or two practical choices given the circumstances previously established.

Business strategies frequently use metaphors from military strategies, except in business strategies we hope we don't have to literally kill anybody. The goal is the "conquest," perhaps a misnomer, of the customer. The goal may not be the annihilation of an enemy army (although you might like to see a competitor laid low) and it might not be the occupation of territory (although you might think of winning market share), but it is growth in customers, sales, and returns. Since most corporations and organizations alike experience rising costs over time, they have to pursue growth just to survive. In most cases, a strategy "to stay the same" over an extended period of time is to court eventual death. Here are six prototype business strategies for growth that are more particular to commerce than to combat:

- Uniqueness. A very common business strategy is to offer a product or service that is unique *and* wanted by customers. This is a business with customers but with virtually no competition. A common example is a store that offers merchandise that cannot be obtained from any other source within many miles. Geography has typically been a vital factor in commerce ("location, location, location"). In manufactured goods, innovation creates products that customers have not seen before. This is the strategy of product and service innovation. Like the historical example of P&G, innovative products can capture the imagination of consumers and dominate shelf space in the stores. However, in a free market successful unique products will not likely remain unique: competitors will offer substitutes and undermine the initial dominance of innovation by offering the same or close to the same to consumers at lower prices. As soon as an innovative product loses its uniqueness and its differentiation, it usually has to compete on price because consumers understand prices better than they grasp product quality if all options look more or less the same. In addition, a unique product or service with many customers and no competition looks like a monopoly, in which case the government will either intervene to regulate it or to break it up. On the other hand, uniqueness can be maintained because the law provides for the protection of intellectual property, such as patents, copyrights, trademarks, and trade names. In addition, practical barriers to competition include proprietary and secret processes, products and services that are difficult if not impossible to reverse engineer, and insurmountable assets.

- Customer Diversification from Existing Products. This strategy involves leveraging existing products and services for growth through new applications, markets, and customers. This is the strategy of market diversification, which can vary in many degrees from previous products and services. The product and service lines may require some adaptations for different customers, but the fundamentals remain the same. A common product platform is developed, from which many variations can be packaged and marketed. An example is Coca-Cola, which diversified into many types of beverages, regular and diet, basic and flavored, which derive from the basic formula of so-called Classic Coke. It is also rumored that the taste of Coke varies between regions and countries with, for example, the use of sugar rather than corn syrup or the varying amount of sweetener used.

- Product and Service Diversification with the Same Customers. This is a complementary strategy to the one above, with the leveraging of existing customers for new products and services. This is another type of diversification built around established customer relationships rather than existing products and services. The emphasis here is on sales and marketing with the products and services being derived continuously. An historical example was the diversification of NCR from mechanical cash registers to all kinds of digital transactional technologies, including computers, which was a highly competitive field. NCR enjoyed a very close relationship with retailers and bankers, who continuously demanded more products and services packaged into more comprehensive systems. NCR grew because of the product and service pull of its customers, but the corporate strategy of responding to numerous customer demands also had the pitfall of leading NCR into products that they could not support and sustain amid the virtual explosion of digital technologies and capabilities in the 1990s.

- Substitutions. This is typically a materials- and process-based strategy. Its basic premise is that customers know and demand certain familiar products, but those products can be delivered in different materials and produced through different ways. The substitution strategy requires the same benefits familiar to the customer with quality control but at lower prices. One example is Rubbermaid, which had the strategy of substituting rubber and plastic products for more expensive products made of metals, wood, or ceramics (containers, trash cans, cooking implements, etc.) The Japanese, Koreans, and Chinese have proven that they can produce a very wide range of products just like, if not better than, American-made products at considerably less cost and at lower prices to consumers. Much of the rapid growth in digital products and e-commerce is due to the substitution of digital for analog products, services, and shopping. In some cases, the product innovation strategy is a substitution strategy in a broad sense, but the substitution strategy is usually narrowly defined to mean direct substitutions with similar if not identical forms and functions.

- Price cutting. The oldest and perhaps the crudest form of competitive strategy is just to undercut the competition by low prices, even so low that the supplier loses money on them. Some price cutting is selective to attract customer attention. Think of "loss leaders" offered by stores to lure in customers, who are expected to buy other products (at a profit to the store) at the same time they are looking for "specials" and "deals." Price cutting was also a strategy of monopolists in the 19th century who would cut prices so low as to drive all other competitors out of the market and then raise prices as high as possible when customers enjoyed no alternatives. The railroads and oil companies were accused of doing this in the late 19th century, resulting in anti-trust laws to restore competition and choices for consumers. In fact, a great deal of government regulation of business practices during the 20th century was to maintain competitive fairness and to protect the interests of consumers. In the early 21st century, some commentators claim that "free trade" as a standard of fairness in international trade has been sabotaged by contrived low labor rates, protectionist quality standards, and unfair currency exchange rates. A skeptic might even go so far as to claim that China today offers so many products at lower prices than American-made products that they are trying to undermine the American economy and drive American products out of markets across the globe.

- More benefits. This strategy is seen when existing products and services become so familiar to customers that they are taken for granted and compete largely on prices. Products and services will experience price erosion over time unless they are improved and updated with new benefits. The quality and differentiation leaders are continuously under pressure to add more benefits just to shore up existing prices (and profits).

Most companies have their hands full trying to implement just one strategy. Only in rare cases will companies attempt to implement multiple strategies at the same time – unless there is an unusual degree of decentralization and delegation of strategies to individual business units. Ideally, companies should have multiple strategies in response to various business conditions, but realistically most companies do not. However, they should have contingencies to cover themselves when the primary strategy seems to be falling short.

Arguably the hardest part of making business strategy is the consideration of the options. Middle and lower level managers tend to over constrain their choices and not seriously consider strategy innovations that they deem "unthinkable" because they deviate from the norm – meaning the past. The default strategy option is usually "more of the same." Manager and staff both want to continue to do what they are most familiar with and comfortable doing (such is the old adage, "If it isn't broken, don't try to fix it," which is an excuse for not doing anything differently unless you have to do so). This is an aspect of both the stability and the inflexibility of corporate culture. After all, many managers and employees do not see themselves as laboratory scientists and they do not enjoy "experimenting" with the business when careers and jobs are at stake. In many cases, there are strategy options that are subtle and creative, often hybrids of strategies that seem abnormal if not impossible ("out of the box").

To stimulate creativity, the generation of potential strategic options should be opened up to several different points of view. An ideal way to approach participatory planning is to hold periodic focus groups of managers, employees, and other stakeholders. With the mission and goals set by senior managers, a facilitator could ask the group to generate ideas in response to a topic question such as "What are the best strategies for achieving our mission and goals by the end of the next calendar year?" The ideas generated become strategic options that can be further refined and evaluated against a set of criteria.

A prototype set of criteria for evaluating strategic options follows:

- *Market conditions:* the degree to which a strategic option fits market conditions, including general economic circumstances, laws and regulations, and consumer behavior. What reasons are there to believe that a strategy would work given general economic and market conditions, both now and in the future?

- *Customers:* the degree to which identified customers will respond positively to a strategy. Do we know who the target customers are, their patterns of behavior, and their value proposition? Will a strategy work with them?

- *Competitors*: the degree to which there is, or will likely be, stiff competition in reaction to a strategy. Do we know who the competitors are and will this strategy be effective against them?

- Consistency with *corporate culture:* Is the strategy compatible with the business mission and definition, the enterprise's vision for the future, its values, and its culture? Does the strategy fit the corporate culture and will the culture support it in order to achieve goals?

- Leverage from existing *corporate assets and strategic competencies and technologies*: the degree to which corporate capabilities, strategic technologies, and assets can support the strategy. Does the strategy leverage existing resources or will new investments have to be made to implement it?

- Existence of *distribution networks:* Does the strategy fit existing distribution networks and systems or would new channels have to be found or created?

- Acceptable levels of risk and attractive *potential returns on investments* (ROI): What are the well considered expectations for expenses of implementing the strategy and the expected returns on that investment?

The filtering of the strategy options generated by a group does not necessarily require the work of the same group. A separate (and emotionally detached) group of analysts can do the research for, and the evaluation of, the strategy options. They may make a report and recommendation back to the manager responsible for a management decision or back to a leadership group for a collective management decision. The process should be documented, but the documentation can be an appendix to the strategic plan document or a separate report.

9. *Resources, Investments, and Budgets*
Every strategy requires an appropriate allocation of resources and investments. Plans have to include budgets, although budgets should not dictate strategies. The difference is that a strategy says "Do what needs to be done to be successful," while a budget-driven strategy says "Do as much as you can with what money we give you to work with." Most situations are a combination of both, but the strategy should come first. Budgets should include such resources as required for manufacturing capacity, locations, raw materials, distribution networks, technologies, and (of course) people. One major reason why strategic plans fail is that, while the strategy may have been well thought out in other respects, insufficient resources and investments were made to achieve the goals of the strategy under both present and future circumstances.

10. *Assignments and Responsibilities*
Each strategy, in addition to identifying required resources and investments, must give specific assignments to identified managers and working groups. Who is going to execute the plan is even more important to success than the mechanics of the how. People must know what they are expected to do and then be held accountable for their performance. Their goals are the goals of the strategy and the accumulated successes of the company.

11. *Schedules, Milestones, and Metrics of Achievement*

The biggest challenge in the planning process is the gap between strategic thinking and day-to-day operations. Crossing the gap is called operationalizing strategic thinking. As thought precedes action, action precedes results. Therefore, each strategy in the plan must have a time schedule with identified milestones and metrics of success. These milestones must be monitored and reviewed periodically, maybe once a month. People need to know that they are or are not on track with the plan. If they are not, management needs to make adjustments, more often than not with the implementers of the plan rather than the plan itself. This puts the plan to work.

12. *Contingencies*

Even the most well considered plans may fail because of inadequate resources, poor execution, uncooperative partners and suppliers, unexpected competitor challenges, resistant customers, and unforeseen changes in markets. Plans rarely work out exactly as intended, so adaptability is vital to reaching goals. Some of the most successful business people are those who have a plan and persist with the basic features of it but remain flexible in day-to-day tactics. They understand the mission and they can adjust to circumstances in its execution. Ideally, a strategic plan should offer contingency plans if the primary plan does not work. Most companies and organizations, however, do not prepare formal contingency plans. One seems to be enough. Great leaders, on the other hand, formulate contingencies in their heads. They anticipate potential changes to the plan and they are willing to move in different directions if necessary. In large corporations with huge asset bases and firm corporate cultures, adjusting strategies to meet new circumstances is very difficult. This is why it is usually easier for entrepreneurs and small companies with fewer constraints to adapt to quickly changing market conditions.

You may be objecting that a plan with as many elements as identified here is a relapse to the past when strategic planning documents were great tomes and largely ignored. Indeed, a large document today is not likely to be read, let alone followed, by very many people. Yet, all of the above elements are important to the process of strategic thinking in real-time. The process of doing comprehensive planning is to become familiar with the steps and speed up the process mentally. Even in the case of an elaborately developed written plan, only abstracts of it may be needed to circulate with others. Certainly a presentation should be shared both verbally and online to summarize the key points of the plan. As you become increasingly familiar with the planning process, you will begin to internalize it. You will learn to think in real-time. In a curious way, you may mentally automate the whole process by thinking through the elements very quickly. You will feel so comfortable with the process that it may become buried in your subconscious and accessed as intuition.

For the futuring manager, the key elements are how to see the external world as it is changing, how to adapt the enterprise to change, how to think strategically as though one had to write out a full-blown business plan, how to best execute the plan, and how to communicate and motivate others to do their parts in achieving goals.

Chapter 8. Managing Applications and Benefits

The central purpose of this book is to demonstrate that, fundamentally, futuring is about taking the opportunity to anticipate and make better futures for ourselves as opposed to doing nothing and taking whatever the future hands us. Businesses and organizations tend to be more reactive to external trends and events than they should be and not as proactive as they can be. In the future, successful managers will become futurists and visionaries by recognizing both the continuities and changes in markets and by learning how to respond to them quickly and effectively.

Operations in many companies and organizations are maybe 95% day-to-day physical, clerical, and managerial work and just 5% cerebral. Of course, thinking always guides actions, but typically the thinking is consistent with routines and repetitive work. This is just as true for corporate executives who have their own daily routines as for shop floor labor. Only rarely do we interrupt our work schedules with such introspective questions as "What is the value of what I am doing for my customers?"

Yet, the 5% cerebral function of business is vital to set strategic context for operations. It is even more important to the survival of the company or organization in times of great stress, often caused by sudden and unexpected changes in customers, marketplace conditions, competitors, and regulations. An analogy from nature might be the animal going about its daily business of eating until it accidently encounters a predator. Maybe the situation could have been anticipated and avoided, maybe not. In any case, it happens. Does the animal remain still and wait out the threat or does the animal cut and run at the risk of being pounced upon and eaten? Does it run in a straight line or back-and-forth at a continuous rate, or stop-and-go to confuse the predator? This may strike you as a trivial analogy, but I can assure you that many individuals and companies felt like a hunted animal in the clutches of a financial predator when stock prices began to plummet in late September 2008, retirement 401(k) portfolios lost at least half of their value, companies laid off workers, unemployment rose quickly, and the government virtually if not officially took over the national banking and financial system.

All through this book I have used anecdotes and case histories to illustrate my points. Although I have already alluded several times to the potential applications and benefits of futuring and visioning, I now turn to a focused treatment of them.

Anticipating Changing Customers, Markets, and Competitors

Countless consumer research studies have demonstrated that consumers can anticipate and articulate whether they would buy a new product or not when they see a fairly advanced prototype. They can respond to specific questions about specific prototype products that they can see and feel. Consumer research based on direct consumer feedback works well for the short term, but it is notoriously misleading for the long term. Consumers typically think in terms of cash flow and immediate purchasing needs. Most American households live from paycheck to paycheck and have more debt than cash. Consumers find it very difficult to imagine what they would or would not buy in the distant future (maybe no more than a year or so) when they cannot anticipate how much money they will have to spend or what they will need or want to buy, and under what circumstances, in the highly uncertain future.

Futuring can provide a surrogate for the voice of the customer in traditional consumer research. The surrogate consists of demographic, economic, and consumer behavior trends that consumers themselves may not be even conscious of. Futuring may also replace traditional market research by anticipating changes using the judgment of experts who understand consumers better than consumers understand themselves.

Trends in consumer behavior have been observed through the research techniques of ethnography and historical research. While each *individual* may be unique and deviate to one degree or another from an observed norm, *groups* of consumers display remarkably consistent patterns of behavior based upon such factors as age, life stage, gender, race, ethnic background and culture, education, work, income, wealth, etc.

Market segmentation and consumer trend forecasts have proven remarkably prescient. For example, traditional middle class Americans have recognizable social and personal values, such as the importance of education, hard work, pride in work, personal and work integrity, respect for debts, and honor. Only in rare moments will they confront any dissonance between their spiritual or ideological beliefs and their material ambitions. Values in the way they conduct themselves set the context for their perception of consumer value in the goods and services that they buy. They conduct their lives and their households in certain ways consistent with their level of education, income, and social status. Their buying habits are consistent with their life styles, which will vary according to their stage of life but will not vary greatly over larger patterns of generational cohort behavior (Boomers will be Boomers). As consumers, this group will look for bargains, just as everybody does, but they are typically willing to pay extra for certain brands in certain stores. They shop in places that make them comfortable. They show signs of brand loyalty to products over their entire lives. They will buy only certain brands and styles of clothes, shoes, jewelry, food, beverages, etc. They look for quality and superior value even if the price may be a little more than alternatives, which they deem as "unsuitable."

In formulating a 50-year forecast of American consumer value in personal transportation, for example, we identified three super-trends that shaped historical American consumer value and behavior:

1. Generational identity and behavior (such as the World War II generation, Boomers, Gen X'ers, and the Millennial Generation) along with behavioral patterns of life stage (child, student, young adult, middle-age, and elderly)

2. General economic conditions

3. National culture.

Using trend analysis going back to 1950 to look for long-term continuities and employing expert judgment to identify potential changes in them over time, we made extrapolations of consumer value from the year 2000 to 2050. The trends in consumer value are not necessarily linear – some strong trends may span decades with little change, while other trends may vary greatly, even to the point of extinction. These changes in long-term trends include shifts in emphasis and even redefinition according to the conditions of the times. Some values decline or even drop off the charts over time (for example high styling and super-power), while other aspects of value (Internet and GPS connectivity) emerge. Some values, such as fuel economy, even appear cyclical in the sense of bouncing back and forth between system extremes.

For example, a long-term changing trend in consumer value has been safety and security in personal vehicles. In the past, however, safety meant primarily the safety of the driver and passengers from death or injury due to accidents. With improving quality, accidents caused by vehicle failures became increasingly rare, while more accidents were caused by operator errors. Now vehicles are introducing features to mitigate, if not prevent, many operator errors. These might take the forms of technologies for enhanced vision at night and sensors to prevent drunks from being able to start their cars. Another aspect of value is that people want more personal security while driving – they want to avoid being robbed or attacked while in their cars. People want to protect their passengers, especially children, too. Hence, there is consumer value in vehicle alarm systems and voice-command calls for help, including voice activated mobile phones, automatic access to 911, and automated emergency messages dispatched to a centralized vehicle monitoring station. Such features gained in terms of their consumer value in the first decade of the 21st century. These are benefits that vehicle consumers want and may be willing to pay more for; when benefits are offered at "reasonable" prices, let alone for no additional cost, they give superior purchasing value to the consumer. In addition, technical improvements in the things that consumers like, such as integrated Internet and voice communications, will provide further value in the future than in the past.

Another changing value – one that has oscillated like a cycle – is fuel economy. When gasoline prices are relatively low, fuel economy is not a high priority with consumers. It was a non-issue before the so-called Energy Crisis of 1973. After years of perceived high gasoline prices, consumers shifted back to less economical vehicles – mini-vans and SUVs – when gas prices fell in the 1990s. As late as 1999, the pump price of a gallon of gasoline went as low as $0.999. In contrast, the price of gasoline skyrocketed in 2008, rising across the country to pump prices in excess of $4.00 per gallon. Suddenly, consumers began to cut back on their driving miles and shifted again to fuel economy models, including hybrids. Fuel economy is highly likely to remain a long-term consumer value for at least up to the year 2050, given expectations for declines in global oil production, increased demand for all kinds of fuels, likely restrictions on carbon emissions, and the phase of alternative fuel vehicles (operating on bio-fuels, batteries and plug-in electricity, and hydrogen for fuel cells).

Moving on to another case study, in 1987-1988 we generated scenarios for the Los Angeles Department of Water and Power (LADWP). The municipal electric utility routinely generated statistical projections of future electricity demand in the Los Angeles service area. Managers knew that their projections had not been particularly accurate in the past; they were also worried about qualitative issues that were not typically included in statistical modeling. Our scenario analysis for 20 years into the future (up to 2007, a date that has now come and gone) raised many interesting and sometimes controversial expectations. A strongly held belief existed that power demand rose linearly, along with population growth. The scenarios suggested, however, that electricity demand in the future may depend more upon technologies than population. The central question became whether the technologies of increasing demand (computers, consumer electronics, home entertainment, automated manufacturing, security systems, office lighting, electric heating and cooling, etc.) would or would not stimulate customer demand further than the technologies of energy efficiency and conservation might lower demand. During the 1990s, both the area population and electricity demand rose, with a substantial increase in the demand for power caused by the various technologies that we anticipated. In light of the scenarios, LADWP increased its electricity generating capacity in the 1990s in anticipation of rising consumer demand beyond what their econometric models were predicting. When the electricity shortage crisis hit California in 2000, LADWP was one of the few electric utilities that had sufficient capacity to meet demand. When San Francisco went dark, Los Angeles was aglow. As we reached the target year of 2007, we realized that we got several details wrong, but we got the fundamental story correct.[99]

Returning to the present, a major question about the future of American consumer value is whether and to what degree there may be structural and long-term changes caused by the Great Recession that began in 2007. We know that the Great Depression changed many consumer habits and preferences for at least two generations. My expectation is that the recession will have significant impacts on consumers, too. For example, when consumers cut back on several types of purchases (gasoline, eating out, clothes, etc.), retail merchants had to cut prices to attract shoppers. Consumers saw deep discounts in the stores at Christmas time in 2007 and again in 2009. Many retail prices remained heavily discounted all through 2009 and 2010. Shoppers are growing used to lower retail prices because of the recession, and they are highly likely to resist price increases in the future. We are seeing continued growth in the large, everyday low-price stores like Walmart. We are also seeing declines in traditional department stores and specialty shops with premium prices. Old department stores are now looking like mass retailers and are in competition with stores like Target and Kohl's if not Walmart. This could be a shifting long-term trend.

A related change may involve the use of credit cards for consumer purchases. Prior to the Great Recession, many people possessed several credit cards. They would max out (borrow to the limit set for the card) one and continue using others. Consumer credit was easy to get and to use. The idea was that consumers could afford anything they wanted to buy on credit as long as they could afford the monthly minimum required payment on their cards. Some worried not at all about the total debt. Then, with rising gasoline and food prices in 2008, some people could not pay the monthly minimum payments on all of their cards. In 2009, when banks themselves were in trouble, the credit card interest rates went up and card credit was tightened. Those people left with high balances in the face of rising interest rates on past as well as future purchases faced potentially severe financial distress, even bankruptcy.

The same was also true about monthly mortgage payments on homes. During much of the first decade of the 21st century, home buyers could get loans at rates below the prime interest rate that were adjustable over time. With low monthly

---

99   Stephen M. Millett, "Los Angeles 2007 Scenarios," *Economics and Policy Analysis Occasional Paper* Number 64. Columbus, Ohio: Battelle, July 1988; Stephen M. Millett, "Los Angeles 2007: Implications of a Scenario Analysis for Energy Forecasting," *Planning Review*, May/June 1992, pp. 38-39.

mortgage payments based on very low interest rates, some people could afford to buy large homes that they could not have afforded at higher interest rates (and higher monthly payments). Yet, with interest rates at historically low levels, house payments with variable interest rates had only one direction in which to change: up. Few people showed any signs of remembering the recession of the early 1980s, when variable home mortgage rates had doubled and even tripled over about two years. In addition, real estate prices were climbing, so that buyers expected to see the market value of their properties rise in just a few years. With higher market values in general, the theoretical equity in any particular house rose, too. The new paper equity created by inflated real estate prices allowed people to refinance their homes later, exchanging a variable for a fixed interest rate on their homes. In addition to home refinancing at fixed interest rates, the additional equity in homes allowed home owners to borrow against it for home improvements and consumer purchases like appliances, furniture, home accessories, cars, boats, vacations, and whatever else people wanted to buy. Life was wonderful – as long as interest rates remained low, credit was easy to get, and home values were rising.

Then the real estate market hit a peak in 2006 and started to decline. For those who believe in business cycles, a "perfect storm" of declining cycles converged. Certainly in American history there have been many periodic booms and busts of speculation and economic development. It is claimed that "ground zero" for the real estate bust was Orange County, California. It spread across the country, hitting some high inflation areas harder than other, more stable, parts of the US. With declining home values over time, equity declined rather than grew. With time, variable interest rates were readjusted upwards by mortgage lenders. Some people could not make their higher monthly mortgage payments as well as pay for higher priced fuel and food. Some people stopped making their monthly mortgage payments; many had to default on their mortgages, resulting in a severe contraction of national home credit. From the point of view of lenders, the home finance industry was over leveraged. New home construction began to decline. Purchases of major home appliances and furniture also declined. The crisis in consumer spending for homes, appliances, furniture, and other home accessories nearly destroyed the national real estate, banking, investing, construction, and durable goods industries over the bleak winter of 2008-2009.

Due to the global economic downturn that began with the financial crises in the US and Europe in 2008, there are several major changes that may occur in the future of consumer behavior over the next decade or longer, including:

- Fewer people will be able to afford to own their own homes, so they will go into apartments, causing demand for new multi-family residential construction.

- People who could not afford the "McMansions" of the early 2000s will seek less expensive homes, creating a new demand for more modest new homes and rehab of older structures. This trend will be reinforced by another trend: the downsizing of Boomers in their 60s and 70s looking for smaller, less expensive and more convenient new patio homes. These trends will likely lead to a new boom in residential construction, but of different kinds of structures than those that were built over the last decade or so.

- People will become increasingly concerned about rising energy prices, especially gasoline and electricity. They will buy vehicles that get better gas mileage. Responding to ever increasing electricity prices, they will seek energy-saving appliances and electronics and become more careful in their use of electric power. They may be willing to pay higher retail prices for items that show long-term cost-savings through energy conservation. When the electric utilities shift to variable time-of-day pricing and real-time meter readings, consumer behavior in the use of electricity could shift dramatically toward conservation.

- People who live in their own homes will attempt to do more home repairs and yard work themselves, avoiding the high costs of home contractors and lawn services. This may result in a higher demand for home tools and yard equipment if they are easy to use, convenient to store, and provide energy cost savings, too.

- There may be a new demand for home appliances and furniture, but at lower prices and longer payment periods to meet new residential needs for comfort and convenience. Consumers will expect lower prices and bargains that they got used to during the tough days of the Great Recession. They may also expect longer periods of time to pay off major purchases.

- People will not borrow nearly as much money from their home equity to finance consumer purchases and they will use credit cards more conservatively.

- More stores will likely offer their own credit cards with extended payment options to avoid the credit restrictions and higher interest rates of the nationally known credit cards.

- Retail stores will make more effort to know their customers personally in order to attract repeat business.

- Retailers will increasingly carry products with their own store brands on them at slightly lower prices than traditional brand name products.

These store brands will be of the same or nearly the same quality as the company branded products, and may in fact be manufactured by the same companies. This will strengthen store loyalty at the expense of brand loyalty.

- There will likely be a reemergence of consumer cooperatives and collective buying; it will not be exactly the same as the cooperatives of the 1930s, but there will be organizations for consumers to join to get group prices. This also means that more consumers may take a small ownership stake in their retailers.

- On-line shopping will grow further, due to lower prices offered to customers around the world, if transportation networks and fuel prices allow.

All of these trends indicate some structural, long-term changes in consumer behavior due to the Great Recession. These consumer changes may not be expressed currently if you were to ask consumers themselves, but they are logically consistent and probable changes because of several trends that can be identified and analyzed using the methods of futuring.

In a recent project, we addressed the future demand for a category of personal products. A few international companies with famous brand names dominated the market for this product category around the world. They had a history of innovative products, but they also were accustomed to competing with each other with premium products and premium prices in a growing global market. The scenarios of the future, however, suggested that there was a distinct possibility that the market dynamics and competitors of the past might change within just the next 10 years. In the scenario with the highest probability of occurring, there arose many new competitors in the form of local labels and store brands selling at pennies below the manufacturers' famous brands. In a recession scenario, companies would likely have to compete more intensely on price in addition to benefits, quality, and reputation, thereby potentially changing the competitive dynamics considerably.

Another uncertainty of the future is to what degree consumers will remain loyal to brands. For decades, consumers showed a distinct preference for certain brands and the quality associated with them. The new economics of recession, however, may tempt consumers to migrate to less expensive brands, especially store brands. We are currently seeing a proliferation of store and Internet branding that we have never witnessed before. Will the big brand manufacturers also produce the store brands, as some already do, or will they fight back with new product benefits or lower everyday prices? Stay tuned.

Just as you can use futuring to frame expectations for future customer demand and market dynamics, you can also use it to anticipate competitors. Futuring can be used for threat analysis as well as for opportunity identification. You need to know who your present competitors are and try to anticipate potentially new rivals in the future. In this respect, emerging technologies create new business opportunities for both you and your competitors.

Futuring may provide a competitive advantage over rivals in the market. In many lines of business and investing, timing is everything. You may make profits by buying certain stocks, securities, assets, and properties at low prices and then seeing them appreciate before others do. The first to market may secure the market. You may also anticipate changes and position yourself well for them when others are caught off guard. Like war, taking the initiative may mean winning the battle. As an historical example, during the American Civil War the Confederate general Nathan Bedford Forrest allegedly attributed his military successes to the principle that he reached a strategically vital position first with the most men. He anticipated successfully where the enemy was going and he reached the best place for his men to fight them, or deter them, before they did. His saying got rendered into the popular adage "Git thar fustest with the mostest." In business and investing today, this means anticipating the place and the time that will gain the ultimate competitive advantage.

Envisioning Potential New Products and Services

In conjunction with anticipating consumer behavior, markets, and competitors, futuring can also be used as a source of inspiration for potential new products and services.

Continuing the previous discussion from above, once you have bounded the uncertainties of trends and imagined disruptive events that may occur with future customers and markets, you can identify emerging business opportunities, including new products and services. The logic runs thus: if I anticipate x, y, and z conditions in the future and if I anticipate the behavior and values of consumers in the future, then there will be an opportunity for a, b, and c products and services.

A debate has raged for years over the sources of inspiration for new product development, especially at the "fuzzy front end." Obviously, one source of inspiration would be customers themselves, if only they had a clue of where they were going and what they would want in the future. As I have mentioned several times before, customers typically do not have an inkling of what they will buy beyond the present and very near term future. This fact, however, does not preclude research that directly asks customers what they want in the future. This can be done through consumer interviews, surveys, and focus groups. You can ask – just be skeptical about short-sighted answers.

You can also ask indirect questions, such as "What aspects of current products displease you?", "If it were possible, what would be the characteristics of a perfect product or service?" The answers to these questions about dissatisfaction with current products and services might provide foresight into new products and services that address the issue of current customer unhappiness.

Another approach to identify unmet consumer demand and potential future products and services is observing consumer behavior. Ethnography – a discipline of observation that borrowed liberally from anthropology– became very popular with European and American consumer product companies in the 1990s, although it had been used extensively by Japanese companies studying American consumer behavior in the 1950s. The theory rests upon trend momentum and extrapolation. It holds that the successful products and services of the future will emerge because they meet the patterns of consumer behavior in the past and present. Knowing how customers shop and how they use products and services in their own environments (as opposed to a corporate R&D laboratory) provides clues to long-term consumer behavior and to the products and services that they will likely embrace in the future.

In the 1980s, with the emergence of Japanese competitive advantages over traditional American companies even in the American market, some business analysts accused the Japanese of merely copying and providing low-cost alternatives to products already proven to be successful by American companies. The analysts dismissed the creative capability of the Japanese (and of other emerging economies in Asia, such as the Koreans, Chinese, et al.) to visualize and develop new products. The Asian corporations, obviously, have learned a great deal about R&D and the methods of new product development and marketing. They can be just as creative and inventive as any companies anywhere in the world.

The Japanese approach to new product development in general is to analyze current products and services, current technologies, and current consumer behavior to establish a baseline. They explore how consumers behave in certain situations and what they want through examining their actions. They seek to understand how consumers use products and for what purposes. What benefits do consumers expect and at what prices? The Japanese also imagine, using techniques like group creativity and quality circles, what the "perfect" product might be in the future, maybe as long as 50 or 100 years away, as a baseline for the future. They then triangulate consumer wants, technologies, and continuous product improvement. They plan to close the gap between today and the future horizon by incremental technology advances and product enhancements. They develop a very clear idea of how one product leads to a better product that will sequentially improve consumer value and therefore market appeal.

I was doing a scenarios project on a major food category for a large, international corporation in Europe in the mid-1990s. I saw that the R&D organization, separate from the marketing department, was conducting its own ethnographical study to gain insights into new and improved products from the behavior of consumers. They invited "typical" homemakers to come into the corporate laboratory kitchens and prepare meals using existing and prototype new food products. The laboratory set up the kitchens according to their own specifications. Some researcher, however, asked the question whether consumers behaved the same way in their own kitchens as they did in the corporate laboratory kitchens. They decided to observe the same homemakers in their own kitchens, and the researchers were shocked to discover that the homemakers behaved differently than they did in the laboratory kitchens. New insights were gained as inputs to the development of both products and their packaging as a result of observing the "real" behavior of kitchen natives. The same R&D organization learned that ethnography complemented well the foresights being gained through futuring processes, namely: multiple trends analysis; studying the interrelationships among trends by cross-impact analysis; and formulating alternative futures generated by analytical scenarios, including simulations of potential corporate strategies to achieve desired futures.

Futuring is another source of inspiration for new product development. It can bound the uncertainties of the future and provide foresights into future consumer behavior based on trends in aging, diversity, mobility, education, shopping patterns, affordability, and consumer value propositions. Futuring is a way to anticipate the voice of the customer, or, said another way, of discovering the unarticulated voice of the customer.

It is unlikely that futuring will ever precisely predict future consumer behavior and value, but it can frame both realistic and imaginative expectations when direct consumer research reveals little or nothing. Its best application is long-term forecasting at the early stages of new product development and R&D. As the proto-product gets closer to market launch, you must switch over to traditional, short-term consumer and market research methods.

Thought Leadership

Having generated a forecast for several purposes within the company or organization, you can also use the forecast for thought leadership in the external market. The forecast becomes a piece of strategic conversation with customers and constituents. Futuring can be used for substantive, informative marketing and client relationship-building. You can frame expectations for clients and explain how you will be a part of their future. One aspect of this is the backward integration of co-product development with customers to co-strategic planning back to co-futuring.

In 1995 we began the so-called "top 10" technology forecasts at Battelle. We generated these lists using the expert judgment of dozens of Battelle scientists and engineers at the Columbus laboratories and with the national laboratories that Battelle managed for the US Department of Energy. We performed at least one top 10 list each year on a different topic from 1995 to 2005. Given a topic question, the experts generated ideas and voted on them to give us a rank order. The first one was called Strategic Technologies 2005. "Strategic technologies" meant those technologies that would lead to products and services that in general would be commercial successes and dominate markets for years to come. This list, by way of illustration, contained the following items:

1. Human genome identification and mapping

2. Super materials (anticipating nanotechnologies)

3. Compact, long-lasting, and portable energy (anticipating advanced batteries and fuel cells)

4. Digital high definition TV

5. Electronic miniaturization for personal use (anticipating ubiquitous cell phones, laptops, and hand-held devices like Blackberries)

6. Cost-effective, automated, "smart" systems in manufacturing

7. Anti-aging products

8. Pinpoint medical treatments (anticipating laser surgery and highly targeted drug treatments)

9. Hybrid fuel vehicles

10. Edutainment (anticipating the convergence of entertainment technologies into education).

Looking back on this list, the Battelle experts proved to be overly optimistic about the rate of technological and market progress in some areas, but surprisingly prescient of developments that they were aware of but most people were not, such as electronic miniaturization, manufacturing "smart" systems, pinpoint medical treatments, and hybrid fuel vehicles (which very few consumers knew about). The accuracy of the forecast was not the central issue; the central issue was that Battelle knew R&D and was willing to exercise thought leadership about future technology directions. Battelle had a point of view that it was willing to share, and in sharing took a little step toward making those expectations for the future happen. We offered the lists to the media, which gave us global news coverage at no cost to Battelle. We invited people to talk with us if they had different points of view, and we had many inquiries and conversations with companies and government agencies, some leading directly to business relationships with Battelle.[100]

I mentioned above that customers typically cannot visualize, let alone articulate, what they want and what they are likely to buy in the middle to long term future. For targeted customers, especially large commercial and industrial customers, you can use futuring as a tool of strategic conversation with those customers. This is called "concurrent futuring" as a precursor to "concurrent planning," the step that comes before "concurrent new product development" or "concurrent engineering."

Is it possible that a forecast can change the very future that it is forecasting? It certainly is. A forecast might be very persuasive and convince audiences to do something that the forecast shows will be desirable or not do something that will likely end in disaster. Forecasts should give people guidance for the future. Plans, too, can have a powerful influence on people's expectations and behavior toward achieving goals. Such is the power of the self-fulfilling prophecy.

Teaching the Learning Organization and Changing Corporate Culture

The concept of the learning organization has been much heralded, but often misinterpreted, since the publication in 1990 of Peter Senge's bestselling book *The Fifth Discipline*. Among many methods, Senge was particularly enamored with the use of scenarios, largely based on Arie de Geus' reported experiences at Shell, to open people's mental models up to new possibilities. Senge astutely observed that managers as well as employees get locked into certain ways of thinking based on corporate culture, past success, and day-to-day routines. As

---

100 www.battelle.org/SPOTLIGHT/tech_forecast/index.aspx

long as business continues to thrive and customers and market conditions do not substantively change, what worked in the past will more than likely work in the future. But enterprises do not continuously thrive and customers and market conditions do substantively change over time, and any company has to recognize change and adjust to it or risk going out of business. Successful companies can fall into the traps of overconfidence and arrogance and totally miss changes in their business environments. To say it another way, a company or organization has to be open to learning in order to adapt to the realities of external change.

Senge asserted that the successful organization of the future would be a learning organization about the future. He defined "the learning organization" as the one that is "continually expanding its capacity to create its future." "Adaptive learning," he argued, is required to get through the tough moments, but "generative learning," or the ability to anticipate the future and create ways to realize emerging opportunities, was required for sustainable success over the long run.[101]

Senge also discussed the importance of team-building and the sharing of common values and a vision of the future. Where does this shared business vision come from? It may come from the visionary leader. It may come directly from customers, if they have a vision for themselves. More likely, a vision will emerge from the employees when they have opportunities to think about the future and their roles in it. The Shell method of scenario generation has proven to excel at all levels of an organization in getting people together to collectively generate alternative futures. The early Shell experience with scenarios was directed at remolding the strategic thinking of executives; the method applies equally well with the strategic thinking of middle managers and employees. My experience has been that the Shell intuitive scenario method may not even be prescient let alone predictive of the future, but it is usually successful in building team camaraderie and encouraging individuals to share with each other their expectations for the future.

In 2006, I conducted a futuring exercise with the State Board of Education in Ohio, of which I was a member, and the senior management of the Ohio Department of Education. The exercise provides a good example of the benefits that can be achieved by changing long-term culture. We generated four alternative scenarios for education in Ohio by the year 2016. Using the intuitive scenario method made popular by Shell, the group decided to build their scenario structures upon the globalization of the Ohio economy and educational achievement. The group broke into four sub-groups, each of which fleshed out a scenario. The four resulting scenarios were as follows:

---

101 Senge, *The Fifth Discipline*, pp. 5, 167-170, 174, and 219. Also see Arie P. de Geus, "Planning as Learning," *Harvard Business Review*, Vol. 88, No. 2, March-April 1988, pp. 70-74.

- High globalization of the Ohio economy and low expectations for educational achievement ("Ohio: The World Passes Us By").

- High globalization of the Ohio economy and high expectations for educational achievement ("Ohio: The Center of It All").

- Low globalization of the Ohio economy and low expectations for educational achievement ("Ohio: The Armpit of It All").

- Low globalization of the Ohio economy and high expectations for educational achievement ("Ohio: Independent and Happy").

Having generated these four scenarios, the entire group generated a list of what they thought were the most important implications of all four scenarios for the future of public education in Ohio and the potential role of the State Board of Education and the Ohio Department of Education. The most profound implications included:

1. While the globalization and growth of the Ohio economy may generate more revenues for public education, the quality of public education can also attract companies from out of state (and even from other countries) and home-grown entrepreneurs and start-up enterprises. Public education cannot sit still and wait for the globalization and the economic growth of Ohio, but rather must be more proactive in trying to create it.

2. We need to review our first generation of education standards and benchmark them against the most effective public education systems around the world.

3. We need to reach out to the business and industrial sectors of society to learn more about what they need in terms of educated employees and managers of the future. We need to identify more specifically how public education can be leveraged for economic growth in addition to educating children to be good citizens and pursue life-long learning.

The conventional wisdom had been that economic growth would generate the tax revenues required to invest in new resources and so to achieve uniformly high educational achievement across the state. It was widely believed in the existing state government culture that no significant improvements could be made in public education without more money. However, having thought about the scenarios and their implications, a new realization emerged: educational achievement could stimulate economic growth by attracting new industries and incubating new enterprises in Ohio. We could be more proactive in leveraging public education for economic growth and less reactive to the economy producing the revenues that we thought were necessary to advance our agenda. We had to move on with our educational goals and not wait for economic growth. In addition, we had to find ways to cut operational costs and overhead in order to free up money for new programs. We had to explore new ways of providing quality educational services at less, not more, cost. We did not foresee that the Great Recession was coming, but we moved ahead with our agenda and so, fortunately enough, were able to anticipate it.[102]

Risk Management

The traditional methods of risk management have involved the tools of financial modeling and projection. There are many tools to calculate hypothetical returns on assets, returns on investments, product development and product costs, future sales, etc. Some of these models are remarkably accurate in their quantified predictions – but under very specific conditions. In the insurance business, for example, actuarial tables and statistical forecasts based on accident data can be very reliable for determining future pay-outs to insured customers and future profits for the insurers. But one challenge that remains for insurance companies is the variability of the weather, especially storms and disasters like severe winds, rains, floods, tornadoes, and hurricanes. The insurance business, in other words, is well prepared to deal with the typical accidents and small disasters of everyday life, but poorly prepared for the low probability but high risk disasters like a Hurricane Andrew or Katrina.

Futuring provides a way to broaden traditional risk management methods to include disruptive events and alternative futures. It elevates risk management to uncertainty management. All types of companies do risk management of one sort or another, as all enterprises have risks of one kind or another. Investment companies (banks, credit unions, credit card companies, stock brokers, and insurance companies, to name a few) deal specifically in risk, and hence have some of the most sophisticated trend analysis and pattern recognition programs. They monitor customer behavior and market trends very carefully. They also use expert judgment to anticipate changes in trends and potential disruptive events. The expert judgment typically comes from successful executives and high-priced industry consultants. The financial industry is learning to expand expert judgment methods to include increasingly broader types of experts in order to open up the perspective on the future with different concerns, information, and even biases. The same companies are adopting scenario analysis to assess future risks under different possible futures, ranging from the continuity of trends to some real wild cards. If new types of risks can be imagined, then they can be managed.

---

102 Stephen M. Millett, "Public Education in the New Global Economy 2006-2016," *Futures Research Quarterly*, Volume 23, Number 4, Winter 2007. pp. 57-81

Strategic Planning

Planning is the junction of futuring and visioning. In the past, too much strategic planning was not very strategic, because it failed to capture external customer and marketplace trends and it leaped to a vision unbounded by realities. The planning was too optimistic – it was full of wishful thinking. A strong strategic plan contains an analysis of the evolving external environment and presents a vision soundly grounded in opportunities along with the alignment of corporate culture, strategic assets and technologies, and resources to execute the vision.

Plans are examples of self-fulfilling prophecies, some of which work out as intended while others do not. Plans increase the probability that a desired outcome will actually occur because we ourselves lay out the path to achieving that which we choose to achieve. To be successful, plans must be well thought out with courage and determination and with the necessary cooperation of others and sufficient resources. To the extent that all important trends and factors, both external and internal, have been considered, expectations have been well considered, and no disruptive events occur, plans can be implemented up to 100%. Plans fail when important trends and factors have not been considered, goals and expectations have not been well considered, and disruptive events, especially black swans and "wild cards," occur to throw our plans off track.

You should never assume that plans will work out exactly as designed without some later adjustments. It is best to expect that something will go wrong. You may not know what exactly will go wrong, but you know that probably something will. Every "Plan A" should have a backup "Plan B." We use those expressions in our everyday language, so the concept is hardly novel. Yet so many corporate and organizational plans, especially the big plans, fail to anticipate problems and adjust accordingly. Every plan should have milestones that are periodically reviewed against new information gathered from the continuous monitoring of trends and events. Every plan should have contingencies so that adjustments to changing circumstances can be anticipated and implemented when necessary. This is a far more effective way of managing than making snap decisions in the heat of an unexpected business crisis.

While every level should have its own plans, too many so-called "strategic" plans are in reality operational in character. This is because budgeting is confused with planning. Budgets tend to be very operational and short-term, such as one or two years. Strategic plans should be conceptual with an emphasis on goals and strategies rather than an emphasis on operational mechanics. They should also be more long-term than budgets. Typical strategic plans should have time horizons of five or ten years into the future. The Japanese may have 50 year plans, but 10 years is plenty long enough for most American corporations and institutions.

Futuring and visioning make "strategic" plans strategic. They provide the "big picture" and the long-term perspective. Futuring addresses the most important external trends and provides well considered expectations (forecasts) for them. Visioning, conversely, deals with the most important internal trends and provides the context for capabilities and operations. Strategic plans provide the documentation for both processes in an integrated and coherent manner.

Visionary Leadership

Finally, arguably the most important application and benefit of futuring and visioning is the extent to which you may develop into a visionary leader beyond a competent manager. It's that extra something that makes you shine above the rest and gives you the boost to higher levels of responsibility. You can use trend analysis, the judgments of many experts, and scenarios to frame your own expectations for the future of your business or operation. You can use this information to visualize what is possible (more likely than not) given alternative sets of conditions. Are the conditions for the success of your business likely and what can you do now to make such a good future happen? If you can visualize an end result and how to get there and if you can convince others, both your superiors and your subordinates, of the merits of your vision, then you can inspire them to help you achieve your goals.

In conclusion, the successful manager of the future will be better prepared to think in the long term and strategically, in addition to (not in place of) acting operationally in performing the short-term work of the enterprise. Different benefits of futuring and visioning will occur due to specific circumstances, but the practice of thinking like a futurist and leading like a visionary will transcend the particulars of the moment and accrue to the success of life-long careers in management.

Chapter 9. Managing Expectations

According to the epic poem *Aeneid* by the Roman poet Virgil and other classic texts, the ancient Greeks finally captured the great walled city of Troy through a very clever ruse devised by the hero Odysseus (Ulysses). After allegedly investing 10 years in the war against Troy, in what is now estimated to have been in the year 1260 BCE, the Greeks were about to give up and return home. Odysseus, however, came up with a last-minute, desperate plan: build a monumental wooden horse as though it were a peace offering to the Trojans. It would be as large as a house on stilts. The Greeks would clear their camps and remove their ships. According to the plan, the Trojans would accept the trophy of war, which subsequently would prove to be the ruin of Troy.

This, of course, is a very old story, possibly true. It certainly has provided material for a lot of great literature over many centuries. But let's look at it from a different perspective – as a very dramatic example of managing expectations.

Odysseus' plan was based on his expectation that the Trojans would see the wooden horse and the collateral evidence of Greek withdrawal and conclude that the war was over. The Trojans would have expectations based largely on their own wishful thinking that would lead them to accept the Greek deceit at face value. Odysseus expected the Trojans to take the wooden horse inside the walled city and make it the center of a great victory celebration. Inside the hollow horse, however, there were some 40 Greek soldiers, who would emerge from it in the dead of night and who would open the gates of the city to a Greek army that was waiting in hiding.

The Greek plan worked like a charm. The so-called Trojan horse was left on the abandoned beaches of the former Greek war camp. All of their men and ships had disappeared. They left one man behind who said that he had been abandoned. He told the amazed Trojans that the Greeks had returned home and left the wooden statue of a horse as a symbol of respect for the Trojans. The Trojans wanted to believe what they were told and what they saw. Their expectations were that they would not have to fight the Greeks again anytime soon and that the Greek siege of the city had failed. They had the horse in their control, but they declined to probe the horse or otherwise gather any more information about it. Instead, they took the horse into the city and made it the center of a great victory celebration, just as Odysseus had intended.

Two Trojans, however, protested the presence of the horse within the city. One was a priest who warned the Trojans, according to the story, "Beware of Greeks bearing gifts." The other was Cassandra, the daughter of King Priam of the

Trojans and the city's soothsayer. She predicted that the horse would be the ruin of Troy. But both of them were dismissed as alarmist and for not appreciating the great tribute that the Trojans had received. At this point, the Trojan leaders would have been smart to have tempered their exaggerated expectations with a lot of healthy skepticism.

The Greek plan worked because the Trojans acted exactly as the Greeks anticipated that they would. The Greek soldiers inside the horse came out without being detected and opened the gates of the city. The waiting Greek army swung into action. The Trojans responded with too little, too late. They were caught totally by surprise and were unprepared to deal with the unexpected Greek soldiers. The Greeks massacred the Trojan people and razed the city so thoroughly that its ruins would remain only in legends for some 3,000 years.[103]

This book has been about how to form well considered expectations and how to manage the future. I retell this old story of the Trojan horse to contrast the Greeks' expectations for the future with those of the Trojans. The Trojans misunderstood the intentions of the Greeks, while the Greeks had a plan well thought out and executed. Today, we are not likely to encounter any situation nearly as dramatic as the Trojan War and the only Trojan horses that we may encounter will be on our laptops, but we can take a lot from the historical point that well considered expectations may lead to desired results while erroneous and exaggerated expectations may lead to disaster.

In the context of early 21st century life, I have offered you many observations on how to anticipate and manage the future. I have based them on my experiences as both a consulting futurist and a manager, and I have related them back to basic theories about the physical nature of time and the future. I have tried to blend philosophy, theories, and practices, because I think understanding the underlying premises of a forecast or plan is extremely important to its prescience and usefulness. My aspiration is to improve the futuring as well as the planning skills of young managers, and people in general, and to encourage them to strive for well considered expectations for the future upon which they can make sound long-term decisions. To conclude this book, I would like to comment more specifically on the nature of expectations themselves. I want to share with you some highly subjective observations and suggestions that are more in the realm of attitudes and emotions than intellect and skills.

---

103 The original epic of the Trojan War was told by the ancient Greek bard Homer in the *Iliad*, which is usually dated to the 8th century BCE. The story of the Trojan horse appears in Virgil's *Aeneid*, which was completed in about 19 BCE, and many other lesser known works from ancient Greece and Rome. For a modern history, see Michael Wood, *In Search of the Trojan War* (Berkeley, CA: The University of California Press, 1998), especially pp. 15, 24-26, 230-231, and 252-253.

Your Expectations for Your Business

The principal focus of this book has been on anticipating the future of your organization, whether "organization" means a for-profit business, a non-profit organization, an institution (such as a school, university, hospital, etc.), or a government department or agency. The management challenges are very similar in all cases: you have to do your day-to-day work, meet your goals, take responsibility for others in addition to yourself, and plan for the future. You need to do more than just *plan* for the future – you need to *manage* the future in order to improve the odds of achieving desired success.

This book has given you much advice on how to formulate well considered expectations for the future. In everyday life, we all have expectations, but many of them are unrealistic and based on little more than our own wishful thinking. Now, having read this book, you know better. You are now sensitive to the trends around you and how to recognize both continuity and change.

Much of the rigor of futuring and visioning may seem to demand too much of your time and resources. Like so many other skills that we learn, futuring and visioning at first seem overwhelming, but with repeated practice we become more comfortable and adept at doing them. We learn to automate processes in our own minds. The objective is not just to consistently form well considered expectations for the future, but also to form them quickly based on learned patterns and intuitive algorithms. We would like to do futuring and visioning in our minds as close to real-time as possible.

The rational benefit of futuring and visioning is to logically and effectively prepare for the future. There are emotional benefits, too. A plan gives you confidence and courage. You think in the present that you know what you need to do and how to do it. You have confidence that you can achieve goals. Planning also gives meaningfulness to your day-to-day work – you feel encouraged that you are "moving in the right direction." You have a sense of continuity and security. You feel as though you are managing your own fate, that you will be more proactive and less reactive to the inherent uncertainties of the future.

Sometimes your expectations and plans will work out just as, or pretty nearly as, you thought that they would (should). Of course, you cannot anticipate everything, so there will always be an element of luck in achieving your objectives as well as good planning and execution. Through your planning and dedication to its implementation, you are well prepared to take good advantage of luck.

But a word of caution: you should never allow yourself to be held hostage by your expectations, even when they have been well considered. You cannot experience the future until it occurs. You can anticipate it through the theory of predictability, but you cannot know it through your physical senses, as you feel heat or see blue. You form expectations all the time, but so many of them, at least with hindsight, seem short-sighted, illogical, even self-centered. Most of us need to improve our skills in managing exaggerated expectations. We naturally want the future to be good to us, but we are not always ready to have to make it good for ourselves. The trick is to craft informed, logical, and well considered expectations for the future and then go out and try to make those expectations come true, to the extent that you can control resources and circumstances. Expectations for the future are always works in progress and subject to updates and revisions. When things do not happen as you expected, then you have to be flexible enough to adapt new approaches to achieving your goals according to changing circumstances.

When you draw up plans according to your well-considered expectations for external trends and internal goals and resources, you must always remember that you are pursuing actions that are always vulnerable to changes, often totally beyond your ability to control. There are always other people pursuing their own objectives in their own ways that may interfere, if not cancel out, your own. In addition, the physical environment in which you live here on earth – what we call "nature" – has its own ways regardless of the affairs of people. That is why you must always have alternative plans in mind. You may not be able to anticipate specific changes, but you can anticipate that some unknown changes may occur before you reach your destination. You need to stay true to your mission and values, but you have to remain flexible over the ways in which you pursue them.

It is relatively easy to prepare logically and emotionally for "good" outcomes in the future, but it is typically very hard to accept the possibility of "bad" things happening. For example, we think that there is a possibility that we could be in a serious automobile accident, and we have some insurance to buffer that potential disaster, but we too frequently dismiss the idea that it will happen. We may know that we are in danger of losing our job, but we wish to think that the loss of jobs will happen to others rather than to ourselves. Even if we were to have a 90% *a priori* probability based on good information that we were about to lose our job, we might still cling to the hope of the 10% rather than do careful planning for the 90% eventuality. It takes a lot of discipline to form well considered expectations for things that we emotionally categorize as catastrophes.

Even well considered expectations should not be assumed to have a 100% probability of occurrence. There are laws of nature, which, given specific frames of reference (boundary conditions), produce results that are virtually 100% certain. We have yet to discover any corresponding laws of history or of human nature that give us anywhere near 100% predictability for the future. Healthy skepticism, therefore, helps us prepare emotionally for surprises. Just thinking about potential changes and their possible consequences helps us prepare for them and react more quickly and cleverly if we have to face them.

The bane of futuring is anticipating the unthinkable. Try as we may, we cannot anticipate every action or accident that might occur in the future. We tend to think of logical outcomes and ignore those things which in our own minds are "unthinkable," both materially and emotionally. We can form well considered expectations for the future and we can draw up and execute plans that really work as long as all things play out according to our thinking. But we are continuously surprised by events that seem very logical in 20/20 hindsight but appeared totally impossible in foresight. Therefore, we can think with intelligence and act rationally, but we also need to prepare ourselves for having to deal perhaps with random craziness, of which this world appears to have an abundance.

Futuring, to be honest, will never assure success with 100% certainty. You can have prescient expectations and do all the right things and still not achieve your goals. But futuring will improve the chances that expectations and goals for the future will enjoy a happy union, producing plans and actions that you can believe in. At a minimum, well considered expectations for the future should greatly reduce, if not eliminate, the chances that foolish moves will lead to self-fulfilling disasters. Futuring will also provide a basis for learning as life happens so that you can react smartly to the opportunities that unexpectedly emerge.

This goes for planning, too.

There are penalties, however, as well as benefits to expectations. We cannot predict the future in detail or with complete certainty, so our expectations can only be hypotheses yet to be validated or refuted. In addition, expectations form shifting frames of reference for "normal." We react to events according to expectations, even when such events might be considerably off the mark of what we thought was going to be "normal." For example, investors might expect the unemployment rate to be 9.2%, but because it gets reported as 9.5% such investors think that the economy is actually getting worse than expected, and so they sell off securities, making the Wall Street stock market prices go down. The Dow Jones industrial average on a day-to-day basis is highly influenced by people's expectations of the future, even for the next day let alone the next year. If economic metrics meet expectations, stock prices may not go up because expectations were met, so no big deal, but when they exceed expectations, then stock prices go up because investors want to take advantage of a good situation. The opposite occurs, too. It's not so much the absolute levels met, but the metrics relative to the expectations that really matter in the market.

There can be a certain tyranny to expectations that we need to resist. We react in response to how we think the world is going according to our own expectations. Our expectations do not by themselves predestine the future, but our actions based on our expectations can influence the course of events as the future is being made.

We can become the victims of our own high expectations. We must remind ourselves that for all great expectations there must also be high preparation and high support. Many times, despite our own plans and actions, there are not the resources and allies that are required for success. High expectations can lead to big disappointments, so we need to continuously strive toward expectations that are balanced with our resources. We need our psychological state of mind to allow us to keep on trying even in the face of failure.

The key point to be made here is that on the whole you are better served by well considered expectations as opposed to relying on reactive spontaneity, even though the most well considered expectations can mislead you. The best that you can do on a sustained basis is to optimize the effects of good luck and minimize the consequences of bad luck through the discipline of expectations. In many cases, the best result that well considered expectations can offer is the prevention of serious mistakes that might otherwise have occurred without the foresight of well considered expectations.

We delude ourselves when we have expectations that rely heavily upon favorable circumstances over which we have little or no control. When things do work out well, we call it "luck." But to make our own best future come to pass, we have to have resources, determination, and a certain control over circumstances in addition to random good fortune.

In your thinking about the future of your business, or even of your life in general, it may help you to consider a matrix of environments and the degree of control that you have in them. One such visualization is Figure 9.1 below. It's a highly simplified model of reality, of course. The traditional x axis represents the environment, ranging, from left to right, from your internal to various external environments. For our purposes here, the "internal environment" is your company, organization, institution, or agency. In a private sense, it might also be your home, household, family, or inner self. The y axis is your degree of control over things, ranging from high at the bottom to low at the top of the axis.

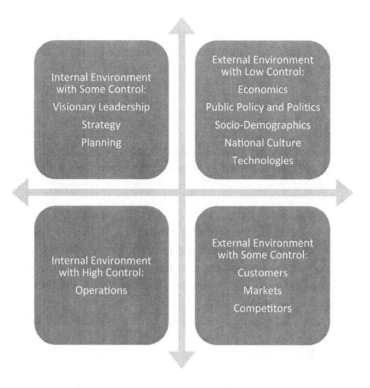

Figure 9.1: Control and Environments

The lower left quadrant of the matrix is the set of conditions in which you have a high degree of control over your internal environment. I characterize this area as "operations." It's your day-to-day work and your corporate culture (or personality). This is largely the area in which predictability is most possible because of the self-fulfilling prophecy – you have extensive information, intentions, and resources. The situation may also be predictable as a (quasi-) closed system with a fixed set of variables. Here your expectations should be highly prescient, as your expectations reflect your intentions and capabilities.

But, moving to the right on the *x* axis, your degree of control and the amount of information with which to form well considered expectations decrease as you move farther into external environments, where you have to deal with other people and macroscopic trends. The system becomes more open and the number of variables with which you have to deal grows beyond a perceived fixed set.

In the lower right quadrant, you encounter your customers (clients, consumers, constituents, patients, service recipients, etc.). You offer them products and services and you deal with them regularly. You know their patterns of behavior well from past experience and you have some influence over them. There are degrees of predictability here, although certainly not 100% as customers and markets can change. There is predictability in trend momentum, along with consistent cause-and-effect relationships, and at least partial, if not complete, knowledge of customers' intentions. You may have confidence in your dealings with customers and market conditions, but you should never allow yourself to fall into the trap of over-confidence and self-delusion. Customers and markets may surprise you someday by questioning your offerings and shifting to your competitors.

As an analogy for competition, even war, the lower-right corner is where you would encounter your opponents. In your engagement with them, you have some control and information, but what you do is very much affected by what others do, too. In the upper right hand corner, you have very little control over macro-trends or the environment of your enemy, but you can have information about them that will help you overcome their resistance to your achieving your objectives.

In the upper right quadrant, you move into extended external environments that are largely, although maybe not entirely, beyond your control. This is the realm of macro-trends in national and global economics, public sector policies (including laws and regulations as well as preferences) and politics, national and global socio-demographics, national and regional cultures, and ever-changing technologies. Unless you enjoy extraordinary power, you will most likely have very little control over these trends. In addition, your information about these macro-trends may be largely incomplete, even wrong. You do not know much about the intentions of others. They may behave with apparent randomness. Their motivations and actions may make good sense to them, just not to you. In such remote environments, you may think of yourself as helpless, as a victim of circumstances beyond your reach. Ignorance colors your expectations for the future and you allow wishful thinking to fill the void of well considered expectations. Nonetheless, you have to think about macro-trends to have any chance at all of anticipating, let alone preparing for, possible outcomes.

Because of the uncertainties of the upper right quadrant, we have to track trends, gather the best available information, and generate forecasts. They are never definitive. They are expectations and working hypotheses. Your thinking about the future, however, can improve if you engage in the theories and best practices explored in this book.

Finally, in the upper left hand quadrant you have the realm of visionary leadership, strategy development, and planning. Your thinking about the macro-trends of the upper right quadrant will feed into your thinking in the upper left quadrant. You have less control here than in operations because you are still in the process of thinking rather than doing, and there is always a gap between the two. This is the challenge of what I have called operationalizing strategic thinking.

Information is a very important aspect of this matrix. When you are in control of a situation, you think you may have access to complete, accurate, and timely information. This should be true in most cases, as personal involvement brings intimate familiarity. But this is not always the case, as your subordinates may not be telling you everything that they know. As you go out to the right of the matrix into environments increasingly out of your control, your need for information increases in importance. In business, this is the need to know your customers, their immediate circumstances, and your competition. Information about them is what gives you any control that you can exercise over them. In military terms, information is called "intelligence." In the upper right of the matrix, you may have little or no control over circumstances, but you need extensive information, which provides warnings of potential threats and opportunities for your business. Gaining accurate and timely information, or what the intelligence community calls "anticipatory, actionable intelligence," is the next best thing to having control.

You may think of futuring and visioning as managing the future. More literally, they are aspects of managing expectations for the future – your expectations for the business, your expectations for others, your expectations for yourself, and others' expectations for you. Your performance evaluation and the progress of your career will depend greatly on how your work measures up, not just according to absolute standards, but to the relative expectations for you over time. In an abstract sense, as a manager working for others, you are somewhat like a commodity, traded in a big market of human talent rather than stocks and bonds.

Your Expectations for Others

In addition to your expectations for your business, you may have expectations for other people. In the business or public life context, as a manager who is responsible for achieving goals with other people, you come to expect things of colleagues, associates, bosses, and employees. Many managers think that other people want the same things that they want. Unfortunately, this is not always true. You may expect your colleagues and associates to work well and effectively with you. You may expect them to act like friends. In many situations, they will. But they have their own personalities and careers, too. They may see you as a potential threat to their personal success. You should always treat your colleagues as though they were friends, but they are business friends, not necessarily personal friends. Be careful. Do not always expect that they will support you in the ways that you wish rather than relative to their own wishes.

You may expect your bosses to be supportive of your work. You may think that they want you to succeed, because your success feeds into their success. Maybe yes, maybe no. Bosses have their own agendas, too, and they may not share information with you about senior corporate politics. You may think that when you get into trouble, and all middle managers have troubles from time to time, your boss will bail you out. Many times they will, but you could just be the future victim of a reorganization or "personnel adjustments" and discover that you are no longer a manager. Treat your boss, of course, with respect, but always with an appropriate distance according to corporate rank, just like the military. Ask for help when you need it, but do not ask for help when you can solve a problem yourself.

I recall an incident when I was a junior officer in the US Air Force. I had personality problems with another officer and I felt that I was not getting the cooperation from him that I expected. I went to our commanding officer, a colonel. I explained the problem to him and inquired how he was going to deal with my problem. He just looked at me with an odd expression, like I had asked him a really stupid question. He said to me something to this effect: Captain, you are confused. I am not here to solve your problems – you are here to solve mine. I sure got put in my place. But the lesson was a good one for my future career in business: your responsibility is to solve the problems of your boss (and your customers) rather than expecting that they will solve your problems.

You very likely have expectations for the people who report to you. You expect them to do their jobs correctly. Of course, they have to know what their jobs are, and training is a huge part of managing employees. So is motivation. Here is the value of visionary leadership. Many of your employees are focused on the present: do a day's work at a time. They get tired and bored, but they need the job and its pay. They have no idea what may be coming in the future. Their only expectation is to come to work tomorrow. So you as their manager have to have the long-term vision and generate excitement about the prospects in the future. You have to talk with your employees and tell them how important they and their jobs are to the enterprise and how they can contribute to even better times in the future. You have to inspire them to want to go above and beyond the norm of the day. They want to work toward better things in the future, too, just like you, but you have to provide the vision and the enthusiasm. And, of course, the enthusiasm for the future begins with you. You set the example as well as the tone for the future.

As mentioned above, your expectations for others are the most uncertain. They may be somewhat predictable from past patterns of behavior, but they can always surprise you. This is precisely where plans, simulations and games most often go wrong. You may have very well-thought-through plans that nevertheless go wrong because others did not do what they were supposed to do. They forgot or they were sick or they just ignored you. Or you count on others, such as competitors, to respond in certain ways and then they don't. They fool you because of your ignorance of their intentions. Or you plan a war game or conduct an elaborate computer simulation and then reality does not play out as it was envisioned. The enemy, knowing that you have plans, will try to destroy your plans by doing things that you don't expect them to do. Especially in the case of the underdog in sports and war, one has to do the unexpected in order to have any chance of winning against perceived superior opposition. If you are the underdog in any business or personal situation, then figure out what would be expected logically by others and do something very different. If you are the superior player, then expect others to do seemingly irrational and impossible things that you never dreamed possible.

Your Expectations for Yourself

What I have observed for professional managers is also true for personal managing. At surprisingly early ages, some people acquire special passions for particular activities, such as playing sports, playing music, riding horses, acting, drawing and painting, collecting, etc. Their intense interests lead them to focused behavior with desired results. Goals then require plans. One cannot expect to compete in the Olympics, for example, without years of preparation. It is typical of a female gymnast, to give but one example, to begin training for the Olympics as early as age six. Boys may start playing organized football also at the age of six. Exceptional musicians often begin by learning how to play an instrument at very early ages. The list of such examples could go on and on.

Just as in business and other aspects of our public lives, your expectations for yourself can vary from ridiculous to prescient. I continuously run into people, both young and getting older, who have no idea what resources are required or what conditions have to occur so that they will realize their expectations, which, of course, are largely based on wishful thinking rather than facts.

Let's consider the self-expectations of a whole generation of Americans: the Baby Boomers numbering about 78 million who were born from 1946 to 1964. It has been claimed that they were the first generation of children who were generally planned and wanted, rather than randomly appearing as natural consequences of intimate adult relationships. They were born after World War II, when millions of men came home to marry, raise families, and have careers. After the hardships of the Great Depression and the Second World War, Boomers grew up in a national environment in which most parents wanted a better life for their family than what many of them had experienced a few decades previously.

In general, Boomers have had high expectations for their lives based on the nurturing of parents and other family members, sustained economic growth with unprecedented standards of living, amazing new technologies, and the fruits of American institutions, traditions, and power. Against the framework of high expectations, Boomers have suffered many disappointments. They gradually lost confidence in their stability at home, as they became increasingly aware of tensions between fathers and mothers. This, in part, led to Boomers experiencing as high as 50% divorce rates for their own marriages. Boomers gradually lost confidence in the wisdom of teachers, many of whom were not well prepared to deal with the large numbers of overly self-confident Boomer students. Boomers doubted that teachers were any wiser than their own parents. Boomers lost confidence in the truthfulness and transparency of government during the Vietnam War and the Watergate political crisis. They lost trust in large corporations because of periodic layoffs. Yet, most Boomers have survived their disappointments and many have enjoyed exceptional lives, even though many of their exaggerated stretch goals have gone unfulfilled.

Many Boomers face yet another big life disappointment due to their exaggerated expectations for retirement. They may survive as they always have, but with elements of bitterness and resentment due to the gap between reality and their own wishful thinking. Their faith in ever-growing 401(k) plans was dashed by the brutal bear market of 2008-2009. They have grave doubts that Social Security will survive long enough to see them through their old age. They are gradually losing their exaggerated expectations of retirement homes, vacations, leisure activities, and good health with youthful vigor.

In 2010, the youngest Boomers reached the age of 46, which is the early stage of their peak earning and spending years. The oldest Boomers turned 64. Some of them have taken early retirement benefits from Social Security, but they have not quite reached age 66 for "full retirement" benefits. By 2020, the youngest Boomers will be 56 and the oldest of them will be 74. Boomers generally expect to continue their standard of living into retirement. But why do they think that they will have enough money to do so? Boomers have long had a behavioral pattern of spending most of what they made and saving little. Many of them overinvested in their homes and experienced a net loss in property values in the Great Recession. Maybe some have idealistic notions that the Federal government will take care of them. Not likely given economic and political conditions existing today and likely to continue for another decade. Yes, the Great Recession will end and there will likely be continued economic growth in the US, but current forecasts are indicating future GDP growth rates at 2-3%, not 5-7% as many Boomers seem to expect. Some Boomers have pensions, but many do not, especially the younger Boomers who chose to work for startup companies promising future rewards in stock options rather than long-term job security and pensions. Many companies dropped pensions in the 1990s in favor of corporate participation in individual employee 401(k) plans.

So it seems very unlikely that most Boomers can maintain the standard of living that they got used to in their 50s and early 60s when they reach their late 60s and older. They cannot likely rely solely upon Social Security, or pensions (when they even have them), or 401(k) plans, most of which temporarily (but as measured in years, not months) lost as much as 50% of their value during the Great Recession. Maybe some Boomers are counting on future financial support from their children – I sure am not. Young people in general resent contributing to Social Security let alone taking on the potential financial burdens of supporting their aging parents.

The Boomers who are best positioned for the future are the ones who formed realistic expectations for their retirement long before that stage was reached. They had well considered expectations tempered by the recognition and tracking of general economic, social, and political trends. They were less optimistic about the future from an early point. The careful Boomers discounted just how clever they were and sought more probable outcomes. They remained employed for long periods of time, often sacrificing some degree of career advancement and pay (including bonuses) in return for long-term security. They tended to live under rather than over their means – they under-spent and limited their use of credit. They lived in houses more modest than they could have financed; they paced their spending; and they invested as much as they could afford in their 401(k) plans, IRAs, and regular savings.

Now the cautious Boomers may be fooled in the future, too. There are still many things beyond their control. The big unknown, of course, for each individual is the check-out time for life. But because of their well considered expectations and planning, they are in a stronger position to achieve their goals and to mitigate the potential reverses of unknown changes.

The principles of futuring and the best practices for managing futuring and visioning as discussed in this book apply to individuals in managing their own lives as well as for managers in companies, organizations, institutions, non-profits, and government. Be careful with your expectations and be prepared for the possibility of being surprised. Have plans and try to stick to them, but also have alternative plans ready to turn to if things do not work out as you expected.

The extent to which you can achieve your expectations for yourself depend upon many trends and events over your life. I will mention just a few of them:

- Education. You need to do well in school to show that you have intelligence, discipline, and ambition. Doing well in school provides options for the future. Not all smart people do well in school, and not all students who do well in school will have wonderful careers in business, the professions, and government – but the odds of success for the future go up with successes in the past. In the past, you were expected to be a college graduate to rise in corporate management. Then managers were expected to earn at least one advanced degree, especially the MBA or equivalent graduate degree in accounting, finance, psychology, physics, engineering, economics, or political science. Many managers have advanced degrees, including the Ph.D. and JD. In the future, you will be expected to earn at least two graduate degrees and continue your education for all of your life. You should have high expectations for your own education and seek the support that you need to achieve your goals.

- Friends and Relationships. There's an old saying that it is not what you know but who you know that counts. I would not go that far, but making and keeping friends is vitally important for your mental health and career. During your years of formal education, you need teachers and professors who will be your champions – who will make introductions and write recommendations and otherwise promote your progress. The same is true when you begin work. You need bosses who like and respect you and who have high (but not exaggerated) expectations for your future success. You need mentors at critical points in your development as a manager. You also need colleagues and friends to give you emotional and intellectual support. Parallel to your work environment, you need the encouragement and support of loved ones and personal friends outside of the work place. Your relationships may last a life time and play a critically important role in your career.

- A Seriousness without Severity About Work. You need to take every assignment and every job seriously. In the theatre, they say that there are no small roles, only small actors. Everybody has to play a support role from time to time. The leads are the ones who make every role seem important. They take their work seriously. Likewise in business and in government, leaders emerge because they took every job seriously regardless of their own pride. The pride comes with achieving even the smallest jobs, and the well-done small jobs will likely lead to larger jobs with more responsibility and pay. But don't go too far with your seriousness. You do not want to come across to others as severe, like some kind of fanatic. Do your work, do it on time, do it well, and do it with a smile.

- Compatibility. You need to learn to blend into every situation and corporate culture in which you have to perform. There is another old saying that states that if you want to get along you have to go along. This means being compatible with your coworkers and playing like a good teammate. Social skills are extremely important in successful leadership and management roles all the way across the spectrum from the shop floor to the White House. Learn and practice good manners and the social rules of fair play with others.

Expectations for You

Finally, you must manage the expectations that others have for you. You want to promise value, but you need to learn the fine art of slightly under-promising and then over-delivering. You want your boss and your customers to expect much from you, otherwise they would have less faith in your ability to achieve their goals and needs. If they did not have good expectations, they would not hire you. On the other hand, you do not want to overstate yourself and promise too much. You do not want to disappoint them by failing to fulfill their expectations. What makes your boss and your customers impressed is your delivering more than you promised, exceeding their well managed (by you) expectations.

Expectations for yourself can be just as exaggerated as your expectations for others. In school, you may have had inflated expectations of high grades; you may have taken jobs that you thought were going to be easy for you; you may have accepted promotions and management positions that you thought you could handle. And then maybe you experience a rude awakening along the way to the future. You have to align your own talents with changing circumstances in your own career just like, as a manager, you have to adjust operations and your immediate corporate culture to the changing realities of the market.

Expectations for the Future of Futuring and Visioning

In 2009 the futuring and planning consulting industry went into recession like so many other industries in the US. You would think that the need for anticipating and preparing for the future would be highly valued in tough times, but they are not. During the Great Recession, many businesses had to cut costs in order to balance reduced revenues. It is typically easier to control your own business operations than it is to control customers, so when customers cut back on their spending for your goods and services, it is faster and easier to cut your own costs than to re-stimulate customer demand. So, many businesses cut budgets for forecasting and long-term planning as expendable overhead costs. What planning that remained in reduced corporate circumstances focused on short-term recovery rather than long-term growth. Survival comes first – growth can wait until troubled times pass.

When economic conditions generally improve, the business community will look back and wonder how they failed to anticipate the global banking and financial crisis of 2008-2009. Where were the warning signs? What trends brought us to the brink of disaster? Why were we so poorly prepared to deal with the recession? They will ask these questions and wonder what happened in September 2008 much like the intelligence community has been asking what happened in September 2001.

In the comfort of recovery, the business community will pay more attention to the future. I expect to see strong growth in the futuring and visioning industry with more companies hiring internal staff for trend tracking and analysis and contracting with more vendors to provide strategic foresight services. I further expect to see more attention given to qualitative trend analysis and alternative futures (scenarios) that convey compelling stories about possible and likely (given certain sets of circumstances) futures rather than a continued reliance on traditional statistical trend projections, such as those that failed to account for the radical changes caused by the Great Recession.

Perhaps the biggest change in the market for futuring and visioning services is that companies will want to acquire those skills for themselves rather than outsource them to consultants. They want those skills added to the portfolio of managers' capabilities. Therefore, the value-added (highly differentiated) market opportunity for consulting futurists, like me, will increasingly lie with corporate education and training of managers in futuring and visioning skills rather than in conducting such projects for corporate clients. Another opportunity might be in providing low-cost services in trend tracking and trend analysis for many clients, who will in turn use such information for their own processes of futuring and planning.

The long-term emphasis on trend analysis will very likely (0.80) continue for decades more. The contemporary corporate function of identifying and monitoring customer, marketplace, and competitor changes dates back to at least the 1960s if not earlier. The growing-up of the Boomer generation, the unprecedented pace of economic growth, and the disruptions of the civil rights movement and the war in Vietnam caused planners to question the market and investment assumptions of the 1950s. Trend analysis was part of the strategic planning function headed by Ian Wilson at General Electric. By imagining the possibilities of completely different outcomes for the future of consumer behavior resulting from the trends coming out of the turbulent 1960s, Wilson and his team by 1970 could visualize alternative futures for the year 1980. Likewise, Shell had a corporate function that they called "environmental scanning." Pierre Wack and his team that generated the first global oil scenarios in 1972 were served well by Shell's library of trend research.

One lesson of the Great Recession is that we need to consider many trends in many different areas of life around the world. Tracking the trends of our specific business arena is not enough. We learned in the autumn of 2008 that rapidly rising oil prices and sharply receding real estate prices combined to threaten the very existence of such divergent conglomerates as General Motors, General Electric, and Bank of America.

One operational model for the future is that companies will have staff members or teams dedicated to monitoring the trends that are closest to their proprietary interests and will contract to specialty vendors the overview of global trends. The external contractors will support the in-house visionary leaders and futuring managers. The internal staff may be assigned to one of many possible functions, such as corporate finance, marketing, and planning. I think it best to have a relatively small futuring and visioning staff assigned directly to the office of the CEO to remove it as much as possible from the competing pressures (i.e. wishful thinking) of corporate politics. I do not think it likely (0.25) that companies, except the largest, will go back to the model of corporate strategic planning that existed in the 1960s. Governments, on the other hand, may move toward that model, but in general the costs are too high for most companies to afford.

Trend tracking was traditionally done by reading newspapers, magazines, and the trade literature; watching TV news; and gathering information (intelligence) from the field. Much of this is still done today, but the big change has been the digital explosion in resources. With the introduction of the World Wide Web in 1995, trend trackers began the transition from analog, printed media to digital, on-screen media. Trend trackers still watch TV news, but they increasingly rely on the Internet news services. They can search for sources of information all around the world in a matter of minutes. Today there is no excuse for not being aware of almost real-time shifts in the patterns of consumer behavior, marketplace conditions, and competitor responses.

The new challenge is not so much finding valuable information but being able to sort so much information into meaningful trend analysis for decision-makers. Analysis based on data became more difficult to do when the amount of data increased exponentially. The challenges of corporate trend trackers are very much like the challenges of the national Intelligence Community, which monitors trends and events for the highest ranking CEO in America– the President of the United States– with potential consequences for the lives of more than 300 million Americans.

Corporate and national intelligence also share a fundamental approach to trend tracking: most of what they do falls into Type II pattern recognition, or the monitoring of specific potential changes. Type I pattern recognition, or the continuous monitoring of background conditions, is still done, especially for short-term security purposes, but it is not as popular as Type II pattern recognition, whereby real or imagined changes (signatures) are looked for with great anticipation, even dread. Many corporations, as well as individuals, assume that Type I pattern recognition is what they already know, so they concentrate on what they do not know. Type I pattern recognition can be very boring – just "more of the same."

Yet, the Great Recession that hit so many Americans with complete surprise in late 2008 proved, by painful experience, that we have not been tracking Type I patterns well enough in order to spot unexpected changes from the norm. And too many companies and individuals monitor Type II changes with predispositions and biases that blind them to significant changes. When trend trackers become aware of changes and potential shifts in patterns, they too quickly assign a Type I pattern to the new data without going to sufficient trouble to array data into potentially new Type III patterns. They fail to distinguish between the statements "it is the same as…" and "it is similar in several ways to…."

Trend tracking requires all three types of pattern recognition to be performed simultaneously.

I foresee substantial growth in the area called "predictive analytics." This includes large scale data mining, modeling and simulation, pattern recognition, and game theory. It is fundamentally Type III pattern recognition, drawn from arrays of large amounts of data gathered day-by-day. Patterns will emerge from the data. In some cases, these patterns will look very much like previous Type I patterns, but some will be new and will become the Type I patterns of the future. They will become increasingly predictive due to trend momentum, well-documented cause-and-effect relationships, laws of nature (including established patterns of human behavior), and (semi-)closed systems and fixed sets, particularly within well defined boundary conditions (or circumstances).

A major question for research in the future is whether there are relatively few Type I patterns (basic backgrounds) that serve as archetypes for many emerging Type III patterns, allowing us to cluster patterns by analogy according to some meaningful criteria, or whether there will be many new arrays of Type III patterns that will be recognized as new Type I patterns.

In the intelligence world since 9/11/01 there has been an emphasis on "anticipatory and actionable intelligence" for the top echelons of civilian and military leaders. The same may be said for the executives of companies and non-profits.

Another challenge for the future is the development of relatively simple methods to integrate many trends into coherent views of the future. I have had success using cross-impact analysis with one particular proprietary software product, but the method needs to be widely available. Cross-impact analysis can be performed either as a systems flow diagram or as a table. It can be used with or without Bayesian probabilities. There should be a common cross-impact software program that is either free or very inexpensive to allow many futurists and planners to access it. In addition, there should be simple template models to help futurists and planners better visualize trends and their relationships with each other that is dynamic and easy to use to perform sensitivity analysis and simulations.

The packaging of forecasts and plans begs for substantial improvements in the future. Many executives are highly visual in their perception style. There is a continuous need to improve appropriate and compelling graphic displays of scenarios and other forms of forecasts beyond the traditional two-dimension graphs or quadrant displays.

Among futurists and planners, there is a need for more professional development and cohesion. In the US, they have emerged from many different disciplines and areas of experience. Only two universities (the University of Houston and the University of Hawaii) have offered a Master's degree in future studies and none has offered a doctoral degree. Most undergraduate and graduate business programs do not offer any courses in futuring, forecasting, and scenario generation. Not surprisingly, with professional futurists and planners coming from many different frames of reference, there is a lack of a common taxonomy of terms and consensus of concepts in futuring and planning. "Forecasting" is still the term most widely used in place of "prediction," but it suffers from mental images of numbers rather than stories. "Foresight," especially "strategic foresight," is being used increasingly. I prefer "futuring." Perhaps "foresight" might be used as the term that covers both the external functions of futuring and the internal functions of visioning. I have used the expression "well considered expectations" to cover both futuring and visioning. But many professionals still do not make the distinction between futuring and visioning as I have in this book.

Professional futurists and planners in the coming years will likely spend less time performing studies for other people and more time exploring new futuring and visioning methods and teaching them to managers, who will become more skilled in doing their own forecasts and plans.

I conclude with the final challenge that faces us: the validation of the fundamental premise of this book that managers will be expected to be their own futurists as well as planners and that the ability to form well considered expectations for the future can be improved through valid theories, applied skills, and better information. We will never be able to accurately and precisely predict the future due to complexity, variability, and uncertainty about things that can happen but have not yet occurred. Having admitted this limitation, I argue that we can do much better in anticipating the future than we are doing now, which in many regards is better than what was being done 50 years ago. We are developing better models and tools to think about the future. We are accessing and organizing much greater quantities of accurate and timely information. We are learning to discern new Type III patterns rather than jumping to the conclusion that emerging patterns are just like well-known Type I patterns. We are also developing better concepts as mental if not physical models of how to manage the inherent uncertainties of the future. Whether or not my expectations prove to be valid remains to be seen.

About the Author

Stephen M. Millett received his A.B. degree from Miami University (Oxford, Ohio) and his MA and Ph.D. degrees in history from The Ohio State University. He served as an officer in the U.S. Air Force before joining the professional staff at the Battelle Memorial Institute in 1979. During his 27-year career at Battelle, Dr. Millett became an internationally respected technology forecaster and futurist. He managed over 100 major futuring and visioning projects for corporate, non-profit, R&D and government clients in North America, the European Union, India, and east Asia. He retired in 2006 and founded his own research and consulting company, Futuring Associates LLC. He is also a faculty member in the MBA program at Franklin University. Dr. Millett served as a member of the State Board of Education in Ohio from 2003 to 2010.

He is the author of five books, seven chapters in compiled books, and 34 articles in professional journals and websites.

His website is: www.futuringassociates.com

Index

About Triarchy Press

Triarchy Press is an independent publishing house that looks at how organisations work and how to make them work better. We present challenging perspectives on organisations in short and pithy, but rigorously argued, books.

Through our books, pamphlets and website we aim to stimulate ideas by encouraging real debate about organisations in partnership with people who work in them, research them or just like to think about them.

Please tell us what you think about the ideas in this book at:

www.triarchypress.com/telluswhatyouthink

If you feel inspired to write – or have already written – an article, a pamphlet or a book on any aspect of organisational theory or practice, we'd like to hear from you. Submit a proposal at:

www.triarchypress.com/writeforus

For more information about Triarchy Press, or to order any of our publications, please visit our website or drop us a line:

www.triarchypress.com

We're on Twitter:

@TriarchyPress

and Facebook:

www.facebook.com/triarchypress

Related Titles from Triarchy Press

Facing the Fold: Essays on Scenario Planning
by James A. Ogilvy
Scenario Planning brought right up to date with case studies and a series of essential essays from one of its foremost exponents – Jay Ogilvy

Systems Thinking for Curious Managers
by Russell L. Ackoff
An insightful, extended introduction to Systems Thinking as developed by Russ Ackoff.

The Decision Loom
by Vincent P. Barabba
Vince Barabba explains an elegantly simple approach to making better decisions, setting out to change our "analytical" habit and inviting enterprises to consider the bigger picture.

Strategy, Leadership and the Soul
by Jennifer Sertl and Koby Huberman
The authors call for "transorganizations" (in permanent transformation) led by "transleaders" (able to adapt constantly) and responsive to customer "experations" (expectations of the business's operations)

Adventures in Complexity
by Lesley Kuhn
Complexity Theory explained, this book shows how the theory can be translated into the workplace – for practitioners and academics.

In Search of the Missing Elephant
by Donald N. Michael
Essays by eminent futurist and polymath Don Michael offer some hope in taking on those messy, seemingly intractable issues, in a world where rapid change means that yesterday's solution no longer works.

The Innovation Acid Test
by Andrew M. Jones
Drew Jones sets out the defining practices and procedures of some of the world's most innovative – and most successful – companies.

The Search for Leadership/The Systemic Leadership Toolkit
by William Tate
Used together, this book and toolkit guide HR and other senior executives through the process of leading an open, effective, repsonsible and empowering organization.

Lightning Source UK Ltd.
Milton Keynes UK
UKOW041012251111

182675UK00001B/2/P